Reading Baudelaire with Adorno

Reading Baudelaire with Adorno

Dissonance, Subjectivity, Transcendence

Joseph Acquisto

BLOOMSBURY ACADEMIC
NEW YORK • LONDON • OXFORD • NEW DELHI • SYDNEY

BLOOMSBURY ACADEMIC
Bloomsbury Publishing Inc
1385 Broadway, New York, NY 10018, USA
50 Bedford Square, London, WC1B 3DP, UK
29 Earlsfort Terrace, Dublin 2, Ireland

BLOOMSBURY, BLOOMSBURY ACADEMIC and the Diana logo are trademarks of
Bloomsbury Publishing Plc

First published in the United States of America 2023
This paperback edition published 2024

Copyright © Joseph Acquisto, 2023

For legal purposes the Permissions on p. vi constitute an extension of this copyright page.

Cover design: Eleanor Rose
Cover image: Megan Holmberg, "the trees are bending down"

All rights reserved. No part of this publication may be reproduced or transmitted in any form or by any means, electronic or mechanical, including photocopying, recording, or any information storage or retrieval system, without prior permission in writing from the publishers.

Bloomsbury Publishing Inc does not have any control over, or responsibility for, any third-party websites referred to or in this book. All internet addresses given in this book were correct at the time of going to press. The author and publisher regret any inconvenience caused if addresses have changed or sites have ceased to exist, but can accept no responsibility for any such changes.

Library of Congress Cataloging-in-Publication Data

Names: Acquisto, Joseph, 1975- author.
Title: Reading Baudelaire with Adorno: dissonance, subjectivity, transcendence / Joseph Acquisto.
Description: New York: Bloomsbury Academic, 2023. | Includes bibliographical references and index. | Summary: "An innovative reading of Baudelaire's poetry and criticism in dialogue with the aesthetic theory of Theodor Adorno"– Provided by publisher.
Identifiers: LCCN 2022048248 (print) | LCCN 2022048249 (ebook) | ISBN 9798765103005 (hardback) | ISBN 9798765103012 (paperback) | ISBN 9798765103029 (ebook) | ISBN 9798765103036 (pdf) | ISBN 9798765103043 (ebook other)
Subjects: LCSH: Baudelaire, Charles, 1821-1867–Criticism and interpretation. | Adorno, Theodor W., 1903-1969–Criticism and interpretation.
Classification: LCC PQ2191.Z5 A54 2023 (print) | LCC PQ2191.Z5 (ebook) | DDC 841/.8–dc23/eng/20221129
LC record available at https://lccn.loc.gov/2022048248
LC ebook record available at https://lccn.loc.gov/2022048249

ISBN: HB: 979-8-7651-0300-5
PB: 979-8-7651-0301-2
ePDF: 979-8-7651-0303-6
eBook: 979-8-7651-0302-9

Typeset by Deanta Global Publishing Services, Chennai, India

To find out more about our authors and books visit www.bloomsbury.com and sign up for our newsletters.

CONTENTS

Introduction   1
1   Dissonance   29
2   Subjectivity   73
3   Transcendence   121
Coda and Conclusion   159

Notes   171
Work Cited   182
Index   187

Introduction

To speak of Baudelaire is to speak of paradox and contradiction. It is to speak of a poet who is modern, amodern, and antimodern, one who vaunts transcendent correspondences and lets his poet's halo remain trapped in the mud of the urban street. Baudelaire's works defy any attempt to characterize them except by way of a seemingly infinite set of qualifications, not because his poetics is incoherent but because he inscribes doubleness into the heart of those poetics in their conjunction with something we could call an epistemology, metaphysics, or psychology. What he—metaphorically? literally?—aligns with God and Satan in the "deux postulations simultanées" present at all times in all people is also a spatial metaphor that appeals to the transcendent by means of the (metaphorical? literal?) material world. "L'invocation à Dieu, ou spiritualité, est un désir de monter en grade ; celle à Satan, ou animalité, est une joie de descendre" ["the invocation to God, or spirituality, is a desire to ascend; the one to Satan, or animality, is a joy of descent"] (1: 683).[1] To try to grasp and enumerate the way these contradictions manifest themselves in Baudelaire is perhaps to give in to the "joy of descent," to pursue the potentially endless ways in which his poetry challenges, but also depends on, what comes before him, in ways that have proven tremendously influential for poetics ever since. The excitement that comes from the attempt to say something adequate about a Baudelaire poem comes partly from the realization that individual poems always send us back to other poems and encourage us to read them in groups that alter the meaning of each individual poem in the light of the other poems we have in mind as we read. The parts and wholes start to reconfigure themselves in ways that resist easy description as we pursue the joy of descent into the art of interpretation, and their unity can seem both intuitively obvious and absolutely questionable. Moreover, any move toward interpretation soon becomes imbricated in larger questions of our relation as readers to the poem, the way it may shape us just as much as we shape it in our attempts to give form to a meaning, appealing to conceptual reflection while being aware of the rift between what conceptual reflection can provide and the experience of the work of art that always surpasses it. We may find ourselves tempted, in that Satanic joy of descent, to claim an overarching unity by which we could make some sort of definitive claim about Baudelaire. We might even come to see that "as soon as unity becomes stable, it is already lost," because "unity and multiplicity are internal to each other." That claim comes not from Baudelaire but from Theodor Adorno, arguably the foremost thinker of the role of dissonance in what we have come to call modern art in the broad sense.[2] It will be my claim in this study that Baudelaire's poetry affects a key transformation in lyric subjectivity that Adorno's conception of subject-object relations both in his esthetics and in his wider philosophical project can help illuminate, while at the same time the poetry of Baudelaire resists, as Adorno recognizes that all genuine artworks do, totalizing attempts to subsume the artwork under the conceptual. Rather, the artwork impels conceptual reflection but also always surpasses it, as it sends us, we might say, further down on the joyous descent.

Adorno's approach to esthetics and to theory resonates with Baudelaire's work, not in the sense of providing a specific and easily summarized conceptual lens, but rather by dynamically mapping a space where ideas and artworks mutually inform each other and cannot exist independently of one another. This is a space that is informed by, but not determined by or reduced to, the social context in which the artist creates, and it is one that takes the autonomy of the work of art and its formal tensions seriously. As Adorno indicates near the start of *Aesthetic Theory*, "the unresolved antagonisms of reality return in artworks as immanent problems of form" (AT 7). In fact, for both Baudelaire and Adorno, the autonomy of the work of art, properly understood, follows from its social relations rather than being opposed to them. Adorno intervenes meaningfully in a "modern" approach to the artwork that Baudelaire could be said to have played a key role in inaugurating and leads us to key questions about what remains of a certain view of the power and potential of art that Baudelaire inherited, but now from the perspective of the ruins of the horrors of the twentieth century when those seeking to articulate what remains of that power and potential of art find themselves asserting, like Beckett's character in *The Unnamable*, "I can't go on, I'll go on" (Beckett 418). Baudelaire, too, is important in no small part because his simultaneous preservation and transformation of approaches to the literary artwork that came before him situate him at a crossroads where he encourages readers to ask how artistic creation and interpreters' understanding of that creation need to be transformed, but will not for all that be annihilated, in the changed social circumstances in which that art is produced.

Sometimes Baudelaire's story is told as a simplified and simplifying move from the elevation of the poetic discourse of the earlier verse poems to the cynical urban visions of the prose poems. Such a linear view is symptomatic of a modern approach to time and artistic development but is hardly faithful to the complexity at work, often simultaneously, in Baudelaire's creative output as the tension between an older and newer approach is one of dynamic or dialectical tension, or what I will call dissonance. Adorno's essay-like approach to esthetics allows for a dialectical approach to art and philosophy that shows them to be mutually illuminating in ways that underscore the insufficiency of either one on its own when it comes to making meaning from works of art. In important ways, both Baudelaire and Adorno, while separated from each other by a century and from us by fifty years beyond that, can still be said to be writers of "our" moment insofar as we can still claim their pertinence for the "modern" world we could still be said to inhabit. In other words, they played a role in illuminating or creating some of the artistic and conceptual categories through which we appeal to thought and literature to illuminate experience. This is a point made by Michael North about what he calls "the afterlife of modernism":

> If the reasons for the persistence of modernism are neither esthetic nor historical, then it may be that they are structural in nature. Modernism persists in the present because it still dictates the ways in which we can discuss the present, because it owns the terms by which we mark off as distinct the time we happen to live in. [. . .] Even if they depart in some particular way from the practices identified with modernism, [later periods] confirm its basic precept by changing. Later periods, then, can never be anything other than variations on the theme of the modern, continuing its essential project even as they update it with a prefix. (North 93)

Such an approach invites us to consider the ways in which Baudelaire plays a role in setting the terms by which we attempt to understand art in his time and beyond, and the ways in which conceptual reflection about art becomes entwined with the new set of esthetic circumstances in which he undertook esthetic creation. If we still have occasion to ask whether and to what extent Baudelaire is our contemporary, it is because of the structure of his relationship to his own esthetic heritage and the way he implies a relationship, even a dissonant one, between art, critical reflection on it, and the sociohistorical circumstances which both bring that art and reflection into being and serve as a source of dissonance or critique.

By claiming that mid-twentieth-century thinkers help illuminate Baudelaire's work in important ways, I am of course writing in the wake of the many critics who situate Walter Benjamin as a crucial figure for understanding Baudelaire. Adorno famously responded with harsh criticism, in 1938, to "The Paris of the Second Empire in Baudelaire," and the exchange is an especially fruitful one in terms of negotiating how key notions derived from Marx can best be applied to the texts that Benjamin places under scrutiny. As Robert Kaufman indicates, Adorno implies that Benjamin's essay "limits not only Baudelaire but himself too—constrains his understanding of Baudelaire's, of advanced lyric's, of modern art's critical value—by adopting an essentially orthodox Marxist-Leninist, resolutely determinist approach to exchange value, the commodity, and human agency" (Kaufman "Lyric" 208).[3] More specifically, Adorno writes to Benjamin that "your dialectic is lacking in one thing: mediation. You show a prevailing tendency to relate the pragmatic contents of Baudelaire's work directly and immediately to adjacent features in the social history, and whenever possible, the economic features, of the time" (Adorno and Benjamin 282). Further on, he adds, in a formulation that has become well known: "if one wished to put it very drastically, one could say that your study is located at the crossroads of magic and positivism. That spot is bewitched" (283).[4] My interest in what follows is not to supplant a Benjaminian reading of Baudelaire with an Adornian reading, nor to add fuel to Adorno's arguments against Benjamin in the correspondence, but, rather, to suggest a different sort of productive engagement with Baudelaire that emerges in other aspects of Adorno's work. I engage chiefly with the later Adorno of the posthumously published *Aesthetic Theory* and, in fact, that engagement with Adorno is oblique in the sense that I am not primarily concerned with his remarks, frequent but often in passing, on Baudelaire in his writings. My guiding concepts of dissonance, subjectivity, and transcendence are ideas he develops in contexts that are not limited to, or even centrally anchored in, his literary criticism but belong instead to his work in philosophy and writings on music.

As such, the poems which are central to my analysis in what follows are for the most part not the poems of urban modernity that form the core of Benjamin's analysis, mainly from the "Tableaux parisiens" and the prose poems, underscoring the role of the poet as *flâneur*, the loss of aura, and the primacy of the experience of shock. My own focus spotlights a different subset of Baudelaire's works where what we could call his dissonant subjectivity plays a central role, in poems such as "L'Héautontimorouménos," "Le Crépuscucle du soir," or "Le Flacon." It is my hope that a focus on the destabilized lyric subject in these poems can complement the abundance of work on the poems that form the core of Benjamin's Baudelaire canon, such as "A une passante," "Le Cygne," and "Perte d'auréole." One aspect of Adorno's critique of Benjamin was that he "leaves the distinction between the subjective experience of the artist and its objective conditions intact" since he does not "adequately account for the manifold connections between them," resulting in an analysis where "subject and object are reified" (McCall 22).[5] My reading takes up the question of the complexity of the subject-object relation in Baudelaire more broadly. I focus less on the phenomenology of urban experience as represented in the poems and more on how the modern artwork, in its autonomy, can lead to something like what Adorno does not hesitate to call the kind of truth that can be found in the dialectical tensions and dissonances instantiated and maintained by the way the lyric subject relates to the poem in which he or she figures and through whose contradictions and negations he or she is formed. As Fredric Jameson has recently written, "we must reckon with a persistent anti-esthetic strain in Benjamin, and one seriously antithetical to Adorno's inveterate defense of the famous 'autonomy of the work of art'" (Jameson *Benjamin* 61). In other words, there may be more to the story of Baudelaire and the critique of modernity than an exclusive focus on Benjamin can reveal.[6] Adorno's focus on the autonomy of the artwork is, of course, far from being a bracketing of political or critical concerns; the point is rather that sustained attention to esthetics has the potential to yield one of the best forms of insight into the modern historical moment precisely on account of its removal from the immediacy of that moment. Such an approach makes room for a dynamic lyric subject as constituted by the artwork and has, perhaps, the potential to avoid the danger of "reif[ying] history into something akin to objective fate that remains utterly distinct from subjective experience, and the relationship between subject and object unquestioned" (McCall 22).

A first glance at how lyric poetry not only registers the shock of the modern but also stands as an implicit, but powerful, source of critique of it is available in Adorno's essay "On Lyric Poetry and Society," written nearly twenty years after that exchange with Benjamin. Here we see an outline of the relationship between the lyric self's necessary division from itself and its critical relation to its natural and social worlds:

> The "I" whose voice is heard in the lyric is an "I" that defines and expresses itself as something opposed to the collective, to objectivity; it is not immediately at one with the nature to which its expression refers. It has lost it, as it were, and attempts to restore it through animation, through immersion in the "I" itself. (*Notes* 1: 41)

In a similar way, the works of poetry are, like the lyric subject, always double in that

> their pure subjectivity, the aspect of them that appears seamless and harmonious, bears witness to is opposite, to suffering in an existence alien to the subject and to love for it as well—indeed, their harmoniousness is actually nothing but the mutual accord of this suffering and this love. (41)

For Adorno, lyric poetry plays a crucial role in the philosophical elaboration of these dynamics of subject and object, one that cannot be accomplished by conceptual thought on its own, and which allows it to stand, apart from any explicitly political content, as a source of opposition to what Adorno often refers to as "identity thinking," aligned in this essay with "scientific logic" and the reductive and undialectical relationship of domination that is implied by an identity of subject and object:

> Classical philosophy once formulated a truth now disdained by scientific logic: subject and object are not rigid and isolated poles but can be defined only in the process in which they distinguish themselves from one another and change. The lyric is the esthetic test of that dialectical

> philosophical proposition. In the lyric poem the subject, through its identification with language, negates both its opposition to society as something merely monadological and its mere functioning within a wholly socialized society. But the more the latter's ascendancy over the subject increases, the more precarious the situation of the lyric becomes. Baudelaire's work was the first to record this; his work [...] did not stop with the sufferings of the individual but chose the modern itself, as the antilyrical pure and simple, for its theme and struck a poetic spark in it by dint of a heroically stylized language. In Baudelaire a note of despair already makes itself felt, a note that barely maintains its balance on the tip of its own paradoxicalness. (44)

Lyric poetry stands in a critical relation to society not on account of any explicit political content but rather because of the epistemological implications inherent in the ways it constructs the relationship of subject to object. On this view, Baudelaire does not so much alter or break the unity of subject and object as to demonstrate that any such unity or fullness that may have been suggested by earlier poets or by some of his own earlier works was always the result of an esthetic illusion to begin with. As Adorno puts it, "the state of reconciliation of subject and object, the subject's full presence within the work of art, was [...] always an illusion, and it is almost appropriate to equate this illusion with aesthetic illusion as such" (*Notes 2*: 105).

To claim that I will appeal to Adorno as I develop my reading of Baudelaire invites clarification about *which* Adorno will play the key role here. Such a wide-ranging thinker and writer is not easily boxed in or reduced to a few key concepts, although Adorno is indeed often reduced to something like a caricature, an elitist or curmudgeon whose main interest resides in his ruthless critique of mass culture or his too famous claim that to write poetry after Auschwitz is barbaric.[7] Such clichéd and inaccurate representations of his approach call for the kind of nuance which he often applied to the subject at hand across his contributions to critical theory, sociology, philosophy, musicology, and literary criticism. I should also indicate at the outset that my focus will not be on his explicit engagement, fairly constant though often fleeting, with Baudelaire, the most sustained instance of which is the correspondence with Benjamin whose main concerns are with wider questions of the particularities of Benjamin's Marxist approach to thought and social critique via the vehicle of Baudelaire. Rather, my engagement with Adorno is oblique, drawing on his *Aesthetic Theory* and other works more broadly, rather than attempting to synthesize an approach to Baudelaire from his own explicit comments on the poet. The grounds on which Baudelaire and Adorno meet in my study are the wider fields of esthetic experience and interpretation more broadly. Adorno's often paratactic style in *Aesthetic Theory* lends itself to an act of interpretation and creation by the thinker who engages with that text, as the text implicitly invites readers to use those ideas as vehicles for interpreting texts. No totalizing blueprint is given, and Adorno's assertion thus makes space for thinking with the text rather than according to its dictates. To follow his thinking through his essays collected in *Notes to Literature*, through major works such as *Aesthetic Theory*, and other writings is to share his deep appreciation of the powers of art and his attempt to articulate how they operate, differently but in a very real way, in a modern period that can feel as though it invites the cynical cancelation of art rather than its persistence and continuing challenge. As Adorno himself puts it in a sentence that captures much of the approach on which I will draw, "Art is what remains after the loss of what was supposed to exercise a magical, and later a cultic, function" (AT 127). To see art this way is to see it under the sign of a productive negation, whereby the older vision is still perceivable in its very impossibility and as the condition of its own transformation as art. It is an approach to art deeply informed by paradox as well: "Aesthetic experience is that of something that spirit may find neither in the world nor in itself; it is possibility promised by its impossibility. Art is the ever broken promise of happiness" (AT 135–6).

A major source of affinity between Baudelaire and Adorno is this particular, complex, and shifting configuration of artistic truth, esthetic experience, and the way that art in its very autonomy and in its very form carries political implications without being dominated by them or featuring them in an explicit way. Esthetic experience for Adorno, as Owen Hulatt summarizes it, "is constituted by a dialectic between an immediate truth of the work and the conceptually mediated element [. . .] that makes this immediate truth viable. [. . .] A complicated dialectical relation is being drawn between the immediate truth of aesthetic experience and the intellectually mediated grounds of that experience" (Hulatt 183). For both Baudelaire and Adorno, art calls out for interpretation while repeatedly demonstrating the inadequacy of interpretation fully to account for or to explain the artwork; there is always something that remains even though art does need conceptual reflection in order for what it expresses to be recognized. Configured this way, "the relationship between the philosophical and the esthetic cannot but have epistemo-political implications," as Gerhard Richter has claimed (*Afterness* 60). Working out exactly what those epistemo-political claims are, within the context of the esthetic, requires the kind of dialectical movement between art and interpretation that Baudelaire's texts call for and deeply reward, even as they defy any attempt at reductivist interpretations emphasizing either the esthetic or the epistemo-political at the expense of the other.

It is precisely because Baudelaire's texts lead to a transformation of thinking that they could be said to be political, in ways highlighted by Gerhard Richter, who observes that "the wager of Adorno's esthetic theory is that a truly political work of art, rather than entering into a specific relation to what is, will inaugurate a moment of reflection that shifts the relation predicated upon the conjunction of presentation and commentary to a different kind of relation, the relation of thinking *to itself*" ("Introduction" 7). What I propose, then, is not an Adornian reading of Baudelaire that would map concepts from the latter onto the works of the former or try to extrapolate a system or method of thinking that would then apply to works of literature, which would be unfaithful to both of their approaches. Rather, I seek to read them together, to establish points of mutual illumination between them, as Baudelaire resonates with the reconfiguration of esthetic experience expressed in terms of dissonance and subjectivity that often plays a key role in Adorno's writings on esthetic theory and experience, and as Adorno's writing, in its essay-like, speculative character, not only leaves room for literature as its own system of meaning making but also insists on the primary role of esthetic experience in conceiving what we could call truth. Indeed, some have pointed to an understanding of Adorno's title *Aesthetic Theory* that would indicate an esthetically informed theorizing, a "certain estheticization of theory as well as being a theory of the esthetic" as J. M. Bernstein puts it (*Fate* 241), a thinking about art that necessitates the same sorts of interpretive moves we would more typically apply to works of art. In that sense, both Baudelaire and Adorno could in some sense be said to be modernist writers, reconfiguring the relation of esthetic subject and object in a way that requires the preservation of an older model of that relation, which both persists and finds itself negated by the reconfigured status of the artwork and the perceiver who would interact with it. Adorno's ideas will thus function as points of resonance in what follows; sometimes I appeal directly to ideas he develops in *Aesthetic Theory* and elsewhere, and at other times it will be a question of what Gerhard Richter has called "thinking with Adorno," following Adorno's lead on figuring out, via Adorno's own idiosyncratic approach to thinking and writing about art and subjectivity, "how to question, and how to fashion a genuinely open yet uncompromisingly vigilant comportment toward the objects of one's inquiry" (Richter *Thinking* 2).[8]

When Adorno reads proto-modernist figures, and here Beethoven comes to mind as an important example, it is often to show how they point both backward to what came before and forward to what comes after in ways that were fully present in their works but that only the ensuing historical time that has passed between their moment and ours can enable us to see. Such an approach is particularly fruitful with Baudelaire. While one might claim that to read Baudelaire in light of what came after him, esthetically and historically, is to ignore the context of what it meant to produce art in his own time, such a narrowly historicist view fails to do justice to the artwork because it, ironically, removes it from larger historical considerations that would allow us to see the esthetic past in dynamic relation to later moments, or to reconfigure such a linear notion of time altogether all the better to articulate the ways in which not only the past is not past but that the future was not entirely future in these prescient works of art. To see in Baudelaire's works a reconfiguration of subjectivity that we would only later have the concepts and language to articulate more fully is not to be unfaithful to the poet's situation in his own time but to recognize that fuller understanding of a work is often possible only via the temporal distance that allows theorizing about art to "catch up" to the artwork, so to speak, to be able to articulate what it does, in ways that become clearer only by the ensuing development of art that allows us to read "backward" toward older works. Such an understanding also leads us, in ways that Adorno articulates, to an appreciation of the insufficiency of conceptual reflection on art, which is a necessary, but eternally inadequate, engagement with the artwork which relies on conceptual engagement and interpretation to bring to light both what it has to say and the realization of the impossibility of fully articulating what it might have to say.

In that sense, Adorno's kind of reflection on art is made possible by the works of Baudelaire, whose *oeuvre* created the imperative for the style of thinking that Adorno adopts in order to make sense of modern art; those ideas spring directly from, and ultimately turn back toward, the artworks. The new configuration of subjectivity and dissonance is precisely what gives rise to a new conceptual configuration of those ideas in Adorno, whose reflections ultimately feed back into the artworks in a way that helps make visible what is there in them and how that may be enumerated historically. The fact that artworks reveal something not only immediately (both in the sense of a non-conceptual immediate reaction to an artwork and in the sense of its immediate moment in time), but also over time, points to the importance of the reception history of a poet like Baudelaire which, on this view, is not supplemental to, or inferior to, the experience of reading his works, but is an absolutely essential part of the process of fully reading them. It is not that his reception history is a set of moves on the path to "getting him right" but, rather, an acknowledgment that what it means to read him well is a gradually unfolding and forever shifting notion in which we participate as best we can in full knowledge that to give anything more than a tentative interpretation is to be unfaithful to the richness of the texts themselves.

It is in that spirit that I attempt to articulate how the notions of dissonance, subjectivity, and transcendence form a constellation that can serve as an important point of entry into his works. At a basic level, we could say that both Adorno and Baudelaire propose tentative, shifting answers to the questions of how art can still be art, what remains of the grander claims about the power of art that emerged in the earlier nineteenth century at the same time as a more fully developed individual bourgeois subject, whose existence was necessary to such an emergence but also the subject of much of what art defined itself against in the romantic period. To call claims to transcendence, which I understand in this study in the broad sense of a reality beyond the immediate sensual world of appearance, via art an illusion or a lie, or to claim that all that remains of such a project is its detritus in the wake of the disenchanting horrors of the twentieth century, or even those of Baudelaire's own time, is to paint an incomplete picture, since that art, and that vision of subjectivity, persists in some recognizable albeit transformed image in Baudelaire and beyond. If the subsequent history of art since Baudelaire allows us better to see the way in which transcendence or harmony can exist only as a kind of nostalgia, it also demonstrates the way in which such notions need to persist in order to make sense of new kinds of dissonant artistic expression, which rely on the persistence of the older model in order to be perceived as dissonances at all, in ways I will go on to illustrate at length. Older models of esthetic subjectivity that persist in Baudelaire cannot be merely dismissed as persistent remnants of what came before him, present in an almost nostalgic kind of way, but need to be accounted for as a full part of his mature esthetics which does not go on merely to cancel or cynically dismiss the older work.

Once again, to claim such a thing would be to appeal implicitly to a linear model of artistic development which would be quite at odds with Baudelaire's own approach both to temporality and to notions of progress. So, in some sense, the work of art as Baudelaire practices it and as Adorno conceives of it is of its time precisely by being not of its time, anchored in its social world not despite, but because of, its autonomy. Rob Halpern has articulated this point of convergence between Baudelaire and Adorno:

> It is important to recall that for Adorno, autonomous art submits to the world *radically*—that is, at its very root—in order to create something that won't reduce to the world as it is. [. . .] If for the sake of their own concept artworks wanted absolutely to destroy this reference back to the empirical world, they would wipe out their own premise. [. . .] But what does it mean for art simultaneously to fulfil and transcend its own concept? [. . .] Art that would, in Adorno's phrase, remain faithful to its own concept would thus be an art committed to a form of self-negating praxis, an auto-immolation whereby art would paradoxically realize its vocation.
>
> Accordingly art can have no sustained rapport with [. . .] "progress," which simply renews the present's claims of the future. (Halpern "Baudelaire's" 11)

The world of esthetic paradox, of retention and negation of artistic transcendence, of an emphasis on the way dissonance depends on harmony, brings us to the heart of the idea of duality that governs so much of Baudelaire's poetic project. He famously writes: "Qui parmi nous n'est pas un *homo duplex* ? Je veux parler de ceux dont l'esprit a été dès l'enfance *touched with pensiveness* ; toujours double, action et intention, rêve et réalité ; toujours l'un nuisant à l'autre, l'un usurpant la part de l'autre" (2: 87).

What Baudelaire defines as duality here can also be described as dialectical tension, an unsynthesizable movement between contrary tendencies held in suspension in a way that drives both subjectivity and esthetic production rather than shutting them down.

In fact, for Baudelaire, the entirety of the poetic project, both his own and others', depends on the impossibility of the ideal or of ever discovering or creating it within the realm of the artwork:

> Les poètes, les artistes et toute la race humaine seraient bien malheureux, si l'idéal, cette absurdité, cette impossibilité, était trouvé. Qu'est-ce que chacun ferait désormais de son pauvre *moi*, —de sa ligne brisée ? (2: 455)
>
> [Poets, artists, and the whole human race would be quite unhappy, if the ideal, that absurdity, that impossibility, were found. What would each one do from then on with his or her poor *self*, with his or her broken line?]

Again, it is not a question of dismissing the idea of unity but rather of maintaining it, in its very impossibility, as the motor of art and of esthetic subjectivity. Baudelaire often speaks in the same breath of an artist and of a human being generally, suggesting a continuity between them whereby esthetic subjectivity has particular revelatory capacity for his conception of human subjectivity more broadly. The act of mediation that marks esthetic activity is also what constitutes the relation of non-unity between subject and world, the process by which a subject comes to understand him or herself as constituted not only by the object to which he or she stands in relation but also by the impossibility of arriving at a non-mediated relationship to it:

> Dans l'être humain l'existence d'une dualité permanente, la puissance d'être à la fois soi et un autre. [...] L'artiste n'est artiste qu'à la condition d'être double et de n'ignorer aucun phénomène de sa double nature. (2: 543)
>
> [In the human being the existence of a permanent duality, the power to be all at once oneself and another. [...] The artist is only an artist on the condition of being double and of not ignoring any phenomenon of his or her doubled nature.]

From this split in the subject comes art's fundamental duality as well:

> le beau est toujours, inévitablement, d'une composition double, bien que l'impression qu'il produit soit une ; car la difficulté de discerner les éléments variables du beau dans l'unité de l'impression n'infirme en rien la nécessité de la variété dans sa composition. [...] Dans l'œuvre la plus frivole d'un artiste raffiné appartenant à une de ces époques que nous

qualifions trop vaniteusement de civilisées, la dualité se montre également ; la portion éternelle de beauté sera en même temps voilée et exprimée, sinon par la mode, au moins par le tempérament particulier de l'auteur. La dualité de l'art est une conséquence fatale de la dualité de l'homme. (2: 685–6)

[The beautiful is always, inevitably, of a double composition, even though the impression that it produces be single; for the difficulty of discerning the variable elements of the beautiful in the unity of the impression do not at all invalidate the need for variety in its composition. [. . .] In the most frivolous work of a refined artist who belongs to one of those eras that we too vainly call civilized, duality shows itself there too; the eternal portion of beauty will be at the same time veiled and expressed, if not by the mode, at least by the temperament of the author. The duality of art is a fatal consequence of the duality of man.]

As Alain Vaillant has underscored, it is Baudelaire's insistence on duality that drives his infamous rejection of nature:

Ce n'est pas que la nature soit laide ou ennuyeuse, ou que Baudelaire ne se complairait par goût que dans les villes. Mais la nature est une et simple ; elle est pour cette raison radicalement étrangère à l'homme, qui ne peut rien en faire comme artiste, sinon la considérer pour vérifier, s'il était nécessaire, son absolue différence. Le rejet de la nature n'est donc pas affaire de sensibilité [. . .] mais une nécessité artistique—vitale, qui dépasse le cadre de la raison ordinaire-- : « la première affaire d'un artiste est de substituer l'homme à la nature et de protester contre elle.» (Vaillant 78)

[It is not that nature is ugly or boring, or that Baudelaire would only take pleasure by taste in cities. But nature is one and singular; it is for that reason radically foreign to man, who can do nothing with it as an artist except to consider it in order to verify, if necessary, its absolute difference. The rejection of nature is thus not a question of sensibility [. . .] but an artistic necessity—vital, and which surpasses the frame of ordinary reason: "the first affair of an artist is to substitute man for nature and to protest against it."]

To intervene in the natural world by artistic transformation is to bring nature within the realm of the human and, fundamentally, to make it available for the kind of mediation that allows us to conceive nature both esthetically and epistemologically.[9] It is to see it as both itself and other, and in that sense, esthetic mediation allows for a dialectical interplay between singularity and plural that is implied also by Baudelaire's notion of the *homo duplex* and of the two *postulations simultanées*. As Richard Burton has indicated, in Baudelaire

> The two "postulations" are only simultaneous because they are, at root, but modalities of one single urge—the urge towards the "absolute," which is to be defined not ethically but experientially. At the heart of Baudelaire's ontology is Desire, not a desire for this or that, but Desire in, so to speak, a pure or absolute state, a primordial sense of lack or deprivation which propels both individual and species *jenseits von Gut und Böse* in its clamouring for satisfaction. (Burton 70)

Simultaneity is a way of positing an interplay between oneness and plurality, or rather of indicating that the oneness of human subjectivity is constituted by plurality. Here again, the doubles of both subjectivity and of the artwork are available simultaneously in time but unable to be articulated in its simultaneity, a fact which points to the necessity of conceptualizing the work of art in a way that helps us articulate its play of oneness and plurality via the dialectical interplay that the work of art demands. Such a temporalized process of interplay between work of art and the act of interpreting it in turn echoes the play between the eternal and the transitory that is constitutive of the modern for Baudelaire. On this view, interpretation's role is not to overcome duality but to account for it in a way that sends us back to the work of art once we realize the necessary insufficiency of conceptualization.

Andrew Bowie has brought these strands of art, historicity, ephemerality, and nature together in his reading of Adorno:

> Adorno's conception [of art] is thoroughly temporalized: the participation in art he talks of is inherently "ephemeral," in the manner that the beauty of nature is necessarily transient, and needs to be understood in new ways in differing situations. His positive relationship to "what cannot be fully grasped" puts him at odds with philosophical positions, like Hegel's in the *Aesthetics*, for which the lack of full determinacy and the fleeting nature of things in art are precisely what philosophy is supposed to overcome. For Adorno such overcoming, though, is part of what drives the "domination of nature," and art's job is to do justice to what is repressed in that domination. That is the source of the meaning expressed by art which cannot be expressed in cognitive or philosophical terms. (Bowie 155)

An esthetics such as Adorno's, then, can help us conceptualize the complexity of the subject's relation both to itself and to human and natural objects in Baudelaire, not by reducing the complexity implied by Baudelaire's perpetual doubleness but by elucidating it in a way that ultimately always sends us back to his poems themselves. Such an approach refuses a simple demystifying approach to exegesis whereby all would be accounted for, while at the same time avoiding a fall into a kind of esthetic quietism that insists on a quasi-mystical characteristic of an artwork that will forever guard its secrets. The artwork is, rather, created in the space between its mute speaking and conceptual attempts to give voice to that speech, articulating the duality between artwork of conceptualization as akin in crucial ways to the doubleness of the subject itself, which one could say assumes "form" in order to come into being as a subject in ways analogous to the form that artworks necessarily assume in order to come into existence as artworks. Articulating the meaning of the subject and the meaning of the artwork is a dialectical and therefore historically transitory task, conducted within the eternal imperative to work out those transitory articulations.

The key role of the subject, but constituted in a complex relationship to objects that is not simply one of domination or totalization, is an important point of convergence between Baudelaire and Adorno. Both insist on the importance of subjectivity in constituting esthetic and other kinds of interaction in the world while at the same time seeking to transform them in light of an alienated modernity that mandates a rethinking of subject-object relations by artworks and their conceptualizations as vehicles for maintaining a reformed subjectivity as a gesture of resistance to that alienated world. To say that the subject is to some extent determined by historical circumstance is only, on this account, further to reinforce the primacy of the subject in terms of coming to consciousness of that dialectical relationship with history. As Shierry Weber Nicholsen indicates, "Adorno insists on the subject and on living, current subjective experience as the fulcrum of any cultural analysis, recognizing at the same time that this experience in both its content and its form is subject to historical transformations that in turn cannot be grasped without reference to subjective experience" (Nicholsen 50). It is through the esthetic, for Adorno, that a subjectivity can be constituted in relation to an object without dominating it or assimilating it to itself:

> Ultimately, aesthetic comportment is to be defined as the capacity to shudder, as if goose bumps were the first aesthetic image. What later came to be called subjectivity, freeing itself from the blind anxiety of the shudder, is at the same time the shudder's own development. [. . .] Consciousness without shudder is reified consciousness. That shudder in which subjectivity stirs without yet being subjectivity is the act of being touched by the other. Aesthetic comportment assimilates itself to that other rather than subordinating it. Such a constitutive relation of the subject to objectivity in aesthetic comportment joins eros and knowledge. (AT 331)

This is a kind of unity in plurality that emerges in Baudelaire's doubleness, fully realized not in the moment of shudder but in the stage of esthetic experience that joins conceptualization to the more primal scene of shudder in order to constitute subjectivity in and through esthetic activity. Shudder operates not only in the immediacy of the experience of the artwork, which for Adorno is necessarily incomplete, but also as an interruption in the moment of necessary conceptual engagement with the work of art.

Owen Hulatt notes that "as the artwork engages and enacts a dialectical critique of concepts just as philosophy does, the art-appreciator's performative engagement with this enactment likewise results in a break being effected in their conceptual structure of experience, and results in an experience of the nonidentical: a 'shudder'" (Hulatt 188). It is in that sense that esthetics takes on, for Baudelaire as for Adorno, an epistemological dimension in that it implies a transformed relation to the world around the subject by the very process of that subject coming into being.[10] The experience of the non-identical that emerges in conceptual reflection on art thus mirrors the relationship of non-identity between the work of art and the social world from which it springs and about which it reveals something that would be inaccessible were it not precisely for this nonidentity. While Baudelaire's lyric subject may register more than he can see or articulate,[11] Adorno's esthetic theory gives us the tools to demonstrate how the Baudelairean subject is not simply stuck in this state of shock. It is by taking the artwork seriously as an artwork, as sensually embodied form, and not just as mere cultural artifact, that this insight emerges from nonidentity. Shudder, on Adorno's account, is a broader category than shock because it is at the origin not just of the trauma of the urban encounter but of any kind of subject-object relation that will go on both to cancel and maintain that initial experience of shudder without which the relation ceases to be dynamic and becomes reified and thus dead to genuine esthetic experience. Artworks are exemplifications of a nonviolent synthesis in which there exists a mutual determination of the forming concept and the sensuous manifold.

As I have begun to suggest, thinking of subjectivity this way implies an impetus, visible in both Baudelaire and Adorno, to see artworks and, in our particular case, poetry, as vehicles for a particular kind of thought, a way of thinking that conceptualization cannot quite arrive at independently. As Robert Kaufman has indicated, "for the Frankfurt School critics, lyric dramatizes with special intensity esthetic quasi-conceptuality's more general attempt to stretch conceptual thought proper; this special intensity arises from lyric's constitutive need musically to stretch conceptual thought's very medium, song, but without relinquishing any of the rigor of conceptual intellection" (Kaufman 145). For Adorno, esthetic experience is incomplete, and the fullness of the artwork unavailable, without critical reflection:

> The truth content of artworks is the objective solution of the enigma posed by each and every one. By demanding its solution the enigma points to its truth content. It can only be achieved by philosophical reflection. This alone is the justification of aesthetics. [. . .] Artworks, especially, those of the highest dignity, await their interpretation. The claim that

there is nothing to interpret in them, that they simply exist, would erase the demarcation line between art and nonart. (AT 127–8)

The other side of the coin is that philosophical interpretation, as Richter puts it, "leave[s] a remainder within the artwork that also resist[s] the translation of aesthetic form into this or that meaning"; otherwise, "the artwork would, in a sense, become superfluous" (*Thinking* 117). If such a mutual dependence of art and philosophy can sound a bit vague, it is precisely because works of art, in their autonomy, continually negotiate and reshape what exactly it would mean to understand them: "Only he understands an artwork who grasps it as a complex nexus of truth, which inevitably involves its relation to untruth, its own as well as that external to it; any other judgment of artworks would remain arbitrary. Artworks thus demand an adequate relation to themselves" (AT 262).

As Owen Hulatt has argued, for Adorno, not only do art and philosophy need each other but also that they operate according to similar patterns or structure. He notes that Adorno's assertion that "art is rationality that criticizes rationality without withdrawing from it" [AT 55] evokes his "characterization of dialectical philosophy as the unlocking of the 'nonconceptual by means of the concept, and the self-criticism of concepts'" (138).[12] Thought arrives at aporias and contradictions just as artworks do, and "it is in the frank display of these aesthetic aporias, contradictions, and internal consistencies that artworks increasingly became incapable of successfully forming flawless wholes," leading Adorno to emphasize "irruptions of disharmony" which are "the unconcealed limits of the artwork's attempt to seamlessly dominate and unify its materials" (Hulatt 178). Thus "the artwork is textually performative in the same fashion as the philosophical text, organizing its materials such that concepts are engaged and induced to fail" (Hulatt 180), which in turn carves out a uniquely important role for the active participant in the artwork or philosophical reflection:

> Adorno posits this role of the agent as necessary in order to avoid falling under the "empty gaze" of the artwork (that is, to not become like those Adorno terms the "art-alien," who are incapable of a genuine relationship to and interpretation of the artwork). Just as in the case of philosophy, art is held to have a content that is not reducible merely to its apparent phenomena, but in fact also requires the agent's own engagement. This strongly suggests that art, like philosophy, is held by Adorno to require a performative engagement from the agent in order to fully disclose its content. (Hulatt 181)

Esthetic experience and critical reflection thus enter a complex play of similarity and difference whereby they operate according to similar patterns or structures to point up moments of mutual insufficiency that can point to something like esthetic truth, often articulated negatively.

For Adorno, while esthetic truth does not remain at the level of negation, it also does not allow for transparent manifestation as definitive content either.[13] Peter Uwe Hohendahl has noted that, for Adorno, "any attempt to get close to the phenomenon in order to grasp it destroys the phenomenon" (*Fleeting* 64), evoking Adorno's remark that "those who peruse art solely with comprehension make it into something straightforward, which is furthest from what it is. If one seeks to get a closer look at a rainbow, it disappears" (AT 122). Hohendahl evokes the potentially paradoxical concept whereby "the search for the truth content as the ultimate exploration challenges the artwork as much as the enigmatic artwork challenges and potentially defeats the quest for the truth content" (*Fleeting* 65). Still, Adorno continues to speak of truth content, not despite but in fact on account of its resistance to articulation in straightforward conceptual terms.

Adorno's evocation of truth or truth content in *Aesthetic Theory* often has an aphoristic quality, more evocative than systematic, and this is part of his strategy: we are left to work out their meaning, and in that sense his pronouncements function in a way akin to the artwork, compelling the active participation of the reader in making sense of the affirmation in a way that still leaves room for what cannot possibly be said in a discursive way about the truth of the artwork. That approach is dialectical and processual rather than goal-oriented because to attempt to articulate truth definitively would be to risk a totalizing approach, or an implication that the truth is totalitarian. Adorno defends fragmentary thought in "The Essay as Form," in terms that resonate with key Baudelairean tropes:

> The customary objection that the essay is fragmentary and contingent itself postulates that totality is given, and with it the identity of subject and object, and acts as though one were in possession of the whole. The essay, however, does not try to seek the eternal in the transient and distill it out; it tries to render the transient eternal. Its weakness bears witness to the very nonidentity it had to expression. (*Notes* 1: 11)

Baudelaire's poetry, as I will have occasion to demonstrate at length, performs the non-identity of the subject and object and figures it also as the subject's non-identity to itself, embodying the kind of dissonant unity in multiplicity that Adorno identifies with a critical function of esthetic and conceptual thought. While Adorno's terms here seem at first directly to contradict Baudelaire's characterization of the function of the modern artist to "tirer l'éternel du transitoire," Adorno allows us a fuller understanding of the project of modern art as Baudelaire articulates it, by inviting reflection on the potential impossibility, within Baudelaire, of the project he himself announces. Such reflection can serve as a corrective to the way Baudelaire is sometimes understood, out of context, as announcing the drawing out of the eternal from the transitory as a mandate, whereas the text itself is far more tentative: "Il s'agit, pour [l'artiste moderne], de dégager de la mode ce qu'elle peut contenir de poétique dans l'historique, de tirer l'éternel du transitoire" ["It is a question, for [the modern artist], to detach from fashion what it can conain of the poetic in the historical, to draw out the eternal from the transitory"] (2: 694). There is, in other words, a dissonance within Baudelaire's own poetic project that does not nullify it but rather invests it with precisely the kind of tension that Adorno claims animates the modern, so that by proclaiming an impossible project, Baudelaire plays a more crucial role in modern art than if his project had been realizable.

Here we have the first sign of what we could call Baudelaire's modernity as it came later to be articulated obliquely by Adorno: he continues to use words such as "eternal" in ways that do not explicitly ironize or turn them away from their original meaning, but in ways that, in the context of his artworks, cause us to assign a new and negative valence to them by identifying the dialectical tension that had always existed between such an effort to tarry with the eternal and the way in which art's efforts to do that demonstrate nothing more than the impossibility of such a thing. It is not enough simply to eliminate or overturn such a project and such vocabulary, however. For a negation to be operative, it depends on a tension that would disappear if one of its animating terms were simply canceled, a situation which would lead to no less a one-sided or dogmatic esthetics than the conception it had sought to replace. Adorno's esthetics resists simplicity at every turn while resisting the elimination of truth from considerations of esthetics: "The truth content of artworks cannot be immediately identified. Just as it is known only mediately, it is mediated in itself. What transcends the factual in the artwork, its spiritual content, cannot be pinned down to what is individually, sensually given but is, rather, constituted by way of its empirical givennness" (AT 129). Examples abound of what we could call the eternal transience of Adorno's characterization of the truth content of the work of art. His notion of truth is one that includes the false as a key element: "Many works of the highest quality are true as the expression of a consciousness that is false in itself" (AT 129), which will mean that inasmuch as artworks can reveal the truth of falsity, they cannot "lie":

> Works unfold not only through interpretation and critique but also through their rescue, which aims at the truth of false consciousness in the esthetic appearance. Great artworks are unable to lie. Even when their content is semblance, insofar as this content is necessary semblance the content has truth, to which the artworks testify; only failed works are untrue. (AT 130)

Such truth is not to be had in a single moment or flash of realization: "The progressive self-unfolding truth of the artwork is none other than the truth of the philosophical concept" (AT 130). Such a flattening of the distinction between artistic and philosophical truth can only be tenable on the condition that neither one is completely identical to itself; it is the eternal transitoriness of the working out of the truth content of both philosophy and art that means that it will never come to rest and proceed by a relation of negation to itself, a condition Baudelaire might identify as that of the "fall" but which is the very motor of the esthetic project and the reason that art cannot simply hand over abstract truth to philosophy as a Hegelian esthetics might have it.

The "unfolding" that Adorno evokes twice in the passages I have just quoted do not, and cannot, suppose a preexisting truth content which can be unlocked if only we have the right key. Understanding this aspect of the artwork is crucial to seeing why a body of work such as Baudelaire's has been such fertile ground for endlessly changing co-creation of the work historically by the active participation of his readers. Conceptualization is, for Adorno, intrinsic to the work of art in the appeal it makes to perceivers in their role as what he terms co-enactment:

> A reflective behavior toward the work of art, I would say, is first of all nothing foreign to the work that comes from without, a philosophical behavior in the true sense. It is not the philosophy of art that first causes such reflection but rather, the co-enactment of the work of art itself. This means that this act of being in the work of art, of co-enacting it, already demands that you go beyond its mere immediacy and become aware of those aspects of the work that are not immediately evident to you as sensual elements. And there you can already see what I keep trying to convey to you from the various perspectives: that the conventional notion of the work of art as something merely sensory is not quite sufficient, but that you can only experience those works fully [. . .] not by simply observing, but always by thinking at the same time. (*Aesthetics* 127)

What Baudelaire's poetry thus invites us to do is constantly rethink the meanings we think we have arrived at, both within each poem and across poems, and both for ourselves as individual readers and as part of a particular historical moment that engages with the prior history of his reception. To do so is to recognize the fragility of the work of art and of the meanings we can make from it, which stems from the instability that comes with the eternally transient. What results is, on one hand, a convergence of art and philosophy that is as necessary as it is impossible according to Adorno, as Hohendahl underscores:

> the convergence of art and philosophy stipulated by Adorno seems to be an impossible task, since the universal element, supposedly contained by both must not be imposed on art by philosophy. In other

words, the redemption of the artwork has to come from the inside. The radical doubt must be overcome with the help of the very fragility that characterizes the artwork. This is the task that Adorno pursues energetically, and by doing so he is forced to revise both the concept of art and the idea of the truth content (not to mention their relationship). (*Fleeting* 67)

To revise the concept along these lines could be said, in the case of Baudelaire, to attempt to be faithful to the consequences of the doubleness that he affirms and performs throughout his work and to try to articulate how that doubleness plays out in ways that implicate not just esthetics but a much larger set of questions about subject-object relations and about how best to engage the work of art as it exists in the world, autonomous but also anchored in a world that it mediates and by which it is in turn mediated in ways visible in the tensions of its form once we are able to see them. The artwork is positioned in a complex relation both to the sociohistorical world from which it springs and the conceptual world to which it leads while remaining autonomous from both the world outside it and the conceptual frame of its interpreters.

Adorno's work, in its relentless insistence on this kind of autonomy that implies a relation to, rather than a separation from, the sociohistorical world in which the artwork participates via its very autonomy, can serve, in the complexity of those relations that it sketches, as an important framework for understanding the nature of Baudelaire's complexities. Adorno underscores that

> art becomes social by its opposition to society, and it occupies this position only as autonomous art. By crystallizing in itself as something unique to itself, rather than complying with existing social norms and qualifying as "socially useful," it criticizes society by merely existing, for which puritans of all stripes condemn it. [. . .] Art's asociality is the determinate negation of a determinate society. (AT 225–6)

Adorno is careful to distinguish such a view from the nineteenth-century concept of *l'art pour l'art*, with which his formulation above may have seemed to have some superficial affinities:

> Art opposes the hopelessly antiquated principle of *l'art pour l'art* not by ceding to external purposes but by renouncing the illusion of a pure realm of beauty that quickly reveals itself as kitsch. By determinate negation artworks absorb the *membra disjecta* of the empirical world and through their transformation organize them into a reality that is a counterreality, a monstrosity; this was Baudelaire's interpretation of the watchword of *l'art pour l'art* when he used it. (AT 321)

There is something intrinsic to Baudelaire's artworks, constituted within their very form, which manifests the emergence of this view of the modern artwork as neither disconnected from the world from which it emerges nor wholly infused by it. And indeed there is a tension in Baudelaire's own writings when it comes to art for art's sake. He writes in his article on Pierre Dupont: "La puérile utopie de l'école de l'*art pour l'art*, en excluant la morale, et souvent même la passion, était nécessairement stérile" ["The puerile utopia of the school of *art for art's sake*, by excluding morality, and often even passion, was necessarily sterile"] (2: 26). But in his writings on Théophile Gautier, where he borrows passages from an essay of his on Edgar Allan Poe, he affirms the autonomy of art:

> La Poésie, [. . .] n'a pas d'autre but qu'Elle-même ; elle ne peut pas en avoir d'autre, et aucun poème ne sera si grand, si noble, si véritablement digne du nom de poème, que celui qui aura été écrit uniquement pour le plaisir d'écrire un poème. [. . .] La poésie ne peut pas, sous peine de mort ou de déchéance, s'assimiler à la science ou à la morale ; elle n'a pas la Vérité pour objet, elle n'a qu'Elle-même. (2: 113)
>
> [Poetry [. . .] has no other objective than Itself; it cannot have another, and no poem will be so grand, so noble, so truly worthy of the name of poem, than the one that will have been written only for the pleasure of writing a poem. [. . .] Poetry cannot, under penalty of death or decay, assimilate itself to science or morality; it does not have Truth as its object, it has only Itself.]

Baudelaire's position itself implies a productive dissonance in this conception of poetry, one highlighted and clarified by Adorno's view of the autonomy of art whereby art can only stand in a relationship of critique to society by standing outside of it.[14] An important part of the tension or dissonance in Baudelaire's poetry is that it stubbornly resists any attempt either to reduce it to a cultural artifact, a symptom of some larger sociohistorical phenomenon, or an escape to a transcendental realm of beauty. My claim is that Adorno provides a key set of tools by which we can become more conscious readers of Baudelaire by being able to articulate the way his esthetic dissonance reconfigures our understanding of poetry by reshaping our understanding of subject-object relations broadly. Such perpetual self-consciousness on the part of readers is itself a kind of doubleness, a non-identity to the reading self which is constantly drawn to evaluate its role in the creation of meaning from an artwork that speaks only fleetingly and only paradoxically, and in ways that invite us to enter the artwork while at the same time maintaining suspicion of anything that may look like it makes a totalizing claim on us.

To "understand" Baudelaire, then, may mean not to have understood him at all; it is to stand in an implicit superiority to the split self he performs in the poetry and to refuse to be implicated along with the lyric subject who addresses us as "mon semblable, -- mon frère" (1: 6). As J.M. Bernstein puts it, "the work [. . .] appears as excessive to rationalized meaning, but nonetheless meaningful; it interrupts what we had till now considered as providing the grounds for recognition" (*Fate* 253). Interrupted absorption is, in this light, not a refusal of esthetic experience but an expansion of it, one that will send us back to the work after conceptual engagement has been exhausted. As Ulrich Plass writes:

> Adorno's phrase "knowledge of the artworks" [*Erkenntnis der Kunstwerke* (AT 347; GS 7: 516)] must be read as a double genitive: On the one hand, the artwork is something to be known (objective genitive); on the other hand, the artwork, as Adorno puts it, "participates" in knowledge (subjective genitive). Artworks are not mere objects of knowledge, things that can be known by a subject exterior to them; they are also personified "subjects" of knowledge, entities that know. This paradoxical double character is at the heart of aesthetic experience—it marks the limit of aesthetic understanding. (50)[15]

Such an approach is a deepening of engagement with the work of art that could plausibly be said to come into its own as an approach to art with the kind of complexity that is operative in Baudelaire's poetry, where the text's meaning lies not so much in its decipherment but in its invitation to account for its own particular incomprehensibility. Like Baudelaire, Adorno holds out a certain space for a transformative esthetic experience, a still accessible power of the artwork over its perceiver that somehow resists the commodification and alienation that mark so much of modern experience. As he puts it in his lectures on esthetics:

> The genuine relationship with works of art is not really one of understanding, because art categorically, by its very nature and constitution, if I may put it thus, initially contains an element of incomprehensibility; because art itself, as a piece of secularized magic, eludes any attempt to make it like ourselves and like the subject, which is what the concept of understanding essentially demands. (*Aesthetics* 124)

Thus the task of a philosophy of art for Adorno is "not so much to explain away the element of incomprehensibility, which speculative philosophy has almost invariably sought to do, but rather to understand the incomprehensibility itself" (AT 347). In that sense, the artist and the perceiver cannot remain at the level of critical reflection, for to do so would be to lose sight of the insight that critical reflection generates when it points beyond itself. Paradoxically, the artist becomes so absorbed by thought that he may be led to reject it, as Alain Vaillant underscores in the case of Baudelaire's notion of an *art pensif*:

> sa vraie nature et d'être littéralement *philo-sophique*, c'est-à-dire d'être animé de la passion de la pensée, pour être à son tour capable de la faire éprouver aussi intensément que possible. Le poète est à ce point rempli de cette passion, il l'instille si systématiquement dans toutes les fibres de son être qu'il *s'abêtit* littéralement d'intelligence. *C'est* pourquoi sa puissance philosophante est exactement proportionnelle à sa bêtise essentielle ; [. . .] « la grande poésie est essentiellement *bête*, elle *croit*, et c'est ce qui fait sa gloire et sa force » (2: 11). (Vaillant 64)

> [its true nature is to be literally *philo-sophical*, that is, to be animated by the passion of thought, to be in its turn capable make it be felt as intensely as possible. The poet is at this point filled with this passion; he instills it so systematically in all the fibers of his being that he literally *becomes stupid* from intelligence. *That* is why his philosophizing power is exactly proportional to his essential stupidity; [. . .] "great poetry is essentially *stupid*, it *believes*, and that it what makes for its glory and its power" (2:11).]

The work of art performs its operations in the dialectical space between critical reflection and the realization of the limits of that reflective activity, which sends us back constantly, stupidly, one might say, to the artwork itself.

The approach I adopt in this study owes much to the notion of constellations, a term which Adorno borrowed initially from Walter Benjamin and which plays an important role as a metaphor for the kind of non-systematic, non-linear thinking he endorses and practices. He writes in "The Actuality of Philosophy":

> philosophy has to bring its elements, which it receives from the sciences, into changing constellations, or, to say it with less astrological and scientifically more current expression, into changing trial combinations, until they fall into a figure which becomes readable as an answer, while at the same time the question disappears. The task of philosophy is not to search for concealed and manifest intentions of reality, but to interpret an intentionless reality. ("Actuality" 127)

J. M. Bernstein underscores the affinity between philosophy and art in Adorno by indicating that "constellations are philosophical 'compositions'; as such they are the philosophical equivalents of modernist works of art" (*Fate* 206). Such an approach is rich in implications for the study of Baudelaire's poetry, on a variety of scales: one can see the form and content of an individual poem, for example, as this sort of constellation, arranged to invite and compel certain kinds of interpretation based on the relative tensions and affinities of the poem's vocabulary and formal characteristics. This fundamental interpretive move involves the active participation of the reader, who assembles poems in various configurations so as to be able to posit meaning that can be constructed from the assembly, bringing the act of interpretation to bear creatively on a reality which is otherwise "intentionless." A particularly important application of the constellation in Baudelaire is also the way the poems can be reconfigured in groups and read in light of each other, whether that be the classic pairings of verse and prose versions of poems with the same title, poems that invite paired readings based on a play of thematic similarity and difference such as "Correspondances" and "Obsession," for instance, or other heterogeneous or more idiosyncratic groupings, some examples of which form the heart of my analyses in the chapters of this study. At yet a larger level, Adorno and Baudelaire's works themselves form intriguing constellations where they may be configured in ways that allow us to identify shapes and meanings that were inherent but not visible in their works when taken on their own.

Such an approach encourages us to reach across not just space but also time, as later philosophical developments such as Adorno's can not only illuminate but in their turn be illuminated by Baudelaire's poetry, an exercise that also destabilizes a sense of linear time and progression and the preeminence afforded to what comes chronologically after over what comes before. Thus a truly historicized approach to critique would see in it not just an attempt to use recent critical models in order to decode older works of cultural production but would point at the same time to the ways in which those critical models themselves emerged in part as formed by the objects of their analysis, a move which subtly disrupts a notion of a chronological relationship between artwork and critical reflection. As Gerhard Richter notes, it is crucial to ask "to what extent critique does not simply put what it criticizes behind it, but continues to be codetermined by it" (*Afterness* 44). In our case, this would be not only to ask how Adorno's thought helps illuminate Baudelaire's poetry but also how Baudelaire's poetry was a determining condition of possibility of coming to think along the lines Adorno outlines in the first place. To take esthetic experience as seriously as Adorno does is to refuse to see artworks merely as cultural production, reducible to their sociohistorical context. It is to see them as having agency when it comes to determining the ways in which they are interpreted, in an act of a temporally unfolding understanding of what is, to some extent, present in the artwork but either invisible or ineffable without an engagement with criticism. In that sense an artwork is "both inscribed in the world in which it was created and simultaneously capitalizes on the specific and each time idiomatic ways in which it refuses to be fully coextensive—which also is to say complicitous—with that very world" (Richter *Thinking* 113). Artworks are thus "enigmatic in that they are the physiognomy of an objective spirit that is never transparent to itself in the moment in which it appears" (AT 128). If they are to at least some degree more transparent via the act of a critical reflection which ultimately sends us back to the artwork in a dialectical process, it is because we as perceivers and interpreters of artworks not only establish the constellations via which the interpretations emerge but also enter the constellation ourselves as readers of both Baudelaire and Adorno.

In that sense we ground ourselves historically by not grounding ourselves in the particulars of a single time that would stand apart from defining moments of the past. Rather, an important sense of an inner life formed and informed by the work of art cannot help but be historical, but not in the sense of rooting an artwork definitively in its chronological moment but precisely by disrupting any sense of the possibility of that kind of temporal isolation and separation of a then from a now. Rather, as Michel Beistegui demonstrates in his work on esthetics:

> the place and time to which we belong, and which art can call its *own*, is not one that we *possess* or in which we were born, something that is part of what could be described as our inner life and lived experience; rather, it is the experience of the process through which we are displaced and dispossessed, alienated from the habitual, familiar world, and engulfed in a richer and more intense reality. (Beistegui 172)

On this view, art is most certainly inside time while also transcending linear conceptions of what that would mean. What Baudelaire's works can reveal when read through a focus on dissonance and subjectivity in Adorno (itself made possible and thinkable, I would argue, on account of esthetic developments in Baudelaire) is the persistence of notions such as harmony or transcendence which must at the same time be understood to mean differently than the ways in which those words generated meanings in Baudelaire's own historical moment, which both is and is not the historical moment of the poems. Baudelaire still "makes sense" to us in important ways because the time of the poems is still our time; they make sense by making *new* sense of something we thought we had perhaps understood before. The move from critical reflection back to the poems enacts that disruptive moment in reified sense-making in order to open it up to as yet unseen possibilities.

To read Baudelaire this way is to situate him historically but in a way that accounts for a kind of temporality that challenges a simple linear conception between a then and a now by seeing a dialectical relationship among the temporalities implied by the texts when they take up but reinterpret past esthetic modes, and between the time of their composition and the moment in which we read and interpret these texts whose autonomy does not preclude, but rather requires, that we play a role in the unfolding of the text's meaning by situating ourselves in a reception history. As Rita Felski has argued, "we cannot close our eyes to the historicity of artworks, and yet we sorely need alternatives to seeing them as transcendentally timeless on the one hand, and imprisoned in their moment of origin on the other" (575). It is my hope that my reading of Baudelaire with and through Adorno will help contribute to such an alternative. Seeing texts this way preserves their status, identified by Adorno, as what Felski calls "non-human actors" and allows us to create "cross-temporal networks" which "mess up the tidiness of our periodizing schemes, forcing us to acknowledge affinity and proximity alongside difference, to grapple with the [. . .] connectedness of past and present" (Felski 579). Adorno makes a similar point in an essay on Eichendorff when he writes that

> it is not the timeless Now that would be contemporary but a Now saturated with the force of the past and therefore not needing to idolize it. It is up to advanced consciousness to correct the relationship to the past, not by glossing over the breach but by wresting what is contemporary away from what is transient in the past and granting no tradition authority. (*Notes* 1: 56)[16]

What Adorno identifies as the task of "advanced consciousness" is of course synonymous with what Baudelaire claimed as the task of the modern artist. It becomes our task as well in our engagement with the work of art via what I likened at the outset to the "joie de descendre," the experience of the invigorating dialectical tension between the work of art and its interpretation, the undoing and reconfiguring of a dissonant subjectivity in and through the work of art.

Each of the chapters that follow will present a concept central to Baudelaire's writings and identify resonances between those writings and Adorno's in order then to provide close readings of key poems. Chapter 1 explores the concept of dissonance in Baudelaire's theoretical and poetic writings, arguing that it serves as a catalyst for the reformulation of lyric subjectivity. The emptying out of the lyric subject is accomplished through its dissonant relation to itself, to a person figured as object in the text, and to language itself. Drawing on Adorno's notion of dissonance as "the truth about harmony," I identify dissonance as fundamentally constitutive of the artwork for Baudelaire. Since dissonance relies on notions of harmony in order to be perceived as dissonance, I propose reading Baudelaire's poetics not as a linear progression from transcendence to disenchantment (or, formally speaking, from verse to prose) but rather as animated by the tension by which dissonance and harmony are mutually constitutive. The dissonance of the lyric subject as a "faux accord" helps delineate the complex subject-object relation in play among the poetic subject, the objects of address, the poem itself, and the reader. I examine these relationships in Baudelaire's writings on Poe, where the former's attempts to create unity in his own analysis reveal the underlying dissonance at play all the more clearly, to such an extent that the moments where Baudelaire evokes the harmony of transcendence come to seem dissonant themselves. I then turn to several poems in the Madame Sabatier cycle in *Les Fleurs du Mal*, notably "Tout entière," "Confession," and especially "Le Flacon," which I read in conjunction with "Le Chien et le flacon," showing how the dissonance that inheres in the lyric poetry, and which depends on the systems which it negates, ultimately effects a change whereby poetic subjectivity passes into the poem itself without annihilating the poetic subject.

Chapter 2 extends the discussion of dissonance to consider how Baudelaire complicates lyric subjectivity, first, by establishing it as a relation to the artwork itself and to some extent a sharing of esthetic agency. Much like the perception of dissonance which depends on the persistence of an older model of harmony, Baudelaire's reconstituted subjectivity depends on older models of subjectivity in order to define itself via negation of that older model of a unified lyric subject. Taking "L'Héautontimorouménos" as a model, I show how the Baudelaire's subject vanishes in the poem by the equivalence the poem establishes between irony and subjectivity; poems such as this one and others such as "La Fontaine de sang" do not so much perform the disunity of the self via fracture as they make manifest a split that was already there in older models but masked by the linguistic falsifications that allow us to conceal the self's disunity under the first-person "I." A reading of "Le *Confiteor* de l'artiste" forms the heart of the chapter. I argue that the dissonance at work in that poem between perceiver and landscape prompts a rearticulation of a network of relationships between an esthetic past and present, art and nature, pain and beauty, and muteness and conceptuality. The chapter concludes by considering poems that establish a dialectic of movement and stillness. I demonstrate that poems such as "Elévation," which at first glance seems to feature a post-romantic conception of the powers of the poet, actually point to the fact that poetic subjectivity depends on the impossibility of such a unified and fully perceptive lyric subject. The harmony of unmediated esthetic experience thus can be seen as inhibiting rather than sparking esthetic experience. The chapter ends with a consideration of "Le Couvercle," which appeals to objects in the poem as a vehicle for the artwork to reveal unity and harmony as a lie and thereby to liberate new ways in which the modern artwork could be said to speak. The pot lid does not replace the infinite sky as a proper esthetic subject so much as it reveals that both lid and sky are always already mediated by the lyric subject in ways that undo simple notions of lyric subjectivity and transform notions of esthetic transcendence as it does so.

Chapter 3 extends our consideration of dissonance and subjectivity by exploring the way those transformed relations also reshape the notion of transcendence in Baudelaire's poetry. By acknowledging transcendence as an effect of the poet's manipulation of language, we do not cancel it in favor of immanence, but rather show how the artwork produces its own transcendence, as an effect of language, via a renewed sense of the agency of the work of art itself that depends on a new dialectical relationship of subject and object. I show through a reading of "Je t'adore à l'égal de la voûte nocturne" how the subject-object and immanent-transcendent relationships are constructed concomitantly here via the assimilation of the love object and the sky and that those relationships are reconfigured and voluntarily confused via the act of violence that the poem stages. The poem configures a simultaneous distance and proximity of self-to-other and to the other as self that is the condition of possibility of transcendent esthetic experience. My reading of "Le Crépuscule du soir" extends the subject-object relation to the world of non-human objects, of landscape and the poem itself as mediated objects endowed with a certain agency that acts on the lyric subject and produces meanings that transcend both ordinary objects and clichéd approaches to "poetic" images in order to evoke a kind of immanent transcendence that is configured through the transformation of agency.

Taken together, I hope that these chapters show how Baudelaire maintains a conception of lyric subjectivity but reshapes the subject-object relation in ways that depend on, and spring from, his conceptual and poetic approach to dissonance. Both his poetry and his conception of art more broadly lead us to pose epistemological questions about the human subject's relation to the external world and the way art mediates and shapes perception and experience both within the work of art and beyond it. Baudelaire's reoriented subjectivity requires both the persistence and the negation of older models of esthetic transcendence in a way that reorients our understanding of subjects in their relation to objects under the sign of dissonance. Baudelaire's modernity thus consists not in simply canceling models of subjectivity and transcendence but in reorienting our understanding of the dissonance and complexity inherent in them. By historicizing Baudelaire's readings of the relationship of art and experience that came before him, in the context of our own historical position as readers, we can unlock the esthetic potential of Baudelaire's modernity that persists not despite what it negates but precisely on account of what it negates and preserves and how it does so.

1

Dissonance

Contemporary poet and critic Jean-Michel Maulpoix includes, in his characterization of Baudelaire's contributions to poetic modernity, the phenomenon of "une écriture de la discordance, de la dissonance de plus en plus accentuée. Le beau et le bien ne vont plus ensemble. Il s'agira d'extraire la beauté du mal comme de rechercher le « bizarre » et le déconcertant" ["a writing of discordance, of the most accentuated dissonance. The beautiful and the good no longer go together. It is a question of extracting beauty from evil and of seeking out the 'bizarre' and the disconcerting"] (Maulpoix, *Du lyrisme* 88). Such an affirmation, expressed as a rupture between the traditionally unified categories of the beautiful and the good, seems simple as an esthetic program; it suggests a re-envisioning of experience so as to see evil in terms of beauty, realigning the traditional categories. Much more is at stake, however, when we attempt to unravel what dissonance might mean for Baudelaire, what a dissonant writing might be, what relation it might bear to the historical circumstances in which it emerged, and what might be the exact nature of its relationship to consonance, to the poetic subject, and to the poems themselves both on their own terms and in relation to other poems in *Les Fleurs du Mal*. In this chapter I seek to elucidate what might be the consequences, in Baudelaire's esthetics and poetics, of Adorno's conception of dissonance as "the truth about harmony" by examining the ways in which dissonance is fundamentally constitutive of an important dialectical tension underlying lyric subjectivity as it plays out in the lyric subject's relationship to itself, to poetic objects (human and non-human) in the poems, and to the poem itself. I examine the tension between harmony and dissonance in Baudelaire's writings on Poe before turning to several poems in the Madame Sabatier cycle in *Les Fleurs du Mal*, concentrating most centrally on "Le Flacon."

Baudelaire evokes a dissonant subjectivity most directly and straightforwardly in the central stanza of "L'Héautontimorouménos":

Ne suis-je pas un faux accord
Dans la divine symphonie,
Grâce à la vorace Ironie
Qui me secoue et qui me mord? (1: 78)

[Am I not a discord
In the heavenly symphony,
Thanks to voracious Irony
Who shakes me and who bites me?[1]]

"Un faux accord" can be a chord out of tune, a faulty chord, or a dissonant chord, one that calls into question whether we might even call it a chord, as the echoes in the potentially equivalent term "discordant" suggests. The French term "faux" also posits a direct relationship not just between harmony and dissonance but rather between truth and falsity as well. The lyric subject is the chord that interrupts the harmony of the divine symphony, perhaps, but the evocation of harmony as metaphor also spurs readers to consider that the Western system of harmony depends on the tension that is provided by dissonance, without which there could be none of the resolution on which that harmonic system depends. On this view, dissonance is not an interruption in consonance but a necessary element within it. The very notion of dissonance invites us to reconsider the true and the false as they may pertain to elements of artworks and to entertain a potentially reversible relationship between supposed opposites such as the true and the false. To do this is to read the language of the poem in a doubled way, which is precisely the kind of reading impelled by irony, which is inscribed in this stanza as well as a causal force. The lyric subject may be discordant, or dissonant, but there may in that very dissonance be falsity that allows us to see the truth of the artwork as being what we may have thought was its falsity. Once we begin to pose these sorts of questions about the role of the modern artwork and the subjectivity that emerges from it, the very simplicity on which this stanza seems to depend in its evocation of dissonance and consonance unravels in such a way that invites us to attempt to unravel the complexity lurking in what was claimed to be simple, the dissonance that stands, unveiled by irony's doubling, as the truth of harmony.

There is already a hint of dissonance in Baudelaire's classic formulation of what it means to be modern, that is, the ability to "tirer l'éternel du transitoire" (2: 694). Baudelaire bears a complicated relationship to modernity, often evoked as one of the leading figures of poetic modernity while at the same time bearing a tendency to resist the esthetic, historical, and social worlds of his time in such a way that to be modern comes to mean, in an important sense, to be amodern or even antimodern.[2] It is not for his innovations in poetic form or versification that Baudelaire is signaled as such an important figure for poetic modernity. To be modern, in his case, is not merely to jettison the past and break out on new paths, and for those seeking to articulate what happens at the dawn of esthetic modernity at Baudelaire's historical moment, it is crucial to pay attention to the complex dynamics at play in the way he intervenes in tradition to transform it while not rejecting it. Like his approach to dissonance, it is no mean feat to attempt to enumerate the mechanisms by which his texts accomplish this, and indeed to claim to have found a simple explanation is to do violence to the never-ending task that esthetic modernity sets out for those who engage with it.

To understand the particular ways in which the dissonance of modernity might best be expressed not by modern but by amodern or antimodern poets, we can look to Theodor Adorno, whose own writings on poetry favor, as Peter Fleming has noted, conservative German poets such as George, Eichendorff, and Borchardt rather than figures such as Rilke, Brecht, and Hoffmansthal. As Fleming indicated, for Adorno, "It seems that to be modern, one must not be modern, at least as a poet" (Fleming 97). An important part of characterizing the "modern" poet is teasing out the complex relation of those poets to the society to which they often oppose themselves and yet of which they are uncontestably a part. It is tempting, but far too facile, to posit a simple antagonism between the poet and an increasingly commercial public before whom poets need to prostitute themselves by entering the market. A similarly oversimple narrative would see the claims of autonomous art as an attempt to reject society altogether, to remove poets from any sort of concern with anything other than the closed sphere of art. Rather, there is something in the form and content of poetry that is substantially transformed by modernity and poets' stance within it that goes beyond such simple binary oppositions. Adorno's reflections on dissonance and his remapping of lyric subjectivity and objectivity can fruitfully inform our readings of Baudelaire. To be faithful to Adorno's approach to art is of course not to claim that esthetic theory holds the key to a definitive interpretation. To find rest in such a privileging of theoretical reflection on art is to remain within the false and to have misunderstood art, which always surpasses attempts to understand it conceptually, and so any attempt to elucidate modern poetics in Baudelaire will always have to return to the poems, not just as they may be partially illuminated by Adorno's insights but also as they may point toward the way in which the work of art will always surpass those insights, will always remain an enigma.

Adorno's approach to lyric allows us a way beyond the dead end of an estheticism that would see autonomous art as some kind of withdrawal from the world into some purportedly pure realm of esthetic experience and cult of beauty or, in an equal and opposite reaction, as mere ideological mystification of the material conditions of poetic production and reception. As Fleming notes:

> The poet's rejection of society is its social content: the refusal to affirm what is. In so doing, the subject doesn't withdraw into a self-contained, proper self [. . .] but rather empties itself out, pours itself into language. The lyric subject sacrifices itself to the idea of language, so that language can ultimately flow back into the empty subject. Lyric is then at once the extreme of subjective expression—language saturated with the subject— and of objective language, language as pure form. (98)

Adorno's insight into the modern lyric thus circulates between the grounding concepts of dissonance and subjectivity, of a subjectivity founded on dissonance and in a dialectical relation to the object. I will have much more to say about the subject-object relation in the next chapter; my aim in this one is to identify the way dissonance serves as a catalyst for the kind of reformulation of lyric subjectivity at work in Baudelaire's poetry. The emptying out of the lyric subject happens, I will argue, via a dissonant relationship to itself, to a person figured as other or object in the text, and to language itself. That dissonance allows for a reorientation of what we mean by subject and object, making room for the poem itself to become subject rather than object, by way of the sacrifice of the poetic subject to language. While this approach has certain affinities with a Mallarméan take on poetic creation whereby the poet "cède l'initiative aux mots" ["cedes the initiative to words"] (Mallarmé 2: 211), there is a crucial next step in Baudelaire that then reconfigures the lyric subject and the poem by maintaining their subjectivity and objectivity in dialectical tension, by retaining rather than resolving the dissonance between them after having dismantled a transparent relationship between the speaking subject and its language. That divorce, that dissonance, that rift in unity, is the site of renegotiating the terrain of the poet and poem in relation to their society. The poem is not an explicit critique of that society, nor, of course, an endorsement of it; by engaging with notions of subjectivity, the poem becomes a sort of common term between the poet, who in the romantic tradition is identified with a speaking first-person subject, and the bourgeois society from which that poetics emerged, with its concomitant commitment to individual subjectivity. The dissonance between those two types of subjectivity, societal and poetic, which may actually turn out to be sprung from similar historical roots, allows us to see the lyric as an imminent critique of the society from which it springs while all the while identifying the ways in which it depends on that society, and on that dissonant relationship to it, for its very existence as lyric subjectivity.

Dissonance is, we might say, fundamentally constitutive of the artwork according to Adorno. It plays an important role from the earliest pages of *Aesthetic Theory*, as in this passage where, with a nod to Baudelaire, he identifies dissonance as a potential, if tense, connection between the artwork and the external world even, paradoxically, as the artwork retains and even intensifies its autonomy:

Dissonance, the seal of everything modern, gives access to the alluringly sensuous by transfiguring it into its antithesis, pain: an esthetic archetype of ambivalence. The source of the immense importance of all dissonance for new art since Baudelaire and *Tristan*—veritably an invariant of the modern—is that the immanent play of forces in the artwork converges with external reality: Its power over the subject intensifies in parallel with the increasing autonomy of the work. (AT 15)

For Adorno, the emphasis on dissonance in modern art and esthetics results from an increasing dissatisfaction with harmony, conventionally understood, as either an ideal or a practice:

The more deeply artworks immerse themselves in the idea of harmony, of the appearing essence, the less they can be satisfied with that idea. From the perspective of the philosophy of history it is hardly an improper generalization of what is all too divergent if one derives the antiharmonic gestures of Michelangelo, of the late Rembrandt, and of Beethoven's last works not from the subjective suffering of their development as artists but from the dynamic of the concept of harmony itself and ultimately from its insufficiency. Dissonance is the truth about harmony. (AT 110)

I will have more to say below about Adorno's claim that dissonance is the truth about harmony and about the way he shifts the discussion of dissonance away from psychological perspectives that focus on the melancholy of individuals artists on to the form and even subjectivity of the works of art themselves. For Adorno, dissonance is central to the modern artwork because "if the ideal of harmony is taken strictly it proves to be unreachable according to its own concept. Its desiderata are satisfied only when such unreachableness appears as essence, which is how it appears in the late style of important artists" (AT 110). The attainment of harmony which some would claim as an ideal of art would, on this view, cancel art entirely, since art depends on the tension between the harmonious ideal and the impossibility of its realization as one of its drivers, a characteristic most visible in those artists, and here Beethoven is a key example for Adorno, who cultivates what he terms "late style," where these tensions are made particularly visible in a way that allows us more easily to see those same tensions operating in a more subtle way in other, putatively "harmonious" works.

These artists thus allow us to have a fuller and more complex understanding not only of their own works but also of those that would initially seem opposed to them as dissonance is to harmony. The tension between a harmonious ideal and the impossibility of its realization is also what we could label a dissonance at the heart of any work, as "the truth about harmony," which Adorno also labels "the coefficient of friction in harmony itself" (AT 110). "The emancipation from this ideal [of harmony] is an aspect of the developing truth content of art," he goes on to indicate (AT 110). On this reading, an emphasis on dissonance rather than harmony, or rather on the dissonance inherent in claiming harmony as an ideal in the first place, is not a debasement of art, a renunciation of its former project, but rather its fulfillment according to its own goals. Such a view will allow for a complex account of Baudelaire's esthetic project in his poetry and prose writings; it allows us to move forward from the temptation of overly simplistic accounts of poems such as "Perte d'auréole" where the poet has lost his halo in the urban mud but is content to leave it there for some second-rate poet to find and wear. It is not that Baudelaire abandons a poetics of transcendence and harmony, forced to do so by the poet's altered status as a hawker of poetry on the market. Rather, a linear move from an earlier to a later, disenchanted poetics can be revealed to be an overly simple and inaccurate representation of Baudelaire's poetics as they emerge across his career: the earlier and later poems do not simply coexist; they are related to each other in ways far more complex than a simple linear vision of the cancelation of the earlier vision by the later, cynical one can account for. Rather than giving in to the debased taste of consumers of poetry on the open market, the dissonance that emerges not just within the later poems but also as revealed as operative in the earlier poems too is an act of resistance:

> Art, whatever its material, has always desired dissonance, a desire suppressed by the affirmative power of society with which esthetic semblance has been bound up. Dissonance is effectively expression; the consonant and harmonious want to soften and eliminate it. Expression and semblance are fundamentally antithetical. (AT 110)

It is this resistance to the affirmative power of society that allows us to see even autonomous works as just as powerful a critique as poems such as "Perte d'auréole." The autonomous artwork, always animated by dissonance, thus stands as a potential source of liberation from social unfreedom in ways that do not need to refer to reactionary approaches to removal from the world in order both to articulate a relation, as Adorno does, between art and freedom and to avoid any facile mere identification of one with the other, as opposed to a freedom that is worked out in dialectical relation to its opposite, via the dissonance that is present in any artwork if we read backward from the way "late" or "modernist" works reveal it.

On this view, the "faux accord / Dans la divine symphonie," as a figure of the poetic subject but also, by extension, as the poem itself, makes space within lyric for a dissonance (represented literally here) that leads to a reconfigured understanding of the relations among the poet, the poetic subject, the poem, the society in which the poet operates, and our own time insofar as we stand in a relationship of continuity or dissonance with Baudelaire's day. The "faux accord" invites a reconsideration of the nature of the subject-object relations among all of the categories of poet, poetic subject, poem, and readers. Dissonance lays out the complexity of these relationships, not least because it points to the fact that there is a dissonance inscribed within harmony as the necessary condition of it, and it at the same time helps us take a first step toward attempting to articulate the relationship of dissonance to harmony and the transformation of esthetics that lies in potential there. Adorno can orient our analysis in a way that pays attention to poetic form as the site of transformation of resistance and autonomy that he advocates. This is, as Mario Farina has indicated, a crucial aspect of Adorno's contribution to our understanding of modern esthetics:

> Already the age of Baudelaire conceived the disturbing element of art as a reaction to the alienated condition of the subject [. . .]. What is groundbreaking in Adorno's theory is the reframing of dissonance—and of all the negative aesthetic categories in general—as means to understanding the relationship between form and content. Dissonance, in fact, should not be seen as a divergence of form and content, as the previous aesthetic tradition would have it, but rather as the way in which the historical content formally sediments itself at the age of the universalization of social suffering. (Farina 72)

Adorno thus, a bit paradoxically perhaps, preserves the notion of the unity of form and content from a more traditional esthetics in order to reorient the kinds of conceptualization of the work of art that might follow from that unity:

> the work of art always produces the identity of form and content—to the point that "form" is "sedimented content" and it is therefore impossible to separate them—despite the fact that sometimes—namely, in modernity—that sedimentation can be executed only by means of disharmony and dissonance, as the unreconciled world cannot be aesthetically sublimated through harmony. (Farina 73)

As Farina suggests here, the status of unity is at stake, but not because of a modernist attempt to fracture the unity of form and content. Rather, unity persists as a category but is subject to a shifted configuration. The issue is not with unity but rather with what we may have taken unity to mean in older forms of esthetics. As Albrecht Wellmer has noted:

> What is rendered problematic is rather a *type* of unity and all-embracing meaning, which in the era of great bourgeois art was represented by both the unity of the self-contained work and the unity of the individual

ego. The aesthetic enlightenment discovered both in the unity of the traditional work of art and in the unity of the bourgeois subject is something violent, unreflected, and inauthentic: i.e., a type of unity that is only possible at the price of the suppression and ostracism of things disparate, non-integrable, and repressed. What is at issue here is the "inauthentic" unity of a fictitious totality of meaning, analogous to the totality of meaning represented by a cosmos created by God. (Wellmer 103)

Attention to one kind of unity (between form and content), then, reveals the dissonance always already present in the purported unity in the bourgeois subject as that subject is constructed through art forms such as that of the lyric. Totality and totalizing meanings, as they can be aligned with notions of esthetic unity and harmony, are themselves shown to be fictitious, to stand in a dissonant relation to their own ideals of unity by having a false claim to unity.

What an approach such as Adorno's does is to reveal the unraveling of the unity of work, meaning, and self simultaneously, and to show meanwhile, again paradoxically perhaps, that work, meaning and self are in fact intimately united such that an unraveling of one will yield the undoing of all three. Harmonious unity of self is revealed, as Wellmer indicates, to involve "something violent," an imposition of a disingenuous unity that forces the false to take the place of the true, and which is only revealed as such by reading dissonance in the context of an ideal of harmony that it supplants in the history of the development of the arts in the modern period. Form is inseparable from the history of perceiving artworks, for Adorno. As he writes of music: "No chord is simply 'in itself' false, because no chord exists in itself and because each chord bears in itself the whole, indeed the whole of history" (*Philosophy* 33). The unity of the work of art, if we are able to refer to such a thing at all, necessarily contains the dissonance between its localized moments and the tensions between those and the individual work as well as the networks of individual works in an artist's oeuvre as they in turn exist in the sociohistorical context that gives them meaning. So while violence may be "estheticized" in Baudelaire, in verse poems such as "A celle qui est trop gaie" and "Une martyre" and prose poems such as "Le Gâteau," "Assommons les pauvres," and "Le Mauvais vitrier" among many others, that very estheticization is, on Adorno's view, already linked to political stakes by its way of liberating the approach to dissonance that would reveal false unity to involve "the suppression and ostracism of things disparate, non-integrable, and repressed."[3] This is a point where Adorno's esthetics and his characterization of subjectivity join his larger political critique of knowledge as domination in *Dialectic of Enlightenment*, not by way of studying explicitly political art or by viewing art sociologically, but, rather, by articulating the inherently political consequences of subjectivity and autonomy inherent even in forms of art that resist explicit thematization of politics.

As I have been suggesting, an approach to Baudelaire that concentrates on dissonance allows us to avoid the temptation of seeing in his work a linear progression whereby to be the initiator of modernism in verse would be to move from an older model of poetics influenced by romanticism and focused on transcendence toward a disenchanted fascination with the new, the urban, and the material. Such an approach, ironically, reproduces the very sort of linear temporal logic that Baudelaire himself seeks to undo on account of its association with notions of linear temporal progress which he rejects. An approach to Baudelaire that challenges linear movement over the course of his works does not seek to identify some kind of timeless eternity in them but, rather, articulates, through dissonance as a revealer of dialectical tension, the way in which older esthetics remain in play across all of his works, transformed by the new in ways that make the older and newer esthetic visions inseparable from each other, since neither would be fully interpretable without the other. To articulate not only *what* remains of the older esthetic but exactly *how* it remains, how it is in play but transformed by contact with the new, is one of the main tasks of the interpreter of Baudelaire. This is not to say that such an interpretation will have a tidy account of this to offer; rather, an effective interpretation will allow us to see the way in which Baudelaire's texts themselves pose (rather than answering) those questions of the dissonant, the modern, and so on.

These considerations lead us to reevaluate common notions of harmony as synonymous with consonance and to see it instead, in the more musically appropriate sense, as the mutually dependent interaction of consonance and dissonance, whereby dissonance is only identifiable and able to be labeled as such by an appeal to consonance. I propose to illustrate this reevaluation by considering Baudelaire together with Ludwig van Beethoven. When compared to his long essay on Richard Wagner, Baudelaire's engagement with Beethoven, via a few references throughout his works, seems scarce. Those references become particularly meaningful, though, when we examine Baudelaire and Beethoven through their shared concern with dissonance. I hope to elucidate the way modern poetry and music function as interrelated signifying practices through the question of dissonance. Both Baudelaire and Beethoven, whose contemporary publics struggled to read, hear, and understand their works on account of purportedly unacceptable treatment of dissonance, complicate what we understand dissonance to be. Dissonance, on this view, depends on consonance in order to be perceived at all, a fact which allows us to read the history of music and poetry not just forward in terms of a break but also backward. Baudelaire's approach to dissonance is both new and dependent on long-standing understandings of dissonance and harmony, and that Adorno's writing on dissonance, in conjunction with Baudelaire's, can make us attentive to the dissonance that operates within harmony rather than standing opposed to it.

Adorno famously writes in *Aesthetic Theory* that "dissonance is the truth about harmony" (110). One important aspect of this claim is that it invites us to reconsider what can come, through centuries of accretion, to seem "natural" in music, to the extent that harmonic consonance becomes the norm and dissonance is seen as an aberrant sonority to be carefully managed and resolved into consonance through a development that comprises forward-driven harmonic motion. As Asaf Angermann notes, Adorno's proposition points to the way in which dissonance

> exposes the lie, or the blind spot, in the ideal of harmony itself, which "proves to be unreachable according to its own concept" (AT 110). [. . .] The dissonant breakdown of the mechanism of pleasure based on recurrence and identification, then, literally emancipates the ear, the senses, from the authority of musical norms and melodic conventions. Once the lie is epistemologically exposed, repressive pleasure loses its appeal; the truth about illusory harmony is incorporated into esthetic experience itself and turns ethical and political in a liberating way. (270)

Beyond this interrogation of the natural that also carves out new routes to the ethical via the aesthetic, there is another implication of this idea that sheds light on Baudelaire's aesthetic project and illustrates an important continuity between that aesthetic production and its continuing dialogue with attempts to bring conceptual approaches to esthetics to bear on it. I refer here to the way that Adorno's formulation allows us to see a dialectical relationship of mutual dependence between dissonance and harmony: either of those terms is only intelligible within the context of the other, and that consonance would cease to have any meaning whatsoever without the dissonance that allows it to constitute itself:

> Only in tension with consonance is dissonance possible; it is transformed merely into a multitone complex as soon as it ceases to stand in opposition to consonance. This would, however, be to oversimplify the situation. For in simultaneously sounding tones dissonance is transcended only in Hegel's double sense of the word, that is, both canceled and preserved. (Adorno *Philosophy* 67)

For Adorno as for Baudelaire, it is not a matter of giving new priority to dissonance by exposing harmony as dissonance but rather of coming to a new understanding of the way the two are imbricated and the way in which articulating that relationship may lead, not to a new valorization of one term over the other, nor even simply a new understanding of what harmony or dissonance is, but rather an articulation of their mutually constitutive relationship.

This is to say that conceiving dissonance as the truth about harmony yields new ways of hearing formerly familiar sounds in ways that have the potential to reveal what was already there in the musical material but blocked from our perception by sedimented, culturally determined ways of hearing.[4] As Adorno notes:

> There are modern compositions that occasionally intersperse tonal sounds in their own nexus. In these instances it is the triads that are cacophonous, not the dissonances. As proxy for the dissonances these triads may sometimes be justified. But it is not merely the stylistic impurity that is responsible for their falsity. Rather, today, the technical horizon against which the tonal sounds detestably obtrude encompasses the whole of music. (32–3)

Adorno's claim is not an attempt to impose sociological conditions on the work of art but rather to delineate the range of options available to us to hear the music, to do justice to the work of art for its own sake by being attentive to the ways in which certain forms of listening are available to us or not at any particular time. What emerges here is that harmony and dissonance are not absolutes, and that they are mutable to the point where what had been perceived as harmony can in other contexts be perceived as dissonant. In the case of the tonal triads that Adorno evokes, they cannot be perceived as otherwise than dissonant given the shifted context in which they appear, in which they violate the norms of the system within which they operate in ways that force listeners to reevaluate where the "harmony" lies.

This is true within the structural harmonic logic of a piece of music but also in the context of historical shifts in the way we perceive music of the past. Listening to the music of the past is not a mere exercise in attempting to recreate the conditions in which its first listeners might have experienced the music; rather, it is to hear the music in a way that is, paradoxically, new, but always already inherent in the music but only gradually, historically, revealed as a viable way to hear the music. Thus Mozart's music becomes an important example for Adorno of the way harmony can sound as, and actually be, dissonance:

> Contradiction vibrates through [art's] most remote mediations, just as the din of the horrors of reality sounds in music's most extreme pianissimo. Where faith in culture vainly sings the praises of music's harmony, as in Mozart, that harmony sounds a dissonance to the harsh tones of reality and has them as its substance. [. . .] Only through the transformation of something that is in any case preserved in negative form, the contradictory, does art accomplish what is then betrayed the moment it is glorified as a Being beyond what exists, independent of its opposite. (Adorno *Notes* 2: 249)

Listening to Mozart this way means revising what we may have thought we knew about harmony; it is to hear the consonant harmonic structures as dissonant, as containing within themselves the potential to sound dissonant while remaining, acoustically speaking, the same sounds. It is a question not of redefining what constitutes a dissonant sonority as of how we understand the relationship between dissonance and harmony to begin with, and it is here that Baudelaire can be read, not in light of Adorno, but coextensively with him, as a creator of the kind of art that has the potential to spark the kind of transformations in the aesthetic sensorium that Adorno is describing.

Like Beethoven and other composers who draw on, but fundamentally transform, the tradition in which they are working, Baudelaire does not simply reject or abandon notions of harmony in favor of a proto-modernist aesthetics of dissonance. Rather, the coexistence of evocations of transcendent idealism with other poems that valorize alienation, fragmentation, and shock invites readers to read the transcendent idealism differently, as perhaps containing its own lie in ways akin to what Adorno evokes in his comments on Mozart. And here we begin to glimpse the way Baudelaire's aesthetic vision, not unlike that of late Beethoven, complicates notions of harmony and dissonance by inscribing harmony within the dissonance itself. The presence of what we might term the harmony of transcendent idealism is what constitutes the dissonance we can identify between that late romantic vision and the new aesthetics of fragmentation. It is not that dissonance replaces harmony but rather that the harmony is a key component of that dissonance, that the dissonance could not be identified as such without the enduring presence of a vision of what has been labeled "harmony." The harmony gradually comes to be perceived as dissonant, so that Baudelaire's poetry calls for, and indeed mandates, a rethinking of our understanding of harmony and dissonance, not so that we can dismiss the latter as false and abandon it, but rather so we can better understand the dialectical relationship between the two terms in ways that force a redefinition of what we thought we understood about harmony and its relationship to dissonance. That is the epistemological work that necessarily happens not within the experience of work of art or the philosophical conceptualization of it alone, but rather in the mutually completing gestures of both.

Such reevaluation of harmony and dissonance is not a later accretion being read back into Baudelaire but is, rather, active in his own understanding of those terms. A crucial angle on the question of harmony and dissonance in Baudelaire is his use of the term "harmony" as a category that is not synonymous with consonance, and which has the potential to include dissonance within it. As Margery Evans (1988) indicates:

> Baudelaire's understanding of the term *harmony* seems on the whole to have been close to the original Greek sense of the word as *assemblage*. But this notion of combination implicit in harmony has frequently been

neglected by critics of the *Petits Poèmes*, who have loosely opposed 'harmony' to 'dissonance' as though the two were antithetical. [. . .] In musical terms harmony does not preclude dissonance, being concerned with the relationship between several superimposed notes, including concords and discords.

Whilst it would be wrong to convey the impression that Baudelaire's statements about harmony at different periods in his career are all perfectly consistent, it is equally misguided to suggest that the sudden shifts of tone so frequent in is later works imply an outright contradiction of his earlier theories. (Evans 318)

The difference across periods involves a shift away from an early emphasis on the individual imagination, which Evans nonetheless argues "could easily accommodate a new stress on dissonance, which would reflect the satanic quality of the modern artists' temperament" (318).[5] Rather than seeing a linear progression where we perceive Baudelaire's position as gradually accommodating dissonance, it is more effective, I would argue, to see his work as complicating the ways in which we understand what dissonance and harmony are, taking our cue from Baudelaire himself when he moves us toward the modern via an older sense of the word harmony as assemblage. To see harmony as assemblage is not necessarily to posit some overarching unity that would subsume dissonance and consonance alike under a larger sense of organic form, but at the same time nothing precludes that approach from remaining operative even as dissonance and fragmentation come to the fore to challenge prior notions of aesthetic unity.

The refusal to craft a poetics that would seek to resolve such tensions is an essential aspect of what Baudelaire brings to modern aesthetics, and the impact of such a tension would be significantly lessened if his approach were simply to cancel prior notions of harmony and unity as opposed to putting them into dynamic aesthetic and historical tension. The dissonant elements in Baudelaire's critical writings and poetry are both of his historical moment and outside it, prefiguring as they do tendencies that guide modernist artistic production and theorizing for which Baudelaire would retroactively be seen as an inaugural figure. In this sense Baudelaire is close to Beethoven in his late style, which, as Edward Said has described it, is "too late for the times, in the sense of superseding or transcending them" (Said 300). Commenting on this remark, Nathan Waddell reminds us that "if this music is 'belated' in the fashion Said claims, it is also the case that this is music peculiarly cognizant of its own place *in* time" (Waddell 170). That is to say that, for both Baudelaire and Beethoven, part of being in one's own time is to be beyond it. One important consequence of this is what Françoise Meltzer has termed Baudelaire's double vision by which "he does not see what he nonetheless records" (Meltzer 8):

> His crisis [. . .] consists in being unable to experience the present. [. . .] Baudelaire's crisis is the rejection of modernity in the sense of the new at the expense of memory. He may talk of *le moderne* and be enraptured by the productions of contemporary art and literature; but he emphatically neither wants nor acknowledges the erasure of the past. (241)

Recording a present historical and aesthetic moment without being able, from within the moment, to identify its full impact is what leaves space open for the kind of theorizing that critics such as Adorno offer, a critical perspective that allows us to see points of commonality between Baudelaire and Beethoven that go beyond what the poet himself explicitly states yet which are there for the finding in his writings.

It is within the framework of a dialectical approach to dissonance that I would like to examine a productive point of commonality between Baudelaire and Beethoven. Baudelaire's references to Beethoven are few.[6] One of them appears in Baudelaire's essay on Théodore de Banville in *Réflexions sur quelques-uns de mes contemporains* (1861): "Beethoven a commencé à remuer les mondes de mélancolie et de désespoir incurable amassés comme des nuages dans le ciel intérieur de l'homme" ["Beethoven began to stir up the modes of melancholy and incurable despair that were amassed like clouds in the interior sky of man" (Baudelaire, *Œuvres complètes* 2: 168). The comment comes in a brief discussion of common characteristics among the arts at the time; Baudelaire underscores a similar tendency in Maturan, Byron, and Poe. Baudelaire opposes this new tendency in art to another conception of beauty that had come before: "Jusque vers un point assez avancé des temps modernes, l'art, poésie et musique surtout, n'a eu pour but que d'enchanter l'esprit en lui présentant des tableaux de béatitude, faisant contraste avec l'horrible vie de contention et de lutte dans laquelle nous sommes plongés" ["Up until a rather advanced point in modern times, art, poetry, and above all music, had no other goal than to enchant the mind by presenting it with tableaux of beatitude, contrasting with the horrible life of contention and struggle in which we are plunged"] (2, 168). Jocelynne Loncke has signaled that Baudelaire's comment on Beethoven represents a commonplace about him at the time, noting the similarity to a formulation about Beethoven by E. T. A. Hoffman (Loncke 30). It suggests a view of Beethoven as romantic hero, remarkable for the depth of negative feeling he is able to unearth and, presumably, inspire listeners to unearth as well. I would claim that while Baudelaire puts his finger on Beethoven as a key figure in understanding a crucial shift in the structure, role, and perception of art, the essay, in its emphasis on melancholy, does not quite fully name in what that shift consists; we might say that Baudelaire registers it without seeing it.

The consternation that Baudelaire identifies by noting the accusation of depravation goes far beyond a mere question of psychological disturbance and melancholy, however, as a broader consideration of Baudelaire's treatment of dissonance elsewhere in his writings can illuminate. In his passing reference to Beethoven, he registers, without naming it precisely, an important shift common to both music and poetry that has to do with dissonance. Rather than abolishing classical notions of harmony, dissonance in fact depends on the preservation of classical notions of harmony in order to be perceived as dissonant, and thus to be perceived as meaningful in that way. A glance at Adorno's remarks on Beethoven makes this point with reference to Beethoven specifically and can prove insightful for understanding Baudelaire's dialectical engagement with dissonance in relation to its still-present historical past:

> Expression in music is valid within its "system," and hardly ever unmediated in its own right. The enormous expressive power of dissonance in Beethoven [. . .] is effective only within this tonal complex and with this array of chords. With more extensive chromaticism it would be rendered impotent. Expression is mediated by the language and its historical stage of development. In this way, the whole is contained in each of Beethoven's chords. And precisely this makes possible the final *emancipation* of the individual element in the late style. (Adorno *Beethoven* 58)[7]

Adorno underscores the paradoxical fact that in twentieth-century music it is not fully possible to experience dissonance *as* dissonance in the same way that we can in earlier music where the tension between consonance and dissonance within functional tonality is maintained. The emancipation of dissonance is thus, in an important sense, the cancellation of dissonance. As he writes in *Sound Figures*:

> This preestablished disharmony makes it very hard to create the configurations that transmit tension. The model here lies, above all in intervals of tension like the major seventh or the minor ninth, which have ceased to be taboo or to induce panic in the citizenry but have driven out the consonant intervals. In the process, however, they scarified their own tension, and since they enjoy equal rights with every other interval, they have been neutralized along with them. But if they have ceased to impart any tension, by the same token they no longer allow the composer to impart any tension to them: this loss of tension dates back to the condition of a material that has divested itself of tension. [. . .] The absence of inner tension converges with the loss of artistic independence; where spontaneity finds itself paralyzed in sheer obedience to standards once achieved, the work simply accepts solutions passed in to it from ready-made material instead of producing them itself. (*Sound* 179–80)[8]

An essential element of commonality between Beethoven's music and Baudelaire's poetry, then, is that their very modernity depends on their being anchored in a dialectical tension with the system of literally or figurative harmony which precedes them and which they do not simply cancel in their work. For Adorno, maintaining that tension is essential in order to avoid any false notion of synthesis or reconciliation, either within the music itself or within the society into which art provides key insight:

> Classicism and Romanticism can only be reconciled, if at all, through their extremes. But even then the idea of a synthesis has its repugnant side, namely the hope that unity and peace can be achieved in art, even though they missed their moment in reality. Music that aims at reconciliation is at its most sensitive when confronted by the illusion of reconciliation [. . .]. What is wanted is not a peacefulness above all conflicts, but the pure, uncompromising representation of absolute conflict. (*Sound* 122)

Thus what Beethoven and Baudelaire force us to reconsider is not just what dissonance is but the very conditions under which we are able to perceive it at all, its inscription in a system of harmony that depends on dialectical tension. As with the theological system on which Baudelaire depends via his idiosyncratic engagement with God and Satan in his poetry, notions of harmony are maintained in his work all the better to allow the dissonance to operate.[9] Rather than being a question of a demonic reversal, or a simple leap out of the logic of the theological opposition between good and evil, Baudelaire's poetry forces a reconsideration of what we understand by those terms and how they could continue to operate under the changing conditions of modernity. The same could be said of Baudelaire's discussions of harmony and dissonance, virtually all of which appear in the metaphorical context of their application to poetry, and it is to these discussions that I now turn in order to illustrate how they help to elucidate the way his poetics catalyzes a rethinking of the relationship of harmony to dissonance.

In the *Notes nouvelles sur Edgar Poe* (1857) Baudelaire turns to questions of dissonance in the context of the threatened unity of the work of art. He identifies the supremacy of the imagination for Poe but describes it as "une faculté quasi divine qui perçoit tout d'abord, en dehors des méthodes philosophiques, les rapports intimes et secrets des choses, les correspondances et les analogies" ["a quasi-divine faculty that perceives first of all, outside philosophical methods, the intimate and secret relations of things, correspondences and analogies"] (2: 329). The short story facilitates this kind of perception because it can be read in one sitting, and the mark of a well-crafted story is, for Baudelaire, a sense of the unity of structure on the part of the writer which can be perceived by the reader: "Dans la composition tout entière il ne doit pas se glisser un seul mot qui ne soit une intention, qui ne tende, directement ou indirectement, à parfaire le dessein prémédité" ["In the entire composition, not a single word must slip in that is not an intention, that does not tend, directly or indirectly, to perfect the premeditated design"] (2: 329). The greater variety of tones and rhythmic freedom of the story give it an aesthetic advantage even over poetry: "Ce genre de composition qui n'est pas situé à une aussi grande élévation que la poésie pure, peut fournir des produits plus variés et plus facilement appréciables pour le commun des lecteurs" ["this genre of composition, which is not situated at as high an elevation as pure poetry, can furnish the most varied and easily appreciable products for common readers"] (2: 330). Baudelaire goes on specifically to identify this greater set of tones and techniques with dissonance: "L'auteur d'une nouvelle a à sa disposition une multitude de tons, de nuances de langage, le ton raisonneur, le sarcastique, l'humoristique, que répudie la poésie, et qui sont comme des dissonances, des ouvrages à l'idée de beauté pure" ["the author of a novella has at his disposition a multitude of tones, nuances of language, the reasoning tone, the sarcastic, the humoristic, that poetry repudiates, and which are like dissonances, affronts to the idea of pure beauty"] (2: 330). To what extent can we uphold an older notion of *beauté pure* in the wake of the new set of techniques and greater range of artistic expression that Baudelaire evokes here? A lot rides on the "like" in "like dissonances": Is this a straightforward indication of a metaphor borrowed from music in order to describe literary technique, or are there other ways to speak about what might be perceived as "like dissonances"? Do these dissonances expand the potential range and scope of harmony? The answer is entirely dependent on the reader's take on whether "pure beauty" is to be upheld as a desirable universal in the classical sense or expanded in order to come upon a new kind of beauty not marred by, but rather enacted through, the multitude of nuances that are "like" dissonances.

One could say that Baudelaire's text on Poe is itself dissonant in its attempt to defend a classic view of the unity of the successful artistic work while also making room for the new. That defense of the new is itself a kind of dissonance within a theory of unity, and thus the critical text begins to mirror the poetic text on which it comments. The notion of unity as an aesthetic value is simultaneously underscored and undermined, forcing an interpretive move that requires evaluating whether "dissonances" in either the critical or poetic text interrupt unity, despite Baudelaire's suggestions to the contrary, or whether they invite a redefinition of unity that accounts for dissonance. To redefine unity that way would, however, also require a reevaluation of what we mean by dissonance, since a dissonance that is then subsumed into unity can hardly be said to be a dissonance in the usual sense, and as such it risks losing any meaning whatsoever. Encompassing the dissonance within a posited higher sense of unity would be to destroy the tension between harmony and dissonance on which this very approach to the work of art depends. He calls unity "la condition vitale de toute oeuvre d'art" ["the vital condition of all works of art"] (2: 332), which he qualifies by indicating that he is not referring to "l'unité dans la conception" ["unity in the conception"] but rather "l'unité dans l'impression, de la *totalité* de l'effet" ["unity in the impression, the *totality* of the effect"] (2: 332). Since Baudelaire remains invested in this higher sense of unity, his theory risks minimizing the radical aesthetic potential of dissonance, which is an unusual position to be in for a poet frequently acclaimed as inaugurating modern poetics. Thus I would claim that a new form of dissonance emerges in this text at the level of aesthetic theory which, in order to remain vital, needs to maintain its implicit tension rather than resolving it.

It is here that a more developed look at the passage in Adorno that contains his claim about dissonance as the truth about harmony can shed light on the tensions I have begun to enumerate in Baudelaire's esthetic theory. Adorno's claim is that what is called harmony in the work of art is always something else: "What is achieved [in the work of art] is never aesthetic harmony but rather polish and balance; internal to everything in art that can justly be called harmonious there survives something desperate and mutually contradictory" (*AT* 109). Artworks therefore operate on a necessary, but impossible, attempt to smooth over contradiction, which brings them closer to the realm of the false:

> According to their internal constitution, artworks are to dissolve everything that is heterogeneous to their form even though they are form only in relation to what they would like to make vanish. They impede what seeks to appear in them according to their own a priori. They must conceal it, a concealment that their idea of truth opposes until they reject harmony. Without the memento of contradiction and nonidentity, harmony would be aesthetically irrelevant. [. . .] The more deeply artworks immerse themselves in the idea of harmony, of the appearing essence, the less they can be satisfied with that idea. (AT 109–110)

Adorno explicitly cites late Beethoven, along with late Rembrandt and Michelangelo, as examples of artists who illustrate this uncovering of dissonance as the truth of harmony, not on account of the "subjective suffering of their development as artists" but via "the dynamic of the concept of harmony itself and ultimately [. . .] its insufficiency" (110). It is thus not that art is false but rather that an emphasis on harmony leads us away from the truth content of art, whereas an emphasis on dissonance can restore a sense of that truth content which harmony cannot help but distort.

It is thus to a sort of listening beneath the surface of the artwork, and by extension of the critical work as well, that Adorno summons us. A critical ear attentive to the ways harmony has the potential to cover over dissonance comes to see how in supposedly harmonious works "corporeal form presents what is not reconciled as reconciled and thereby transgresses the very postulate of the appearing essence at which the idea of harmony aims. The emancipation from this ideal is an aspect of the developing truth content of art" (AT 110). Art and critical reflection on it are thus always engaged in reevaluating truth and lie in relation to harmony and dissonance and, by extension, a reevaluation of a sense of unity that is prompted, as musicologists such as Daniel Chua have argued, by works such as the late quartets of Beethoven, whose logic is one of "structured disruption" which "forces analysis away from the allowed concept of unity toward paradox, ambiguity, and disconnection" (Chua 5). One important consequence of this shift toward a "coexistence of these contradictory elements [i.e., unity and disunity]" is that "the work will never quite coincide with itself—the ideas cannot be fully grasped within a unified framework, even through the totalizing tendency of analysis" (AT 106).

With this perspective in mind, we can turn back to Baudelaire's text on Poe to see the way in which his own attempts to create unity in his own analysis reveal the underlying dissonance all the more clearly. For if Adorno links dissonance directly to the truth of the work of art taken on its own terms—Adorno had claimed, immediately before the passages I have cited above, that "no work of art [. . .] is directed toward an observer, [. . .] no artwork is to be described or explained in terms of the categories of communication" [AT 109]—Baudelaire attempts to exclude truth from the consideration of the artwork entirely. As we have already seen, he writes that "la poésie ne peut pas, sous peine de mort ou de défaillance, s'assimiler à la science ou à la morale; elle n'a pas la Vérité pour objet, elle n'a qu'Elle-même. [. . .] L'Intellect pur vise à la Vérité, le Goût nous montre la Beauté, et le Sens moral nous enseigne le Devoir" ["Poetry cannot, under pain of death or weakness, assimilate itself to science or morality; it has only Truth as its object, only itself. [. . .] Pure Intellect aims at Truth, Taste shows us Beauty, and the Moral Sense teaches us Duty"] (2: 333). Baudelaire's attempt to impose classical order in his tripartite division of the good (masquerading in classical garb as duty here), the true, and the beautiful could be seen as an attempt to smooth over the dissonance inherent in such neat categorizations and to resist what would presumably be the contamination of one of these areas by the other. And yet to deny truth value to the work of art arguably robs it of a key aspect of its value. While Baudelaire is presumably arguing against the tendency of some literature to present philosophical concepts barely disguised as literature, Adorno's analysis suggests a different way of conceiving the relationship of art to truth that has nothing to do with presenting philosophical concepts in artistic form but rather affirming a kind of truth specific to the work of art that criticism is insufficient, on its own, to elucidate. Such a reconception of truth is consistent with Baudelaire's own aesthetic theory and practice but in ways that can only be presented as a dissonance in Baudelaire's text because he is still operating, at least on the surface, with a conception of classical unity that can make no explicit room for dissonance as truth.

The three domains are both separate and connected, a position that introduces a dissonance that gives the lie to the conception of harmony that would see them as distinct. Dissonance becomes a term in the dichotomy of virtue and vice, but the introduction of dissonance is itself a dissonant note in the supposedly unified system that Baudelaire is attempting to defend, one which would claim to see art as its own domain that does not intersect with truth:

> Le vice porte atteinte au juste et au vrai, révolte l'intellect et la conscience; mais, comme outrage à l'harmonie, comme dissonance, il blessera plus particulièrement certains esprits poétiques ; et je ne crois pas qu'il soit scandalisant de considérer toute infraction à la morale, au beau moral moral, comme une espèce de faute contre le rythme et la prosodie universels. (2: 334)

> [Vice undermines the just and the true, revolts the intellect and the conscience; but as an offense against harmony, as dissonance, it will more particularly wound certain poetic spirits; and I do not think it scandalous to consider all infractions against morality, to the morally beautiful, as a kind of sin against universal rhythm and prosody.]

Baudelaire now brings together what he had claimed to separate, and establishes a division between harmony and dissonance rather than an expanded characterization of harmony that could include it. He goes on to develop this view of poetic harmony in ways that ultimately end up framing this classical and transcendent portrayal of poetic beauty as itself dissonant with the more complex view of beauty he had already offered. He marshals both music and poetry as revelatory of eternal splendor, via an effective, psychologizing response:

> C'est à la fois par la poésie et *à travers la* poésie, par et *à travers* la musique que l'âme entrevoit les splendeurs situées derrière le tombeau; et quand un poème exquis amène les larmes au bord des yeux, ces larmes ne sont pas la preuve d'un excès de jouissance, elles sont bien plutôt le témoignage d'une mélancolie irritée, d'une postulation des nerfs, d'une nature exilée dans l'imparfait et qui voudrait s'emparer immédiatement, sur cette terre même, d'un paradis révélé. (2: 334)

> [It is at once by and *through* poetry, by and *through* music that the soul glimpses the splendors situated beyond the grave; and when an exquisite poem brings tears to the eyes, these tears are not the proof of excess enjoyment but rather the proof of an irritated melancholy, a postulation of the nerves, a nature exiled from the imperfect and would like immediately to seize, on this very earth, a revealed paradise.]

Here the affective realm of melancholy is conjoined with metaphysical concerns that suggest that the melancholy stems from the inaccessibility of full transcendence. What a presumably harmonious music or poetry gives rise to here is its own lie; by the reader or listener's participation in making meaning from the artwork, the lie of harmony is revealed through the perception of dissonance revealed as metaphysically infused melancholy presumably akin to the kind that Beethoven was said to stir up. If the work of art is completed by the perceiver,[10] then that experience is part and parcel of what exists in the work as properly understood, and thus there is a rift between the harmony that the beautiful work projects and the dissonance it contains as the truth of that harmony. This is not a didactically conceived, transparently communicable truth, but rather one that is worked out in the process of aesthetic perception and interpretation, in such a way that truth can no longer be said to be separable from the work of art as Baudelaire seems sometimes to claim, thus introducing a productive dissonance at the heart of his aesthetic postulates. To jettison either harmony or dissonance is to reject the entirety of Baudelaire's aesthetic project as it emerges in its development across his texts. Moments of description of aesthetic harmony barely cover the dissonance that sits deep within his characterization of aesthetic experience, in such a way that those moments where he evokes the harmony of transcendence come to seem dissonant themselves, like Adorno's major triads in an atonal work.

Seeing Baudelaire's conception of harmony as itself dissonant sheds light on the way the poet goes on to characterize the relationship among passion, beauty, and truth:

> Ainsi le principe de la poésie est [. . .] l'aspiration humaine vers une beauté supérieure, et la manifestation de ce principe est dans un enthousiasme, une excitation de l'âme, --enthousiasme tout à fait indépendant de la passion qui est l'ivresse du cœur, et de la vérité qui est la pâture de la raison. Car la passion est *naturelle*, trop naturelle pour ne pas introduire un ton blessant, discordant dans le domaine de la beauté pure, trop familière et trop violente pour ne pas scandaliser les purs Désirs, les gracieuses Mélancolies et les nobles Désespoirs qui habitent les régions surnaturelles de la poésie. (2: 334)

> [Thus the principle of poetry is [. . .] the human aspiration toward a superior Beauty, and the manifestation of this principle is in an enthusiasm, a rapture of the soul; the enthusiasm is totally independent of passion, which is the intoxication of the heart, and of truth, which is the pasture of reason. For passion is a *natural* thing, too natural even, not to introduce a wounding, discordant tone into the domain of pure Beauty; too familiar and too violent not to scandalize pure Desires, gracious Melancholies and nobles Despairs that dwell in the supernatural regions of poetry.]

If the principle of poetry lies in its aspiration, it is necessarily impossible to fulfill, and thus the poetic principle contains within itself a dissonance that comes about from the realization of this impossibility. So while Baudelaire goes on in this paragraph to differentiate between the aspiration toward superior beauty and both passion and truth, the very fact that superior beauty depends on what we could reasonably call a dissonance between aspiration and possibility suggests more of a harmony or parallel between that description of unattainable superior beauty and the experience of the "intoxication of the heart" which, as we recall from Baudelaire's evocation of Beethoven, aligns with the "modes of melancholy and incurable despair that were amassed like clouds in the interior sky of man" (2: 168). This dissonance between what Baudelaire claims about these two experiences being distinct and this similarity that seems to unite them suggests something like an aesthetic truth, at which we arrive through aesthetic experience. And if it is the case that something like truth emerges through dissonance, then it is not the case that truth is, as Baudelaire claims, entirely independent of the realm of the aspiration to superior beauty. Rather, his conception of that human aspiration toward harmony contains dissonance as its precondition and the source of tension that animates his very characterization of that beauty through negation and opposition.

This reconfigured relationship of harmony and dissonance allows us to make sense of some of Baudelaire's claims in *Les paradis artificiels* as well, where he seems yet again to appeal to an unbroken unity or harmony of humanity underlying what appears to be dissonant at the level of the individual: "Quelque incohérente que soit une existence, l'unité humaine n'en est pas trouble. Tous les échos de la mémoire, si on pouvait les réveiller simultanément, formeraient un concert, agréable ou douloureux, mais logique et sans dissonances" ["As incoherent as an existence may be, human existence is not troubled by it. All the echoes of memory, if we could waken them simultaneously, would form a concert, pleasant or painful, but logical and without dissonances"] (1: 506). It is an extraordinary claim that all (metaphorical) sounds resounding simultaneously would produce a harmony rather than a harsh dissonance, so extraordinary in fact as either to call the status of the metaphor itself into question or to force a reevaluation of what dissonance is. Baudelaire's model is not one of dissonance resolving to consonance; in this he takes a radical step away from the fundamental notions of tension and resolution that guide tonal music and presents, even in what at first glance appears to be an appeal to transcendent unity, a new way of thinking about consonance and dissonance that depends both on our retaining those terms as conceptual tools and on our reevaluating them such that all tones sounding together produce something which he does not allow us to label dissonance. This approach is itself a dissonant approach that is so at odds with conventional notions of dissonance and harmony as to make of Baudelaire a dissonant sonority within that discourse. While he makes a distinction here between individual experience and an underlying, and distinct, nature of the "human" more broadly, it is precisely this "dissonant," particular exposition of a dissonant aesthetics which leads us to the "truth" of that supposedly underlying harmony as a productive dissonance that allows us to "hear" Baudelaire's metaphysics and aesthetics in a new way. The individual, the "faux accord," is revealed to be the truth of the human via what we might call listening attentively to what Baudelaire's texts do by the way the dissonance of their claims reveals something that subverts conventional notions of harmony. Dissonance, that is, is written into the heart of Baudelaire's arguments for harmony, in a way that is both markedly new and also dependent on standard understandings of dissonance and consonance as they exist in mutually dependent relationships without which neither of them would be meaningful.

Adorno's approach to dissonance as the truth of harmony allows us to continue to hear the dissonance in nineteenth-century works; it allows us to reconsider how our habits of listening and reading have made us potentially inattentive to the shock and disruption that is best expressed within, rather than outside, systems of harmony and ideals of unity. As Lydia Goehr writes in a commentary on Adorno's take on Beethoven which can easily apply to Baudelaire as well:

> Consider the apparent familiarity we feel when listening to Beethoven. Is our familiarity based on the fact that our ears have simply gotten used to Beethoven's dissonances? [. . .] Are we just waiting for them to catch up with contemporary forms? Turn the thought around. Is it not odd to think that our ears find something that is already two centuries old easier to listen to than music composed in our own time? Do we not generally assume we know best what we are closest to [. . .]? [. . .] Perhaps not. Perhaps our contemporary sounds are not our new sounds. (233)

Baudelaire, the "faux accord," allows us to see the old as the new, and thereby to reexamine what we understand by the modern. Such a reflection introduces dissonance both into a linear model of moving from one style or period to another and into any notion of canceling or redeeming dissonance through resolution. Reconsidering the relationship of dissonance to harmony not only allows us to articulate a more complex and dialectical, perhaps even a truer, relation between them, it also reminds us of the necessary persistence of unity in order for the dissonance to be operative at all.

I turn now to an exploration of how dissonance plays out, in a number of ways, in Baudelaire's poems. We may speak of dissonance at a number of different levels as it applies to poems or collections of poems, whether that be dissonance within poems, across poems, within the lyric subject, between the subject and the poem, between form and content. Defined this broadly, the idea of dissonance can serve as a structural element for analysis of virtually Baudelaire's entire corpus. And to adopt this lens is not to seek a single definitive interpretation or interpretive strategy, of course. Rather, a focus on dissonance highlights the precariousness of any interpretation as well as the way in which it depends on interpretation as an unfolding process taking place within a history of reading practices. That history, like the history of musical listening, will influence our judgments about which practices are indeed dissonant with each other in Baudelaire by impacting our notion of what harmony and dissonance could be said to be at any particular point in time. To limit the scope in a way that still allows us a multifaceted glance into the way dissonance functions in Baudelaire's poetry, I'd like to turn first to some of the poems belonging to the cycle dedicated to Madame Sabatier, from "Tout entière" to "Le flacon," a section which included "A celle qui est trop gaie" in the 1857 edition before the poem was censured. These poems present a particularly rich site of investigation of the way Baudelaire engages dissonance in the context of reconfiguration of lyric subjectivity and the tension between romantic notions of transcendence and an approach that calls it into question while depending on its persistence in order for the tension to be operative. I begin with "Tout entière," which, in the first three of its six stanzas, portrays a sort of drama with two characters:

> Le Démon, dans ma chambre haute
> Ce matin est venu me voir,
> Et, tâchant à me prendre en faute
> Me dit: « Je voudrais bien savoir
>
> Parmi toutes les belles choses
> Dont est fait son enchantement,
> Parmi les objets noirs ou roses
> Qui composent son corps charmant,
>
> Quel est le plus doux. » (1: 42)

[The Devil into my high room
This morning came to pay a call,
And trying to find me in fault
Said: "I should like to know,

Among all the beautiful things
Which make her an enchantress,
Among the objects black or rose
That compose her charming body,
Which is the sweetest." (*Flowers* 143)]

DISSONANCE

Fragmentation is represented as a temptation here, as the poem is structured around the opposition of parts and wholes and the question of privileging one over the other. The dissonance or tension between the two is played out in the form of the poem itself, a dialogue between the Demon who poses the question and the poet whose reply constitutes the rest of the poem:

> — Ô mon âme!
> Tu répondis à l'Abhorré:
> « Puisqu'en Elle tout est dictame
> Rien ne peut être préféré.
>
> Lorsque tout me ravit, j'ignore
> Si quelque chose me séduit.
> Elle éblouit comme l'Aurore
> Et console comme la Nuit;
>
> Et l'harmonie est trop exquise,
> Qui gouverne tout son beau corps,
> Pour que l'impuissante analyse
> En note les nombreux accords.
>
> Ô métamorphose mystique
> De tous mes sens fondus en un!
> Son haleine fait la musique,
> Comme sa voix fait le parfum! » (1: 42)

> [— O my soul!
> You answered the loathsome Creature:
> "Since in Her all is dittany,
> No single thing can be preferred.
>
> When all delights me, I don't know
> If some one thing entrances me.
> She dazzles like the Dawn
> And consoles like the Night;
>
> And the harmony that governs
> Her whole body is too lovely
> For impotent analysis
> To note its numerous accords.
>
> O mystic metamorphosis
> Of all my senses joined in one!

Her breath makes music,
And her voice makes perfume!" (*Flowers* 145)]

The poem's dialogical form is in tension with the lyric subject's affirmation of the unity of the lover's body, for while the speaker frames his reply as the avoidance of a temptation, a refusal to be taken "en faute," the inscription of the opposition between part and whole compromises a simple affirmation of wholeness and causes a cleavage in the poem itself whereby the temptation to affirm fragmentation, if we consider the poem as a whole, remains active, since to remove the temptation would be to fragment the poem, to make a monologue of what had been an exchange. Wholeness, or harmony, thus becomes a term in the dissonance of the poem, which undermines the affirmation of harmony in the penultimate stanza. If, on a surface level, the poem moves linearly toward an affirmation of Baudelairean "correspondences" in the final stanza, the fact that the entire second half of the poem is phrased as direct citation of a situated speaking subject moves us away from a more generalized lyric voice and relegates it to one voice responding to another that would challenge it. Unity does not so much triumph over fragmentation so much as closing down the response.[11] Furthermore, the penultimate stanza, where harmony is explicitly invoked, underscores the impossibility of containing, or expressing, that harmony in language. The harmony, in other words, is simply posited, and posited in a way that rejects the possibility of enumeration. That which is, on this view, cannot be expressed, thus creating another dissonance between what readers are asked to conceive (the exquisite harmony) and what is available for presentation (a demonstration of that harmony that would verify its existence). The language of the poem serves not to expound the unity of the beloved's body but rather to call it into question as, perhaps, anything more than the dream or wish of the speaking subject, a mere hallucination rather than a demonstrable reality.

As Eliane DalMolin notes, in the second half of the poem, "spatial and temporal elements completely disappear, and the poet, left alone in his deepest meditation, [. . .] exposes [the woman's body] in poetic figures with which he is familiar" (DalMolin 87). In order to posit unity and the transcendental "métamorphose mystique," the lyric subject needs to remove himself not just from the dialogue but from any situatedness in time and space, so that the poet creates what we might call a dissonance between the space of lived experience and the conceptual realm where that reality is transformed or, perhaps, falsified, in yet another move within the language of the poem that points to a dissonance just as the speaking subject would posit unity. DalMolin questions whether the woman's body can "sustain the fragmentation inflicted by the dramatic query of the Devil, or can it be preserved whole by the poet's will?" (87) and goes on to question whether, reading backward in the poem, we may not even wonder whether the Devil and the poet are distinct characters, "or are they one and the same, the double face of a lyric self tortured by his own duality?" (87). On this reading, the woman simply dissolves, not only into the sensual confusion figured at the end of the poem but also into the poet himself, not in some sort of mystic union but into his fantasy of her unity and her being more generally. Furthermore, the reduction of the dialogue to monologue and of the poetic subject/love object pairing to the poetic subject alone multiplies duality rather than canceling it once we entertain the possibility that the speaker may have been alone from the start, having hallucinated and exteriorized an inner demon. Even that unified subject is called into question by the curious self-address in the second person in the third stanza: "O mon âme ! / Tu répondis à l'Abhorré." DalMolin notes that until this point, the speaking subject had referred to himself in the first person, and that "this sudden separation of the 'I' and the 'you,' of the poet and his soul, occurs at the very moment when, to fight the suggestion made by the Devil about the fragmented body of the woman, the poetic self asserts her totality" (93–4). Likewise, the more we attempt to impose unity on the poem, the more it resists, as the poetic subject begins to disappear into the language of the poem itself, a phenomenon that will be more explicitly and dramatically rendered in "Le flacon," which I consider below.

While we began with identifying unity and harmony as a thematic aspect of the poem, these considerations brought us to the question of form, via the dissonance of the two parts of the poem which led us to consider the possibility that the entire poem is unified, paradoxically, by its refusal to let us affirm esthetic unity. The "métamorphose mystique" may turn out to have been mere illusion or fantasy, on the speaking subject's part as well as on the reader's, as we are left with no way to affirm that unity unconditionally as anything more than a volition or a fantasy. We are left perhaps with our own wish to read unity and coherence in this poem laid bare, an untenable approach to reading Baudelaire that is exposed as untenable only *because* unity and harmony were thematized in the poem rather than jettisoned. It is the preservation of harmony which allows us to articulate the dissonance, which in turn prevents us from affirming the harmony. The whole of the poem, in other words, cannot be captured except through its parts, which never quite get us to the whole, thus revealing the dissonance at the heart of the hermeneutic circle itself. The exquisite harmony remains only under the sign of its negation. J.-D. Hubert sees the woman as a caricature of the transcendent unity of God himself in a kind of reversal of Platonism whereby the Ideal is shown to be nothing more than a posited illusion:

> La maîtresse n'est ici qu'une image caricaturale de Dieu qui est l'unité suprême où se confondent la beauté et la bonté, la toute-puissance et tous les autres transcendentaux ou Noms divins. Les deux derniers vers ne représentent ainsi que la parodie de cette unité divine chère aux théologiens. Il ne s'agit donc pas d'une synesthésie véritable [. . .] mais

d'une image « métaphysique » qui rappelle la manière de John Donne. (198-9)

[The mistress is here only a caricatural image of God who is the supreme unity where beauty and goodness are mixed, along with all-powerfulness and all the other transcendentals or divine Names. The last two verses thus represent only the parody of this divine unity dear to theologians. It is thus not a question of true synesthesia [. . .] but of a "metaphysical" image that is reminiscent of the manner of John Donne.]

The possibility of reading the poem parodically opens up yet another source of dissonance, this time not within the lyric subject but in the poem itself, as it stands simultaneously as an affirmation of a transcendental poetics and the calling into question of that same vision. The form of the poem, its hesitation between dialogue and monologue, its reported speech, its removal of spatial and temporal markers, undoes the content or, rather, undoes any simplistic affirmation of what the speaking subject claims to be claiming here about the unity of the woman's body or of esthetic experience more broadly.

Even if we were to affirm some kind of higher unity operating in form or content of the poem that would cancel the kinds of dissonance I have identified, the fact that the unified reading exists as one option among others suggests that dissonance remains, that Baudelaire intervenes in transcendental poetry in a way that makes it impossible to cancel dissonance because of the way the poetry, in part by way of yielding to language and dissolving the lyric subject, is always open to a reading that calls that transcendence into question; dissonance is thus built into the very structure of reading and writing these poems. The poem "Tout entière" is itself neither whole nor fragment; affirming either one would do violence to the way the poem operates. Engaging with Baudelaire's poems thus becomes a question of accounting for and responding to that dissonance, in a way that maintains rather than canceling it, and attempts to draw the consequences for lyric subjectivity and the role of the reader when it comes to holding on to enough of the transcendent vision to be able to see the violation of that transition as dissonant and not simply the affirmation of a new paradigm.

A clear manifestation of dissonance across poems in *Les Fleurs du Mal* occurs in in Baudelaire's love poetry, which features idolization of the beloved and fantasies of sadistic violence against her. The excision of "A celle qui est trop gaie" from the 1861 edition of *Les Fleurs du Mal* significantly alters a reader's impression of the Madame Sabatier cycle. Following "Tout entière" in both the 1857 and 1861 editions is "Que diras-tu ce soir . . .," with its reference to the "chair spirituelle" of the beloved and her imagined invocation of the Beautiful, as her ghost says:

« Je suis belle, et j'ordonne
Que pour l'amour de moi vous n'aimiez que le Beau;
Je suis l'Ange gardien, la Muse et la Madone. » (1: 43)

["I am fair, I command
That for your love of me you love only Beauty;
I am your guardian Angel, your Muse and Madonna." (*Flowers* 147)]

"Le Flambeau vivant" follows, and it is at this point that "A celle qui est trop gaie" appeared, before "Réversibilité." "A celle qui est trop gaie" thus sounds a dissonant note by its move to sadistic violence. That dissonance is played out in microcosm in the poem as well with its shift from the rather vapid description in the first stanza ("Ta tête, ton geste, ton air / Sont beaux comme un beau paysage; / Le rire joue en ton visage / Comme un vent frais dans un ciel clair" [1: 156] ["Your head, your bearing, your gestures / Are fair as a fair countryside; / Laughter plays on your face / Like a cool wind in a clear sky"] (*Flowers* 151).) to the wounding in the final three stanzas. The dissonance plays on continuity with poems such as "Tout entière" the better to sound its dissonance. The enumeration of the body parts of the beloved in the first two stanzas—head, face, arms, shoulders—echoes the Demon's request in "Tout entière" to identify a preferred body part, with the erotic undertones implied by the "objets noirs ou roses" (1: 42). The turning point comes with the affirmation: "Je te hais autant que je t'aime" (1: 157) ["I hate and love you equally!" (153)], announcing not a move from love to hatred but a simultaneous coexistence of dissonant emotions. The language of the poem takes a turn here not only from the idyllic tone of the first stanzas to the darker representations of violence in the last ones but also from the clarity of expression in the description of the woman to an increasingly mysterious depiction of action. Clarity is inscribed in the poem in the "vent frais dans un ciel clair" of the first stanza, the better to be compromised in the two acts of violence: how exactly did the lyric subject "puni[r] sur une fleur / L'insolence de la Nature" (1: 157) ["punish[] a flower / For the insolence of Nature" (153)]? There is also a dissonance between the reported past act of violence to the flower and the scene of imagined or projected violence to the woman, represented as a wished-for action by "je voudrais."[12] The murkiness of the imagined violence is striking in contrast to the clarity of the first stanzas; the metaphorical sexual act is disfigured and displaced onto the "lèvres nouvelles" that the poet carves into her flesh, and the poem ends on the highly ambiguous wish of the lyric subject to "t'infuser mon venin, ma soeur" (1: 157) ["infuse my venom, my sister!" (153)]. A note published with the poem famously affirms that we are to understand the venom as spleen or melancholy, a reading that would yield a simple interpretation of the poem whereby the woman whom the speaker finds too cheery would be "infected" with melancholy so as to match his tastes more closely. The very need for such an explanatory note points to the obvious fact that such is not the only interpretation to which readers are led here, given the erotically charged nature of the scene; the venom is just as plausibly the poet's semen, perhaps infected with syphilis, with or without a figurative dose of anger or hatred (figured commonly as venom).

What we might want to describe as undecidability here could also be configured as dissonance: contrast between literal and figurative images, love figured and manifested simultaneously as hatred. The imagined violence played out on the woman (and the flower) points also to the violence through which Baudelaire attempts to re-form the poetic tradition not through an act of destruction and rebuilding from nothing but rather through a reshaping of its existing elements. The violent act is one of displacement, an injection of something different into an extant body that sounds a dissonant note within it and potentially violates the wholeness or harmony or integrity of that body. In the midst of this highly corporeal poem would lie the seed of a poetics, the poem serving as a dissonant tone that forces reconsideration of other poems in the cycle and the collection more broadly. The metaphysical confusion of "tous mes sens fondus en un" (1: 42) in "Tout entière" becomes the corporeal confusion of the doubled lips and the ambiguity of the "venin" of "A celle qui est trop gaie." The effect of the dissonance of the latter poem is not merely to see it as an aberrant anomaly, a dissonance to be resolved, but rather to see the dissonance that it figures as a key to approaching the other poems as well, a way to make visible the dissonance that they hold both within each poem and across poems. Excising "A celle qui est trop gaie" through censorship does nothing to change the dissonance operating, in subtler ways perhaps, throughout this cycle and the collection more generally. "A celle qui est trop gaie" is an outburst, a dissonant chord that reveals the truth of the harmony of the poems around it and begins a process, completed by the end of the cycle, whereby the lyric subject begins to dissolve and yield agency to the poem itself, the kind of force that impels the enumeration of the various interpretive possibilities inherent in the infusion of venom. We have already seen the dialogic form of "Tout entière" contributing to such a decentralization or splitting of the subject; a dialogical structure is also operative in "Confession," two poems on from "A celle qui est trop gaie."

The scene of a late stroll in Paris with a beloved is painted at the start of "Confession" in terms even more idyllic than the portrait of the woman in "A celle qui est trop gaie":

> Il était tard; ainsi qu'une médaille neuve
>   La pleine lune s'étalait,
> Et la solennité de la nuit, comme un fleuve,
>   Sur Paris dormant ruisselait. (1: 45)

> [It was late; like a newly struck medal
>   The full moon spread its rays,

And the solemnity of the night streamed
   Like a river over sleeping Paris. (*Flowers* 159)]

The walk is interrupted by a "tout à coup" that marks the intervention of the woman's speaking voice represented as music:

Tout à coup, au milieu de l'intimité libre
   Eclose à la pâle clarté
De vous, riche et sonore instrument où ne vibre
   Que la radieuse gaieté,

De vous, claire et joyeuse ainsi qu'une fanfare
   Dans le matin étincelant
Une note plaintive, une note bizarre
   S'échappa [. . .] (1: 45)

[Suddenly, in the midst of that frank intimacy
   Born in the pale moonlight,
From you, sonorous, rich instrument which vibrates
   Only with radiant gaiety,

From you, clear and joyful as a fanfare
   In the glistening morning light,
A plaintive note, a bizarre note
   Escaped, faltering [. . .] (*Flowers* 159)]

The sonorous scene marks a contrast with the silence in which the final scene of "A celle qui est trop gaie" plays out, where the speaker wants to "ramper sans bruit" (1: 157) and does not represent any sound associated with the scene of inflicting the wound. There are multiple levels of dissonance implied in "Confession": the silence is broken by the unexpected interruption by the voice, and the timbre of the voice itself, "riche et sonore," contrasts with the nature of the message itself, "une note bizarre." The content of the bizarre note is then revealed:
   Pauvre ange, elle chantait, votre note criarde:

«Que rien ici-bas n'est certain,
Et que toujours, avec quelque soin qu'il se farde,
   Se trahit l'égoïsme humain;

Que c'est un dur métier que d'être belle femme,
   Et que c'est le travail banal

> De la danseuse folle et froide qui se pâme
>   Dans son sourire machinal;
>
> Que bâtir sur les coeurs est une chose sotte;
>   Que tout craque, amour et beauté,
> Jusqu'à ce que l'Oubli les jette dans sa hotte
>   Pour les rendre à l'Eternité !» (1: 46)
>
> [Poor angel, it sang, your discordant note:
>   "That naught is certain here below,
> That always, though it paint its face with utmost care
>   Man's selfishness reveals itself,
>
> That it's a hard calling to be a lovely woman,
>   And that it is the banal task
> Of the cold and silly danseuse who faints away
>   With a mechanical smile,
>
> That to build on hearts is a foolish thing,
>   That all things break, love, and beauty,
> Till Oblivion tosses them into his dosser
>   To give them back to Eternity!" (*Flowers* 161)]

The woman and the note are blurred by the grammatical structure of the presentation: "Pauvre ange, elle chantait, votre note criarde," where the poor angel is not the subject of the verb *chantait* but rather an apostrophe, with the pronoun *elle* preceding what turns out to be its antecedent, *note criarde*. The words, figured as music, are thus divorced from the human subject pronouncing them and a dissonance is established between the "riche et sonore instrument" and the "note bizarre" and "criarde," yet another instance where dissonance stands both on its own (as the bizarre note) and as a term in relation to harmony (the dissonance between the melodious voice and the theme of the message). Whereas in "Que diras-tu . . ." the poetic subject had wondered what to say "à la très belle, à la très bonne, à la très chère" (1: 43) ["To the kindest, dearest, the fairest of women" (147)], here she responds that playing that role is a job, demystifying the aura of Beauty by expressing it in terms of the labor market. There is an implicit critique of the unified lyric subject that would objectify her as beautiful in her indication that "l'égoïsme humain" is always operative, although sometimes disguised. We can read the dissonant message here as the truth about the harmony of beauty and as a reminder that any particular moment in Baudelaire's poetry should always be read in dialectical tension across poems, not so that one poem can cancel the other but so that the dialectical relationship between them can emerge. If, in "Le flambeau vivant," two poems prior to "Confession," the lyric subject had evoked "ces Yeux pleins de lumière" (1:

43) ["those eyes aglow with light" (149)] which shine with "clarté mystique" (1: 44) ["mystical clarity" (149)]. When the person who personifies clarity speaks, it is to call into question not only the kind of harmonious beauty that the male speaking subject had evoked throughout this cycle but also to reduce such celebration of beauty to the possibility of a manifestation of ego.

The dissonant note remains hanging, without further commentary from the lyric subject in the final stanza:

> J'ai souvent évoqué cette lune enchantée,
> Ce silence et cette langueur,
> Et cette confidence horrible chuchotée
> Au confessionnal du cœur. (1: 46)

> [I've often evoked that enchanted moon,
> The silence and the languidness,
> And that horrible confidence whispered
> In the heart's confessional. (*Flowers* 161)]

The poetic subject plays the role of mere reporter here, both of the scenes and of his own reflections on them, without giving us further insight into the context of those reflections, as if the woman's confession had begun to undo the lyric self and make him more of a transparent storage receptacle for the memory of the exchange. And yet the final stanza introduces two more sources of dissonance: what the poet refers to as "ce silence" had not been evoked explicitly as such; readers are sent back to the first part of the poem to confirm that when the woman speaks, it does break an unnamed silence that had been evoked paradoxically via two references to hearing. The speaking subject had indicated that "la solennité de la nuit, comme un fleuve, / Sur Paris dormant ruisselait » (1: 45) ["And the solemnity of the night streamed / Like a river over sleeping Paris" (159)], a comparison that suggests a sound, since flowing river water is indeed audible. One stanza later, he describes cats passing by, "l'oreille au guet" (1: 45) ["with ears pricked up" (159)], an image that prepares our ears too to be attentive to the unnamed silence and the way it will be broken "tout à coup" in the following stanza. Beyond the dissonance between silence and sound, there is also the tension between memory and forgetting. While the woman had ended her confession with the reminder that "tout craque, amour et beauté, / Jusqu'à ce que l'Oubli les jette dans sa hotte," ["That all things break, love, and beauty, / Till Oblivion tosses them into his dosser"], the poetic subject seems to give the lie to that claim by commenting immediately afterward that he often thinks of that moment, a reprise of the parenthetical affirmation in the first stanza that "ce souvenir n'est point pâli" (1: 45) ["that memory is not faded" (159)]. And yet, despite the poetic subject having the last word, the woman's affirmation remains, reminding readers that neither the lyric subject nor the poem is immortal, despite the lyric subject's efforts to preserve the memory. As Claude Pichois notes, the "hotte" in the lines just quoted is to be understood as that of the ragpicker (Baudelaire, *Œuvres complètes* 1: 917–18), suggesting that that the appropriate site of metaphorical landscape is not the idyllic moonlit cityscape of the first part of the poem but rather the dustbin of the collectors of refuse, those who remove waste precisely so that the illusion of an idyllic cityscape becomes possible. The truth that reveals the illusion of the lyric is the woman's confession, in all that it reveals about the lie of natural beauty and the potentially irredeemable transitory nature of art, contained in the poem in the sense that it appears within the poem but is not "contained" in the sense of mitigated or attenuated. The poem presents the impossibility of the vision of beauty, eternity, and memory that it inscribes both within itself and by reference to other poems in the cycle, in a way that prepares the melting away of the lyric subject and a shift to the interactive play of the words that simultaneously build up and tear down a transcendent esthetics, an affirmation of beauty in human and artistic form.

An excellent example of what I have been calling "reading backwards" can be found in the relationship between the prose poem "Le chien et le flacon" (1862) and the verse poem "Le flacon" (1857). The prose poem is among those that seem utterly transparent at first: a dog is rebuked for preferring the smell of excrement to the odor of fine perfume, and the speaker (literally a speaker, as the narrator represents himself as addressing the dog in direct speech except when describing the dog's actions) goes on to explain a straightforward comparison between the dog and the public, rendering the meaning of the prose poem supposedly transparent:

> Ainsi, vous-même, indigne compagnon de ma triste vie, vous ressemblez au public, à qui il ne faut jamais présenter des parfums délicats qui l'exaspèrent, mais des ordures soigneusement choisies. (1: 284)

> [Because of this, you, unworthy companion of my dreary life, you resemble the public, which must never be offered delicate perfumes that exasperate them, but only meticulously selected garbage.][13]

There is, obviously, more to say about what is going on in this poem, however.[14] Upon a closer look, for instance, we see that the speaker describes the dog as "reculant soudainement avec effroi" before the fine perfume. What is it about the object that inspires that kind of fear, horror, or anguish? It is not mere indifference or even disgust, but rather a deeper, quasi-metaphysical repulsion. Perhaps the dog is on to something about the horror that a fine object can provoke. Julien Weber has argued that Baudelaire is playing out a Kantian distinction between the pleasurable and the beautiful in the prose poem:

> L'expérience à laquelle le narrateur voudrait exposer son chien [. . .] vise [. . .] à représenter la réception de l'œuvre d'art comme l'expérience d'un

plaisir esthétique désintéressé, conformément à la conception kantienne de la perception du Beau. [...] Or l'expérience échoue, ce qui confirme que chien et public préfèrent définitivement l'agréable au Beau, la jouissance de ce qui flatte leurs dispositions particulières à celle d'une œuvre qui pourrait toucher à l'universel. (246)

[The experiment to which the narrator would like to expose his dog [...] aims [...] to represent the reception of the work of art as the experience of a distinterested esthetic pleasure, conforming to the Kantian conception of the perception of the Beautiful. [...] Now the experiment fails, which confirms that the dog and the public definitively prefer the pleasant to the Beautiful, the enjoyment of what flatters their particular dispositions to the enjoyment of a work that could touch on the universal.]

And if we are to understand the perfume as analogous to poetry or other artworks, does Baudelaire's esthetic not make room for, and even privilege, notions of the abyss and the horror it provokes? Is "effroi" not in fact a viable esthetic reaction? And what about the way the perfume is first presented, as "un excellent parfum acheté chez le meilleur parfumeur de la ville" (1: 284) ["an excellent perfume purchased from the best perfumer in the city" (12)]? It is as a commodity that we are invited to consider the perfume, which is rather astonishing given that Baudelaire is taken, rightly, to rail against the prostitution of the artist on the free market and the transformation of the artwork into a mere commercial good to be bought and sold. Could an artwork be both? Are the poems that the poet puts before the public simply high-end consumer goods that the speaker here mistakenly assimilates to pure artworks that should not inspire fear or horror? Or is there something to be said about the proper "consuming" of the artwork, an active attempt at interpretation that resists passive consumption as it eschews surface-level meanings and judgment?

By engaging with these questions, readers remove themselves from the position of the vulgar public precisely by refusing to take the allegory at what at first seems to be face value.[15] As we consider these questions, we can be led back to the *flacon* without the *chien*, as it appears in "Le flacon," a poem notable for its complexity and resistance to straightforward interpretation. In other words, it seems to be the opposite of what the seemingly didactic "Le chien et le flacon" was; there will be no explanatory moment at the end where the poetic subject proposes an interpretation. The contrast is even more striking once we see that, formally, the two poems share a similar structure: a proposition followed by a comparison announced by an "ainsi." In the prose poem the "ainsi" introduces the comparison of the dog to the public. In "Le flacon," it sets up a far more complex comparison between the bottle and the poet whereby the nature of poetic subjectivity is called into question by the ways in which the poem only haltingly allows for the emergence of a first-person subject in the last two of its seven stanzas. Critics have provided exigeses that underscore the simultaneous simplicity and complexity of the poem. Claude Pichois offers a paraphrase that he reduces, "en termes [. . .] trop simples" ["in terms [. . .] too simple"] by his own account, to the following analogy: "Le parfum est au flacon ce que l'amour est au poète" ["The perfume is to the bottle what love is to the poet"] (Baudelaire 1: 921). Antoine Adam summarizes critical approaches that have seen in the title's *flacon* an image of *Les Fleurs du Mal* themselves, "ou l'âme corrompue de Baudelaire ou encore—chose à peine concevable—ils ont cru que le poète faisait allusion à sa prétendue passion pour l'opium et le haschich" ["the corrupted soul of Baudelaire or—and this is hardly conceivable—they thought that the poet was alluding to his supposed passion for opium and haschish"] (in *Les Fleurs* 332). For Adam, however, the right interpretation is clear: "Lorsqu'un jour, plus tard, des hommes ouvriront *Les Fleurs du Mal*, ils y retrouveront le parfum de cet amour que Baudelaire a voué à sa Madone [. . .] mais « ranci, charmant et sépulcral »" ["When one day, later, men open *The Flowers of Evil*, they will once again find the scent of that love that Baudelaire consecrated to his Madonna [. . .] but 'rancid, charming, and sepulchral,'" like the scents in the bottle. There is ambiguity in the poem according to Adam, however, stemming from the fact that "Baudelaire s'identifie à son livre, qu'il se voit survivant en lui, gardant parmi les hommes l'existence que lui conservera quelque exemplaire de ce recueil" ["Baudelaire identifies with his book, he sees himself surviving in it, keeping among men the existence that some copy of this volume will preserve for him"] (332).

As Adam has already (perhaps unwittingly) signaled, there is a tension between unity and disunity that one could say structures the poem, where the initial interpretive act of establishing the kind of analogies that Pichois identifies in order to make sense of the way the poem's images hang together yields to a complexity that undermines such attempts simply to unravel the poem's meaning. The regular form of the poem, with its seven stanzas of rhyming alexandrine couplets, is itself a kind of container that holds in the potentially unruly elements that it contains. At the very center of the poem, the fourth stanza unleashes or unbottles a stormlike vertigo that pushes toward an abyss:

Voilà le souvenir enivrant qui voltige
Dans l'air troublé; les yeux se ferment; le Vertige
Saisit l'âme vaincue et la pousse à deux mains
Vers un gouffre obscurci de miasmes humains; (1: 48)

[That is the bewitching souvenir which flutters
In the troubled air; the eyes close; Dizziness

Seizes the vanquished soul, pushes it with both hands
Toward a darkened abyss of human pollution: (*Flowers* 169)]

The coherence of the poem stands threatened by abyss at its center, as the apparent simplicity which some critics have signaled in the poem is put into question by the complex system of metaphors that cannot be swept away; the bottle that is the poem's form holds the bottle itself (which is said in the first stanza to be porous because there are odors that "pénètrent le vers") along with thoughts, memory, the abyss, and the biblical Lazarus. The poem's coherence risks being swept away like that "âme vaincue" into an abyss where the neither fully dead nor alive Lazarus stands as a figure of the ambiguity that increasingly dominates the poem. The unity of a fully coherent whole thus stands in contrast to the dissonance of the other imagery, the unruly associations unleashed by the scent that refuses to be contained. Unity and dissonance thus become terms in a dissonance that govern the poem, whereby the dissonance is itself both part of the tension and the result of that tension. The unity becomes the precondition of that dissonance, since without the suggestion of unity, the dissonance would not be perceivable *as* dissonance. This is a point on which Adorno insists several times in *Aesthetic Theory* and elsewhere:

> Although art revolts against its neutralization as an act of contemplation, insisting on the most extreme incoherence and dissonance, these elements are those of unity; without this unity they would not even be dissonant. Even when art unreservedly obeys the dictates of inspiration, the principle of harmony, metamorphosed to the point of unrecognizability, is at work because inspiration, if it is to count, must gel; that tacitly presupposes an element of organization and coherence, at least as a vanishing point. (AT 158)

It is not enough to say that unity and incoherence, or harmony and dissonance, exist in dialectical tension in poems such as this one; rather, we need to recognize that the unity is the necessary condition of the dissonance as dissonance; the poem's newness is entirely bound to the persistence of the very codes it is undoing.

A potential unifying element, a source of coherence, would be the lyrical "I," and it is notable that it is absent for most of the poem. The generalized "âme vaincue" is not allied with any particular subject, and indeed it is not until the sixth of seven stanzas that the "je" appears. Along with the rest of the images in the poem, the "je" is presented under the sign of metaphor:

Ainsi, quand je serai perdu dans la mémoire
Des hommes, dans le coin d'une sinistre armoire
Quand on m'aura jeté, vieux flacon désolé,
Décrépit, poudreux, sale, abject, visqueux, fêlé,

> Je serai ton cercueil, aimable pestilence !
> Le témoin de ta force et de ta virulence,
> Cher poison préparé par les anges ! liqueur
> Qui me ronge, ô la vie et la mort de mon cœur ! (1: 48)
>
> [Thus, when I'll be lost to the memory
> Of men, when I shall be tossed into the corner
> Of a dismal wardrobe, a desolate old phial,
> Decrepit, cracked, slimy, dirty, dusty, abject,
>
> Delightful pestilence! I shall be your coffin,
> The witness of your strength and of your virulence,
> Beloved poison prepared by the angels! Liqueur
> That consumes me, O the life and death of my heart! (*Flowers* 169)]

But as was already suggested in Adam's commentary, the lyrical subject is the source of dissonance and dispersion rather than coherence in this poem. The I is a coffin, but the I is both the speaking poetic subject and the book. The fragrance is a poison, both life and death. This end of the poem, rather than resolving the tensions developed in the middle, exacerbates and extends them in ways that also underscore the dissolution of the lyric subject. As Pierre Laforgue notes, "Une des caractéristiques les plus visibles du second romantisme, celui des années 1850, est la difficulté, voire l'impossibilité de tenir un discours poétique à la première personne. Le *je* semble être entré dans une crise qui interdit son emploi" ["One of the most visible characteristics of the second romanticism, that of the 1850s, is the difficulty, or even the impossibility to have a first-person poetic discourse. The 'I' seems to have entered a crisis that prohibits its use"] (245). What we see in this poem, according to Laforgue, is Baudelaire's poetic labor to "rendre possible cette prise de parole à la première personne, par toute une série de dispositifs" ["make possible this first person speech, by a whole series of devices"] (246), namely, metonymy and metaphor, which mediate the articulation of the subject, making of it "un simple effet rhétorique" ["a simple effect of rhetoric"]:

> Tout montre, en effet, que le poème se construit à partir [du *je*] non comme sujet, mais comme objet. De fait, il s'agit d'élaborer le *je* comme objet rhétorique afin de le constituer ensuite, et ensuite seulement, comme sujet textuel. Aussi ce *je* est-il moins une donnée du discours qu'une de ses résultantes. (248)
>
> [Everything shows, in fact, that the poem is constructed from [the *I*] not as a subject but as an object. In fact, it is a question of elaborating the *I* as a rhetorical object in order to constitute it then, and only then, as

a textual subject. Thus this *I* is less a given of discourse than one of its results.]

Just as the poem both establishes and destabilizes coherence via its complex network of images that threaten to hover over the conceptual and sensual abyss, it both grounds and questions the possibility of the lyric I, the conditions of possibility of poetic subjectivity. The question is further complicated by the ambiguity of the *je* as identified both with the poet and with either the poem or perhaps the whole collection. In that sense, the place of the lyric subject yields to the poem itself which becomes subject rather than object. Thus the newness of Baudelaire in this case stems not from rejecting poetic subjectivity but rather from redefining it in a way that depends on the old for the coherence of the new; poetic subjectivity passes into the poem itself without annihilating the poetic subject, a move which resonates with Adorno's characterization of esthetic experience. As Shierry Weber Nicholsen has argued, "Genuine or adequate aesthetic experience [. . .] transcends itself and moves into the work of art. In coming alive, the work of art in turn becomes subject rather than object [. . .]. [T]he quasi-logical and quasi-sensuous characteristics of subjective aesthetic experience inhere equally in the artwork itself" (*Exact* 22). The impossibility of saying *I* uncouples the poet from the poem, or, rather, suggests the dissolution of a clear subject-object relation between them so that the alienation of the subject is at the same time and by the same gesture the affirmation of the autonomy of the work of art, a reforming of autonomous art that depends on the very relation to the modern world that it denounces, and without which there would be nothing to denounce, and thus no grounds for affirming autonomous art in the first place. This, then, is the kind of dialectical critical tension that operates in poems like "Le Flacon" and animates Baudelaire's lyric project more generally. The poetic subject, we might say, both goes away and remains, or stays by virtue of the fact that it is represented as vanishing into the poem via the voluntary confusion effected by the poetic device of the metaphor, "je serai ton cercueil." The self is confounded with the poem by its textual reconstruction as a metaphor, itself the figure of relationality that depends on the cognitive gesture of a reader in order to make sense of the statement that is simply false when taken literally.

Such reflection on subjectivity as portrayed, or, better, enacted, by the work of art resonates with Adorno's writings on the relationship of artworks to philosophy as being completed by a philosophical reflection which at the same time in no way cancels or supersedes the artwork but rather remains dependent on it for what always exceeds philosophy's ability to articulate:

> Every artwork, if it is to be fully experienced, requires thought and therefore stands in need of philosophy, which is nothing but the thought that refuses all restrictions. Understanding [*Verstehen*] and criticism are one;

the capacity of understanding, that of comprehending what is understood as something spiritual, is none other than that of distinguishing in the object what is true and false, however much this distinction must deviate from the procedure of ordinary logic. Emphatically, art is knowledge, though not the knowledge of objects. Only he understands an artwork who grasps it as a complex nexus of truth, which inevitably involves its relation to untruth, its own as well as that external to it; any other judgment of artworks would remain arbitrary. Artworks thus demand an adequate relation to themselves. They postulate what was once the aim of the philosophy of art, which, in its present form, it no longer accomplishes, neither vis-à-vis contemporary consciousness nor vis-à-vis current artworks. (AT 262)

It is apt to consider "Le Flacon" in this context as questions of truth and knowledge could be said, in the spirit of Adorno, to overflow their container, just as the scent both is and is not contained by the perfume bottle which has become porous. The poem depends on its form as container but also operates to show that the constraint of the strict metrical form and the basic structure of the comparison announced by the "ainsi" are what allows for the overflowing to occur and to be perceptible as an overflow of meaning. The confusion among scent, bottle, poet, poem, love object, and so on establishes the conceptual reconfiguration of the metaphorical mapping of images in the poem; the correspondences are ultimately not of the type, prevalent in Baudelaire, that are based on intermingling of the senses (although we do have an echo of that in the description of "mille pensers [. . .] / Teintés d'azur, flacés de rose, lamés d'or") but, rather, of broader categories of subjects and objects, sensual forms like odors and conceptual structures such as thoughts. The subject here speaks as object ("Quand on m'aura jeté, vieux flacon désolé") which becomes a subject, and subject in turn to its own metaphorization as the *flacon* becomes a *cercueil*. The coffin, we might say, holds the remains of poetic subjectivity while also remaining, like the bottle, porous, so that the remains of that subjectivity are not simply invisible. The dynamic relation among objects in the poem is indicated further by the fact that the liquid held within the poet/bottle eats away at it, "liqueur / Qui me ronge, ô la vie et la mort de mon coeur," in a way perhaps akin to the natural process of decay to which both a wooden coffin and the body contained within it would both be subjected.

As noted earlier, critics have often seen this poem as a love poem, and indeed it is among those that Baudelaire wrote for his lover Madame Sabatier. There are only the slightest traces of a love poem here, however, with the apostrophe to the "aimiable pestilence," also called "cher poison," which could arguably refer to either love or a lover. The genre of the poem thus likewise also both decomposes and allows for a framework by which to shift the poem away from hackneyed considerations of romantic love and toward questions of the possibility of subjectivity in relation to objects. That relation is configured here not as other people but as literal objects, including the poem itself which reduces the poet, metaphorically and perhaps more than metaphorically, to an object in the sense of a thing. "Le Flacon" both is and is not a love poem, then; it depends on the persistence of that genre in order to go beyond it in an intelligible way. It is perhaps the non-parodic counterpart to "Une charogne," a poem that plays explicitly with the tradition of the Renaissance *blazon* and the *memento mori* in the way it establishes equivalence between the love object and the horse carcass. The final stanza of "Une charogne" indirectly echoes the complex figuration of poison and decay at the end of "Le Flacon":

Alors, ô ma beauté! dites à la vermine
Qui vous mangera de baisers,
Que j'ai gardé la forme et l'essence divine
De mes amours décomposés! (1: 32)

[Then, O my beauty! say to the worms who will
Devour you with kisses,
That I have kept the form and the divine essence
Of my decomposed love! (*Flowers* 103)]

In both poems, love has been decomposed, or revealed to be what it already was in lyric poetry, a vehicle for reshaping poetic subjectivity, an annihilation of the usual subject-object distinction and its reconfiguration as a poetic discourse that overflows both its form and readers' attempts to understand it via appeal to philosophical distinctions between subject and object. To interpret this poem is to grasp it as "a complex nexus of truth, which inevitably involves its relation to untruth, its own as well as that external to it," as Adorno put it in the passage I quoted earlier. The "untruth" of the metaphor yields an esthetic truth that can only be revealed by the groups of images in the poem, which reduces itself to conceptual analysis and paraphrase only with great difficulty and in a way that suggests that such paraphrase is untrue. Likewise, reductive attempts to articulate a simple analogy at work in the poem, such as Pichois's avowedly oversimplified "Le parfum est au flacon ce que l'amour est au poète," are both untrue to the complexity of the poem and untrue in the sense of failing to provide an adequate account of what is happening in it. The necessary failure of any attempt to paraphrase is more than just an esthetic remainder; it is what signals to us the dependence of the poem on the systems that it negates, including the lyric subject, form as "container," and the love poem as model of subject-object relation. If "artworks [. . .] demand an adequate relation to themselves," the impossibility of articulating that adequate relation is both the result of the attempt to define that relation and the dynamism that fuels the kind of back and forth between the artwork and conceptual interpretation that poems such as this one set in motion.

This dynamism is what Adorno suggests when he claims that "under patient contemplation artworks begin to move. To this extent they are truly afterimages of the primordial shudder in the age of reification; the terror of that age is recapitulated vis-à-vis reified objects" (AT 79). While such artworks stand as a powerful potential source of negation and critique, they also serve as a reminder that their very existence as artworks, the very thing that fuels esthetic reconception of subjectivity, depends on the terror of the age of reification.[16] At the same time, the decoupling of artworks from their social context in the sense of harmony with that context liberates the artwork while at the same time exposing it to the risk of emptiness and failure:

> It is incontestable that artworks have, as die-hard reactionaries never cease to repeat, lost their social embeddedness. The transition from this security into the open has become, for them, a *horror vacui*; that they address an anonymous and ultimately nonexistent audience has not been just a blessing, not even immanently: not for their authenticity and not for their relevance. What ranks as problematic in the esthetic sphere has its origin here; the remainder became the plunder of boredom. Every new artwork, if it is to be one, is exposed to the danger of complete failure. (AT 158)

Adorno's *horror vacui* sends us back to the "gouffre obscurci de miasmes humains" at the center of "Le Flacon," not in a way that would seek to allegorize the poem as a mere illustration of what Adorno indicates here but rather as an invitation to read between the poem and the criticism, risking the danger of complete failure of that enterprise but valuing it precisely on account of that risk, without which both art and criticism becomes at best simplistic and at worst banal. What points to art's alienation also points, in this instance, to its power, and all of this within the context of a decomposition and recomposition of what are otherwise fairly conventional "poetic" ingredients, the world of perfume bottles, memory, and Baudelaire's particular approach to the vaporization and centralization of the self that is entirely bound up with the vaporization and centralization of the poem as well.

The possibility of failure is thus one of the conditions of the modern work of art, which brings us back to "Le Chien et le flacon." As I have suggested, a look back at "Le Flacon" opens up new interpretive possibilities in what we might call "reading backwards," a process whereby Baudelaire's prose poems do not simply demystify or debunk a poetic vision prevalent in the verse poems but rather open up sources of dialectical tension between the two that is not easily assimilable to a simple cancelation. I have already indicated that the "effroi" in the prose poem aligns it with the *horror vacui* present in the abyss of the verse poem and that a straightforward allegorical reading of the poem does not likely do justice to the prose poem and could even be seen as a trap for a superficial reader. I framed this as a question about what a proper "consuming" of the poem would be, a question that reduces the distance between artwork and commodity. Jérome Thélot's masterful reading of "Le Chien le le flacon" suggests that similar kinds of blurring are operative in the poem, with the poet exhibiting certain characteristics of the bourgeois he is criticizing in the poem, for instance.[17] Likewise, according to Thélot it becomes difficult to distinguish between author and public in this poem where "le mépris des 'ordures' [. . .] bute sur l'insubstantialité de la différence entre elles et les 'parfums délicats'—ces oeuvres où les artistes se mirent" ["the hatred of the *'ordures'* [. . .] abuts the insubstantiality of the difference between it and the 'delicate perfumes'—those works where artists admire themselves"] (35). Such a blurring forces a reconsideration of esthetic perception that is not involved in establishing an opposition between the beautiful and the ugly, nor a reversal of the value of those terms. Nor is it a question of simply eliminating those esthetic categories altogether, however: "La réponse qu'attend l'agression baudelairienne, c'est au total de n'apprécier « Le Chien et le flacon » ni comme un parfum ni comme un paquet d'excréments. Ce poème n'est ni beau ni laid : sa violence fait sauter les critères du jugement esthétique" ["The reply that Baudelairean aggression is expecting is to appreciate "Le Chien et le flacon" neither as a perfume nor as a packet of excrement. The poem is neither beautiful nor ugly : its violence blows up the criteria of esthetic judgment"] (36). I would argue that we cannot simply jettison esthetic categories in the case of a poem such as "Le Chien et le flacon" because our very perception of the poem as acting on these categories depends on their existence as categories. Without the kinds of transcendence sometimes evoked by Baudelaire in his poetry, the attempt to think beyond that transcendence in poems such as this one would be a moot point, which risks rendering the prose poem meaningless.

The prose poem thus depends on several kinds of dissonance, not just that between the artist and a philistine bourgeois public but between the artist as both bourgeois and critic of the bourgeoisie, as both distinct from and allied with the reader. Being attentive to that dissonance by a careful working through of a prose poem that poses at first as a straightforward and fairly simplistic allegory can in turn condition the way we read verse poems such as "Le Flacon," where the opposite seems to be the case: the poem presents a complex web of images and metonymic and metaphoric relations that challenge conventional notions of lyric subjectivity, yet as we have seen, many readings of the poem attempt to synthesize those images into a consonant whole, often one that depends for its organizing structure on the genre of the love poem. Beyond the biographical fact of the poem having been dedicated to Madame Sabatier, however, precious little in the poem supports seeing love poetry as the best interpretive frame. While in "Le Chien et le flacon" readers need to be wrested from the temptation to follow expectations and see in it a facile allegory, in the case of "Le Flacon" the violence that the poem's structure does to the coherence of the images, even within the basic comparative structure of the "ainsi," should move us away from attempts to impose harmonious coherence on the poem, so that we can be more effectively attentive to the dissonance from which a reconfigured poetic subjectivity emerges, one that blurs the boundary between subject and object by conflating poet and poem.

By a curious reversal, those who see an unmitigated affirmation of classic or romantic notions of beauty in Baudelaire are just as taken in by the temptations of the texts as those who would see the prose poetry as a cynical rethinking either of those notions of beauty or as establishing a clear distinction between artist and bourgeois public. Some of Baudelaire's theoretical writings are so imbued with notions of poetic beauty that phrases such as this one made not one but two appearances in his work: "le principe de la poésie est, strictement et simplement, l'aspiration humaine vers une beauté supérieure" ["the principle of poetry is, strictly and simply, the human aspiration toward a superior beauty"] (2: 334 and 2: 114). But as Thélot notes, "il utilise ce thème de la beauté, en le dégradant, pour attirer à lui le destinataire. Il blasphème sa transcendance théorique en l'attribuant servilement au public, l'approbation de celui-ci lui étant autrement nécessaire que la beauté supérieure" ["he uses this theme of beauty, while degrading it, to draw his recipient toward him. He blasphemes his theoretical transcendence by attributing it slavishly to the public, its approbation being necessary to him otherwise than superior beauty"] (26). Perhaps nothing traps us better within the kind of bourgeois taste that Baudelaire condemns than an investment in precisely the kind of beauty that Baudelaire himself sometimes seems to endorse. The poems invite us to take a step beyond that notion of beauty by neither affirming nor negating it but to think simultaneously within and beyond it, to carve a space for the negation of a bourgeois approach to art from within that very approach, as a kind of thinking against itself, an esthetics of dissonance that is also an esthetics of attentiveness to the way art is conceptualized and made, in Baudelaire's time and our own.

2

Subjectivity

It is no secret that subjectivity plays an important role in Baudelaire, the writer who famously noted in his autobiographical notes: "De la vaporisation et de la centralisation du *Moi*. Tout est là" ["Of the vaporization and the centralization of the *Self*. All is there"] (1: 676).[1] The simultaneity of opposing actions highlights the duality that fuels Baudelaire's poetic production, its working through of the "deux postulations simultanées, l'une vers Dieu, l'autre vers Satan" ["two simultaneous postulations, one toward God, the other toward Satan"] (1: 682), are central to his esthetic project. There is, however, far more to Baudelaire's intervention into poetic subjectivity than a simple positing of simultaneous opposites. In this chapter I attempt to articulate the way in which Baudelaire reconfigures subjectivity by emptying it, notably by figuring it as related to liquid, and filling it up in such a way that the poetic terrain of poetic subject and poetic object is rewritten in ways that distribute subjectivity and objectivity differently across the lyric subject and the poem. The poetic process in Baudelaire is not one that simply centralizes or vaporizes the self but one that entirely reconfigures it. In this chapter I will demonstrate how poems such as "L'Héautontimorouménos" and "La Fontaine de sang" could be said to reveal a fractured, ironic subjectivity that was already operative in earlier poems that appeared under the guise of a unified or harmonious lyric subject. The violence of the reconfigured understanding of lyric subjectivity is perhaps most clearly visible in "Le Confiteor de l'artiste," the subject of an extended analysis at the heart of the chapter, which goes on to consider how object-oriented poems such as "Le Couvercle" illustrate not only such a transformed subjectivity but also the mediated nature of the lyric's relation both to the mundane and to what had been considered transcendent on the earlier models of subjectivity on which Baudelaire depends at the same time as he reveals the dissonance at their heart. Subjectivity in Baudelaire goes beyond the mere doubling that an approach oriented by the *homo duplex* or even one that underscores the vaporization and centralization of the self would suggest. The complex subjectivity that plays out across Baudelaire's poetry suggests a mutually constitutive play between subject and object that I will appeal to Adorno's dialectical thinking about subjectivity in order to help elucidate. For both Baudelaire and Adorno, subjectivity is established in a complex relation to an object but never reduced to it, defined sometimes by negation but never eliminated by that negative constitution.

As I have suggested, artworks themselves have an important role to play in reconceptualizing the kind of lyric subjectivity that has haunted popular (and less popular) conceptions of lyric subjectivity since Romanticism, namely, the lyric I as a transparent and whole subject writing the lyric as a vehicle for expression of subjective (often affective) states. As Stephanie Belmer has argued in a commentary on "shudder" in Adorno: "Artworks [...] have the power to break down the illusion of a closed subject. I see such a breakdown as addressing the ability of art to puncture a subject's illusion of solidity with the destabilizing effect of something jarring, surprising, and unknown" (Belmer 37). This model reserves an important task for modern poetry, which is not necessarily to undo the subject but rather to become the site of disclosure of the nonexistence of the individuated, solid, self-positing bourgeois self as modern philosophy in the wake of Fichte and the idealist tradition had conceived of it. On this view, Baudelaire does not so much perform an undoing or fragmenting of the self so much as he makes visible a sort of fragmentation that was already present in the Romantic lyric self but covered over by other assumptions about the unity of the "I."

> On a trop tendance [...] à interpréter le lyrisme romantique comme l'expression de l'impérialisme du Moi. Or tout en exaltant le sujet, il a travaillé à le destituer de son autonomie, de sa souveraineté et de son identité. Pour Lamartine, le sujet lyrique n'est qu' « un instrument sonore de sensations, de sentiments et d'idées » [...] provoquées en lui par « la commotion plus ou moins forte » qu'il reçoit des choses extérieures ou intérieures. Il se constitue au point de rencontre de l'intérieur et de l'extérieur, du monde et du langage. Et c'est en ce point que Baudelaire situe aussi « l'art moderne » capable de créer « une magie suggestive contenant à la fois l'objet et le sujet, le monde extérieur à l'artiste et l'artiste lui-même » [...]. Cette ouverture remet en cause et peut mettre en crise l'identité du sujet romantique. (Collot 117–18)[2]

> [There is too great a tendency [...] to interpret romantic lyricism as the expression of the imperialism of the Self. But even while exalting the subject, it worked to deprive it of its autonomy, its sovereignty, and its identity. For Lamartine, the lyric subject is only "a sonorous instrument of sensations, sentiments, and ideas" [...] provoked in him by "the more or less strong commotion" that he receives from external or internal

things. It is constituted at the meeting point of interior and exterior, of the world and language. And it is at that point that Baudelaire also places "modern art" capable of creating "a suggestive magic containing at the same time object and subject, the world external to the artist and the artist himself" [...] That opening reintroduces and can put into crisis the identity of the romantic subject.]

Poetry thus has the potential to become the site of legibility of the non-stable self that was already present but not quite visible, a subject that Jean-Louis Cornille associates especially with the prose poems and describes as "hautement ironisé et en décalage par rapport à soi-même et à la société" ["highly ironized and out of synch with both itself and society"] (Cornille 135). There are echoes here of something that I claimed about dissonance in the last chapter, namely, that dissonance reveals the falseness of harmony that was already there in classicist esthetics but only made particularly visible by subsequent esthetic developments that allow us to read backward and hear consonance differently. In a similar way, it is not that we move in poets such as Baudelaire to a new conception of a fragmented and tenuous self, but, rather, that his poetry might help us see and articulate the ways in which the modern bourgeois self, which he both perpetuates and transforms, was already only the fiction of a solid totality.

Orienting subjectivity along the lines of questions about the solidity of earlier modern models of selfhood allows us to see that it is a site of questioning where philosophy and art (and specifically literature in this case) intersect. As J. M. Bernstein notes:

> Because it is idealism that represents the fulfilment of metaphysics, what Adorno terms "identity thinking," then the overcoming of idealism requires an overcoming of the standpoint of the devouring subject: "our aim is total self-relinquishment" (ND 13). Negative dialectics and esthetics are the two roads to self-relinquishment. The goal of the former is "to use concepts to unseal the non-conceptual with concepts, without making it their equal"; this it can accomplish only by changing the direction of conceptuality, giving it a "turn toward non-identity," which is the "hinge of negative dialectics" (ND 10, 12). (Bernstein, "Why Rescue Semblance" 188)

Adorno identifies a split in the self that allows it to conceive of itself as other in the first place, which is an essential aspect of reflection or thinking to begin with. As he writes in *Negative Dialectics*:

> Only if the I on its part is also not I does it react to the not-I. Only then does it "do" something. Only then would the doing itself be thinking. Thinking, in a second reflection, breaks the supremacy of thinking over

its otherness, because it always is otherness already, within itself [. . .]. The mind's nonbeing moment is so intertwined with existence that to pick it out neatly would be the same as to objectify and falsify it. (ND 201–2)³

Here Adorno describes the self as always already split, in the very act of recognizing itself. Moreover, the difference between subject and object for Adorno cannot be suppressed because the two are mutually constitutive: "The difference between subject and object cannot be simply negated. They are neither an ultimate duality nor a screen hiding ultimate unity. They constitute one another as much as—by virtue of such constitution—they depart from each other" (ND 174).⁴

When we turn to split selves in poetry, such as the reduction of the subject-object relation in poems such as "L'Héautontimorouménos," these poems could be said on this model not to perform the disunity of the self by fracturing it but rather to make manifest, in the grammar and form of the poem, a split that was already there and that is simply hidden by the falsity of linguistic simplifications such as the one that allows us to say "I" as if that referred to a solid and unified subject. Baudelaire suggests such complications of subjectivity in his critical writings; he quotes music theorist Auguste Barbereau, for instance, who groups philosophers and poets together by their ability to be subject and object simultaneously: "Les grands poètes, les philosophes, les prophètes sont des êtres qui par le pur et libre exercice de la volonté parviennent à un état où ils sont à la fois cause et effet, sujet et objet, magnétiseur et somnambule" ["Great poets, philosophers, and prophets are beings who by the pure and free exercise of will arrive at a state where they are at once cause and effect, subject and object, magnetizer and sleepwalker"] (1: 398). Baudelaire adds : "Je pense exactement comme lui" ["I think exactly like him"] (1: 398). What is notable here is that the subject-object distinction does not disappear: being both simultaneously necessitates the preservation of the distinction and resonates with Adorno's characterization of the subject-object relation as mutually constitutive. What Baudelaire endorses is an essentially dialectical subjectivity that maintains and complicates the subject-object relation rather than obliterating it. Even in his talk of the non-self, it is not a question of a simple disappearance of the self. He writes in "Le Peintre de la vie moderne" about the "amoureux de la vie universelle" ["lover of universal life"] that "on peut aussi le comparer, lui, à un miroir immense de cette foule; à un kaléidoscope doué de conscience [. . .]. C'est un *moi* insatiable du *non-moi*, qui à chaque instant, le rend et l'exprime en images plus vivantes que la vie elle-même, toujours instable et fugitive" ["one can also compare him to an immense mirror of that crowd, to a kaleidoscope endowed with consciousness [. . .]. It is a *self* insatiably thirsty for the *non-self*, who at each instant renders and expresses it in more lively images than life itself, always unstable and fleeting"] (2: 692). Far from disappearing into the crowd or collapsing the subject-object distinction, the artist is figured here as shaping his consciousness by the desire for non-self, a desire that can only be operational if the self is ultimately maintained and shaped by that desire rather than obliterated by it, represented in the poem even as a dialectical subject constituted in important ways by the object and defined by that relation.[5]

Such a blurring of our definition of what constitutes the individualized self opens up a space not only for the "I" to be foreign to, and object to, itself, but also for it to be bound up imperceptibly with other people, other selves, as well, again in both a philosophical and literary sense. This location of others, not only as objects of, but as constituent parts of, the self, also has political consequences, and it is in this way that subjectivity as enacted in literature begins to take on political stakes. Literature is, of course, highly political for Adorno, but not on account of explicit thematization of politics. Rather, the political structures and critique are inscribed more abstractly within the form and grammar of the artwork, not least of which is the system of subject-object relations as they play out grammatically. Adorno's reflections on the I and not-I in *Negative Dialectics* echo his discussion of the self and the artwork in *Aesthetic Theory*, where he assigns a certain subjectivity to the artwork itself insofar as it has an ability to undo what we would typically call the subject or the "I":

> the labor in the artwork becomes social by way of the individual, though the individual need not be conscious of society; perhaps this is all the more true the less the individual is conscious of society. The intervening individual subject is scarcely more than a limiting value, something minimal required by the artwork for its crystallization. The emancipation of the artwork from the artist is no *l'art pour l'art* delusion of grandeur but the simplest expression of the work's constitution as the expression of a social relation that bears in itself the law of its own reification: Only as things do artworks become the antithesis of the reified monstrosity. Correspondingly, and this is key to art, even out of so-called individual works it is a We that speaks and not an I—indeed all the more so the less the artwork adapts externally to a We and its idiom. (AT 167)

Here Adorno develops an idea we first encountered last chapter, that autonomous art is not a withdrawal from politics but an articulation of politics as critique, a resistance to sociopolitical reality by the crafting of an imaginative space of literature where subject-object relations are reconfigured in such a way that the individualized solid "I" on which bourgeois society stands is showed to be shaky ground at best if not totally untenable. It is a space closed off to the world so as to better concentrate on reading the words, and in a way that will reveal that "I" is "we," in an intensely concentrated reading of the text that inscribes the social not despite, but because, it closes off the text from the world in order to pay better attention to the way it reveals social relations and reconfigures the self accordingly. Fragmentation of the self is at the same time bound up with consideration of parts and wholes of the artwork itself, as there is never a precise alignment in terms of the way parts add up to wholes, a classic problem for hermeneutics:

> Traditional aesthetics possessed the insight that primacy of the whole over the parts has constitutive need of the diverse and that this primacy misfires when it is simply imposed from above. No less constitutive, however, is that no artwork has ever been fully adequate in this regard. Granted, the multiplicitous in the esthetic continuum wants synthesis, yet at the same time, being determined extra-esthetically, it withdraws from synthesis. (AT 169)[6]

The artwork thus seeks the very same wholeness by which it would cease to be an artwork; we saw a similar situation in the case of harmony in the last chapter whereby the striving for harmony on the part of the artwork would be meaningless if dissonance were not a constituent part of the artwork that at some level claims to want to negate that difference. The modern artwork, and also earlier artworks which we can now read differently after the emergence of the modern, depend on a certain kind of failure in order for them to succeed.

Vaporization and centralization are not the only ways to conceive the actions performed on the self in Baudelaire. I turn now to a consideration of the way the Baudelairean lyric self is not vaporized but rather liquefied, as a form of what we might even call liquidation, an emptying out of a common, unified notion of the lyric self the better to fill it up again in reconfigured ways that incorporate language, the other, and language as other in a more nuanced conception of subjectivity. First, we will consider "Sed non satiata," where a woman is drunk by the poet: "Bizarre déité [. . .] / Je préfère au constance, à l'opium, au nuits, / L'élixir de ta bouche où l'amour se pavane"(28) ["Bizarre deity [. . .] / I prefer to *constance*, to opium, to *nuits*, / The nectar of your mouth upon which love parades" (91, translation amended)]. Several characteristics emerge from these first images of drinking the (fragmented) woman as liquid: first, the action is not performed in order to assuage thirst, since, as even the title of the poem indicates, this particular thirst is perpetually renewed despite, or perhaps because, it is constantly indulged. Second, it is not traditionally drinkable beverages which are ingested but, rather, in both cases, bodily fluids: blood and saliva. Lastly, the drinking relationship is dynamic, as poet and love object take turns from one poem to the next being drinker and drunk.[7] Bodily exchange of natural fluids fuels poetic creation at this local moment of *Les Fleurs du Mal*, where already the kind of displaced subjectivity that would find its fullest expression in poems like "L'Héautontimorouménos" is already at play, not at an abstract conceptual level, but in the act of living from the borrowed energy of another's fluids, either given up voluntarily or robbed by a vampire.

In "Sed non satiata" what is remarkable is not only the complexity of the drinking images and the role reversal between drinker and drunk, but also the permeability of gender roles in it. The poet laments the fact that he cannot transform himself, first into a liquid ("Je ne suis pas le Styx pour t'embrasser neuf fois" ["I'm not the River Styx to embrace you nine times"]) and then into the wife of Pluto ("Je ne puis [. . .] / Dans l'enfer de ton lit devenir Proserpine" [1: 28]) ["I cannot [. . .] / In the hell of your bed turn into Proserpine!" (91)]. By their evocation in the poem, these transformations are in fact given a kind of poetic reality, an existence within the universe of the poem itself. The poem is thus both the performance of eternally unquenched thirst and the virtual transformation that creates an imaginative space where the poet might satisfy his desire of becoming the drinker and the drink, the seducer and the seduced. This is precisely the space, theorized by Yves Bonnefoy, of "la réalité intérieure, celle où a lieu le rapport de la personne à soi-même" ["interior reality, the one where the relation of the person to him or herself takes place"] (216). These poems perform a circulation among spaces of various kinds that is not unlike the procedure of the *flâneur* and the poet of urban life who would become manifest in the 1861 "Tableaux parisiens." Both involve evoking and transforming a set of spaces, and negotiating between lived reality and a set of mythical references.

It is useful in this regard to consider Zygmunt Bauman's theorization of "liquid modernity." While Bauman's analysis situates it chronologically in the period that most would refer to as postmodernity, his theorization of many features of liquid modernity resonates with the kind of fluidity we have been tracing in Baudelaire's poetry:

> Fluids, so to speak, neither fix space nor bind time. While solids have clear spatial dimensions but neutralize the impact, and thus downgrade the significance, of time [. . .], fluids do not keep to any shape for long [. . .]; and so for them it is the flow of time that counts. (2)

In Baudelaire's poetry, the passage to liquid metaphors accompanies a reduction in geographical specificity. From the country house of his childhood in "J'aime le souvenir. . .," the poems expand to a vaguely evoked "cité." In the midst of the breakdown of such formerly solid structures as the domestic interior and the body of the poet, it is, significantly, poetic form that remains solid. Baudelaire's regular forms, meters, and rhymes serve as the only anchor in this poetry where dimensions of time and space are reduced to the same kind of liquid state as the poet's blood, fertilizing a new kind of modern poetic territory while at the same time preserving a discourse of metaphysical evil as the impetus behind this birth of the modern, a sort of "metaphysical modern" which, unlike the Paris poems, expands the notion of time and space to envelop even such decidedly premodern notions as original sin. The original "fall," then, is like a waterfall, eternally the same in its constant change, challenging any attempt to fix it in time. It is through an act of allegorization, Baudelaire will reveal, that we can synthesize these newly reconfigured relationships among time, space, solid, liquid, body, and spirit.

The boundlessness and protean shapings of liquid, then, serve as a figure for both the lyrical self and lyrical language, as it outflows the boundaries of mimetic representation of the unified self into as yet uncharted poetic territory. We have already seen a similar scenario in the last chapter in "Le Flacon," which presents a voluntary confusion between poet and poetry. In this sense, we can say with Adorno that poetic language liberates the rigidity of the reified self. As Ulrich Plass notes, "Adorno cannot speak of language other than in metaphors of stream, current, and flow. The reason is that he views the emergence of subjectivity as bound to a process of reification during which the ego becomes rigid and hard" (Plass xxxvii–xxxviii). Some aspects of Adorno's analysis of lyric language's effect on subjectivity in the poetry of Joseph von Eichendorff apply to Baudelaire as well: "His poetry is not 'subjectivistic' in the way one tends to think of Romanticism as being: it raises a mute objection to the poetic subject, a sacrifice to the impulses of language" (*Notes* 1: 65). Such emptying of self into and through language functions not as a permanent liquidation or weakening of the self, or a complete giving over of the self to language, but, rather, an opportunity for its reconfiguration as a site of resistance to the reified bourgeois lyric self:

> The poetic subject that gives itself up to language is paradoxically a strong subject; in contradistinction, the hardened subject suffers from, to use another one of Adorno's frequent terms, ego-weakness—one of the greatest obstacles an education to political maturity has to confront. (Plass xxxviii)

Adorno's figure to represent the flow of language in which the subject loses itself is *Rauschen*, the flow or babbling of wind or water. As Plass indicates: "If Eichendorff's poetry suspends the ego and casts aside the humanist ideal of Bildung, what does it offer in its place? Nothing but language—Rauschen—in which the subject loses itself" (xxxviii). This is not to say that Adorno defends some kind of deconstructionist approach whereby there is nothing outside the text, or even the Mallarméan notion of the *disparition élocutoire du poète*.[8] Something else is at work in Baudelaire, a more dialectical approach to ego-weakening that becomes strong not only by its potential for implicit political resistance to anything like a communicative function for art (this is, as we have seen, the way in which autonomous art has progressive political potential as critique) but also by the way it reconfigures the relations of subject and object in terms of the lyric subject, the human other, and the artwork as participating in that subjectivity as well, via its "critical power to undo subjectivity" (Belmer 37).

To liberate the flow of subjectivity, then, and to begin to see what was already there behind the façade, is to start to conceptualize a complex notion of subjectivity. The self, on this view, would not be permanently dissolved but never again fully individuated either; the dissonance between full dissolution and full individuation is what constitutes the model. This kind of self becomes individuated in its loss of individuation and its reconstitution, but that reconstitution itself depends on the preservation of the former self in order to be defined against it and to preserve a certain nostalgic sense of loss for the unified strong self that never really was to begin with. This is a subjectivity that is possible only on the condition of its impossibility or, rather, how that subjectivity is rearticulated in ways that account for a dynamism among lyric subject, the other, and the artwork as itself a subject. Such a view expands a more simplistic notion of a lyric self as simply mediated by its social context.[9] Colleen Shu-Ching Wu enumerates this complexity:

> In the dialectical relation between the lyric self and the other, if the other is not only society but also the other composed within poetry (such as a world, a concept, someone, memory, etc), then the lyric self is not simply mediated by an external social context but also by the other composed within a poem, an instance of poetic discourse. [. . .] In the discussion of the lyric, both sides, the individual and the "representedness" of what is, are not simple realities delineated by a transcendent observer but are constructed within their positional, complementary, and interweaving relations. (345)

To say that a self and other are constituted by discourse in the lyric is not to reduce their reality to a mere effect of language but rather to assert lyric poetic language's power to define our very ways of knowing and referring to self and other, to acknowledge the way lyric language can act in the world so as to create a subject who enters into dialectical relation with that language. To say that is to affirm a certain power of language and, in so far as language can act, to assign it a subjectivity that can enter into relation with, altering and being altered by, the subject who reads and writes it. As Adorno puts it:

> Art's linguistic quality gives rise to reflection over what speaks in art; this is its veritable subject, not the individual who makes it or the one who receives it. This is masked by the lyrical "I," which in confessing has

over the centuries produced the semblance of the self-evidence of poetic subjectivity. (AT 166–7)

In other words, the more the lyrical "I" became confessional, arguably reaching its height in the Romantic period, the more it belies lyric subjectivity as the transparent communication of a unified self. Adorno here accords subjectivity to the work of art itself by characterizing it as speaking: the work speaks through the subject rather than vice versa.[10] Thus the work of art is no longer merely an object but also becomes a subject in dialectical relation both to the lyric "I" and to the other, a "you," who may appear in the poem and who may or may not be fully distinct from the "I," since now all three, that is, the poem, the I, and the you, are mutually constituted and inseparable.

To conceive of lyric subjectivity this way is in one sense to reduce it to nothingness; after all, if the bourgeois stable individual subject evaporates under this conception, arguably nothing is left. But as Adorno signals, this nonbeing of the subject then paradoxically forms the basis for its rearticulation:

> The idealist construction of the subject founders on its falsely taking subject to be objective in the sense of something existing in-itself, precisely what it is not: measured against the standard of entities, the subject is condemned to nothingness. Subject is all the more the less it is, and all the less the more it believes itself to exist, to be for itself something objective. As an essential moment, however, it is ineradicable. Upon the elimination of the subjective moment the object would come apart diffusely like the fleeting stirrings and twinklings of subjective life. (*Critical* 257)

Adorno thus argues not for the eradication of the subject but for a reimagination of what subjectivity would be, in a context shared by philosophy and esthetics. As Terry Eagleton has noted, the centralization of the bourgeois subject is ultimately self-undermining, since there would be no objective criteria by which the subject could measure its relative importance:

> The more the world is thus subjectivized, the more this all-privileged subject begins to undermine the very objective conditions of its own pre-eminence. The wider the subject extends its imperial sway over reality, the more it relativizes that terrain to its own needs and desires, dissolving the world's substance into the stuff of its own senses. Yet the more it thereby erodes any objective criteria by which to measure the significance or even reality of its own experience. The subject needs to know that it is supremely valuable; but it cannot know this if its own solipsism has cancelled out any scale by which such value might be assessed. What is

this subject privileged *over*, if the world has been steadily dwindled to no more than an obedient mirror image of itself? (Eagleton *Ideology* 70)

Once again, we can see a parallel between what we said about consonance and dissonance and the centralization of the bourgeois self: that centralization only makes sense against the backdrop of an objective world by which we could affirm the self as central; dismantling the objective world thoroughly would leave the centralized subject without a center, just as dissonance is only recognizable as such within the context of consonance and the tensions between them that are implied by the system of tonal harmony.

Thus the decentralized self depends, fundamentally and paradoxically, on a community of others, a shared sense of meaning by which turns of phrase such as the vaporization and the centralization of the self would have any meaning at all. The work of art becomes the site of evaluating the truth of these claims, the site where language performs its work independently of either a vaporized or centralized speaking subject, necessitating the work of the interpreter in order to make any claims about the relation of the self to the text. It is above all a vampiric notion of the self, as Eagleton notes:

> The bourgeois subject would seem in this sense a tragically self-defeating creature, one whose very self-affirmation turns inexorably back upon itself to eat away at its own enabling conditions. [. . .] It is vital that the world confirms my subjectivity, yet I am a subject only in so far as I bring this world to be in the first place. (*Ideology* 70–1).

"All is there" in the vaporization and centralization of the self, but the question remains of what to make of what is there, and on this dialectical view of the kind of bourgeois subjectivity on display in lyric poetry, the affirmation that all is there comes to seem more of an invitation to work out what such a claim might mean rather than a formula that would close down any further affirmations about subjectivity. Baudelaire's statement is the starting point rather than the end of reflection on the way subjectivity is operative in poetry; Adorno can help us understand the way in which these questions need to be worked out in the context of the lyric itself, rather than seeing it as a mere illustration of either the centralization or the vaporization of the self. To ask such questions about subjectivity is thus to blur the line between esthetic and philosophical activity and to see them as deeply interwoven. It is an act of the imagination that was so important to Baudelaire. In the chapter on imagination as "la reine des facultés" in *Le Salon de 1859*, Baudelaire offers a critique of those who want artists to render nature "as it is" precisely on the grounds that those who would affirm that they know "*toute la nature*, tout ce qui est contenu dans la nature" ["*all* of nature, everything that is contained in nature"] (2: 620) would be giving an affirmation that is "la plus fanfaronne et la plus extravagante des réponses" ["the most swaggering and extravagant of replies"] (2: 620). Rather, what is called for, in this absence of objective criteria by which we could affirm that what we see is indeed all of reality, is a creative act that involves disassembling and reassembling the parts of the whole: "[L'imagination] décompose toute la création, et, avec les matériaux amassés et disposés suivant des règles dont on ne peut trouver l'origine que dans le plus profond de l'âme, elle crée un monde nouveau, elle produit la sensation du neuf [. . .]. L'imagination est la reine du vrai" ["[Imagination] decomposes all of creation and, with materials amassed and arranged according to the rules whose origin we can only find in the most profound depth of the soul, it creates a new world, it produces the sensation of the new"] (2: 621). Baudelaire's claims resonate with Adorno's constellatory approach whereby philosophical reflection develops from the artwork but always finds itself undone in creative ways by that artwork which surpasses reflection and shows it to be always incomplete. Truth is found in creation undertaken by the imagination on Baudelaire's view, and thus to go about attempting to make truth claims either about the artwork or the world in which it participates is to engage questions of subjectivity as it too is decomposed and recreated in the process of reading and writing lyric.

By affirming a certain kind of subjectivity for the work of art itself, we can see important parallels in the changing status of both the work of art and the subject that constitutes and is constituted by the modern work of art as inaugurated in Baudelaire. As Terry Eagleton has noted in a discussion of Adorno, the role of the modern artwork is paradoxical in that "culture is deeply locked into the structure of commodity production; but one effect of this is to release it into a certain ideological autonomy, hence allowing it to speak against the very social order with which it is guiltily complicit" (Eagleton 349). Because "art can only be authentic if it silently acknowledges how deeply it is compromised by what it opposes [. . .] it would seem that art must now either abolish itself entirely [. . .] or hover indecisively between life and death, subsuming its own impossibility into itself" (349). However, "it is this internal slippage or hiatus within the art work, this impossibility of ever coinciding exactly with itself, which provides the very source of its critical power, in a world where objects lie petrified in their monotonously self-same being, doomed to the hell of being no more than themselves" (349). Both the lyric speaker and the lyric poem are subject to this potential for autonomy from within the limits of their own compromised nature and the potential for critique that such a position instantiates through yielding to the flow of poetic language. As we have seen, this kind of weakening of the subject is, paradoxically, its strength because liquefying the subject frees it from its reification and the fictional unity that it may have tried to claim for itself.

Thus the work of art facilitates a liberating decentering of the lyric subject that serves as a corrective to the kind of ultimately constraining concentration on the self that drugs such as hashish provoke according to

Baudelaire: "Le hachisch ne révèle à l'individu rien que l'individu lui-même. Il est vrai que cet indvidu est pour ainsi dire cubé et poussé à l'extrême" ["Haschich reveals nothing to the individual but the individual himself. It is true that this individual is so to speak cubed and pushed to the extreme"] (1: 440). Hashish actually compromises the faculty of the imagination that one might think it enriches: "il accorde d'un côté ce qu'il retire de l'autre, c'est-à-dire l'imagination sans la faculté d'en profiter" ["it gives on one hand what it takes back with the other, that is, the imagination without the faculty to gain from it"] (1: 440). Baudelaire thus implicitly accords a certain authenticity to the artwork, which does allow the full benefit of recombinatory creation and something that Baudelaire does not hesitate to call truth, as we saw above. On this view, the centralizing of the self would be an impediment to artistic creation rather than the vehicle of it, and Baudelaire thereby moves away from a Romantic concept of genius; his approach, by weakening lyric subjectivity in order to yield more power to poetic language, echoes Adorno's emphasis on "the centrality of the artwork as mediated through the subject (producing and receiving) and the material (as content)" (Hohendahl 53). It is not a question, then, of merely getting beyond the subject, since the subject is ineradicable, but rather of accounting for the ways lyric subjectivity was able to project a false image of a solid subject and how that same lyrical language can serve as the vehicle of a new flowing subjectivity. This new conception of subjectivity takes center stage precisely by being next to nothing, becoming "all the more the less it is" through the reconstitution of subjectivity that we can see at work, I will claim, in Baudelaire's poetry, which depends on the older view of the lyric subject precisely in order to define itself against it, to show the lie which can become the esthetic truth of his poetry.

Such a reframing of lyric subjectivity identifies it as mediating and mediated by the poem itself, rather than simply serving as unified consciousness of which the poem would be a transparent expression or imitation. The poem, as subject and object, becomes the site of reflection of a lyric subject who is also both subject and object, liberated by a splitting that allows for reflection by its very breaking apart, along the lines of Adorno's model, quoted above, of the I which is also not I, which enables a doing which would be a thinking that "breaks the supremacy of thinking over its otherness, because it always is otherness already, within itself" (ND 201). With this in mind, we can turn to "LHéautontontimorouménos":

Je te frapperai sans colère
Et sans haine, comme un boucher,
Comme Moïse le rocher
Et je ferai de ta paupière,

Pour abreuver mon Sahara,
Jaillir les eaux de la souffrance.

Mon désir gonflé d'espérance
Sur tes pleurs salés nagera

Comme un vaisseau qui prend le large,
Et dans mon cœur qu'ils soûleront
Tes chers sanglots retentiront
Comme un tambour qui bat la charge!

Ne suis-je pas un faux accord
Dans la divine symphonie,
Grâce à la vorace Ironie
Qui me secoue et qui me mord ?

Elle est dans ma voix, la criarde!
C'est tout mon sang ce poison noir!
Je suis le sinistre miroir
Où la mégère se regarde.

Je suis la plaie et le couteau!
Je suis le soufflet et la joue!
Je suis les membres et la roue,
Et la victime et le bourreau!

Je suis de mon cœur le vampire,
— Un de ces grands abandonnés
Au rire éternel condamnés
Et qui ne peuvent plus sourire! (1: 78–9)[11]

[I shall strike you without anger
And without hate, like a butcher,
As Moses struck the rock!
And from your eyelids I shall make

The waters of suffering gush forth
To inundate my Sahara.
My desire swollen with hope
Will float upon your salty tears

Like a vessel which puts to sea,
And in my heart that they'll make drunk
Your beloved sobs will resound
Like a drum beating the charge!

Am I not a discord
In the heavenly symphony,
Thanks to voracious Irony
Who shakes me and who bites me?

She's in my voice, the termagant!
All my blood is her black poison!
I am the sinister mirror
In which the vixen looks.

I am the wound and the dagger!
I am the blow and the cheek!
I am the members and the wheel,
Victim and executioner!

I'm the vampire of my own heart
— One of those utter derelicts
Condemned to eternal laughter,
But who can no longer smile! (*Flowers* 263–5)]

Lyric subjectivity has a most unusual status in the poem, for the first person hides more than it reveals about the subjectivity it putatively represents. What happens to the "je" here is far more than simple doubling or splitting of the self in two. The poem quickly assimilates the "tu" to the "je," thus performing the vanishing of the second person by establishing its equivalence with the "je." While some may assume a relationship between two people in the first three stanzas, nothing in the text suggests that the "te" is a person other than the lyric subject himself. If anything, the title encourages us to see the lyric subject standing alone in the poem, since it implies the kind of autoreflexive violence that is played out from the very first line. Why, then, are we tempted to see the first part of the poem as representing a relationship between two people?

It is true that Baudelaire initially conceived the first part as representing an intersubjective violent relationship between the lyric subject and a lover. The poem as we know it could in some sense be called a fragment; Baudelaire had initially planned for it to be an epilogue to his verse collection. An 1855 letter to Victor de Mars enumerates an outline where the speaking subject asks that his lover be "cruelle, menteuse, libertine, crapuleuse et voleuse; --et si vous ne voulez pas être cela, je vous assommerai, sans colère. Car je suis le vrai représentant de l'ironie, et ma maladie est d'un genre absolument incurable" ["cruel, lying, libertine, villainous and a thief ; --and if you do not want to be that, I will take you down, without anger. Because I am the true representative of irony, and my sickness is of an absolutely incurable type"] (1: 985). An early manuscript copy places the word "Sinon" before the start of what we know as the full poem, suggesting that the violence in the first three stanzas does take place between two people and is not the work of the speaking subject on himself. But this key does little to account for the poem as we actually have it in *Les Fleurs du Mal*, where instead of such a clear intersubjective relation, we have a completely ambiguous suite of three stanzas where subject and object could very well be the same person, an interpretation that is confirmed by the title we have read at the head of the poem.

So as we read the poem as it is presented in every printed version, it should be obvious that *je* and *te* are the same person. Why then do so many critics take it for granted that the first part of the poem is about a pair of lovers? Jean Starobinski, for instance, argues that in the latter half of the poem "le rapport à soi a supplanté le rapport à l'autre: il aura fallu, pour cela, que s'opère le dédoublement, grâce auquel *se frapper soi-même* devient un geste représentable, homologue et inverse du geste de frapper l'autre" ["the relation to the self has supplanted the relation to the other: for that it was necessary for a doubling to have occured, thanks to which *to hit oneself* becomes a representable gesture, homologue and inverse of the gesture of hitting the other"] (34). What is at stake in positing an interpretation of the poem is exactly what action it represents and when. While there is a turning point of some kind in the central stanza where the speaking subject labels himself the "faux accord," we would still lack evidence for the presence of a lover in the first three stanzas. And in fact there are, strictly speaking, no literal violent actions at all in the poem: all of the acts of violence in the first part are presented in the future tense, one that never spills over into an immediate present. When the tense shifts to the present, it is an iterative present. The poem is structured to perform the vanishing of time, as the future tense of the first three stanzas disappears in favor of an eternal iterative present. These shifts are mirrored by the structural changes from simile in the first part to metaphor in the second, from a verse structure favoring enjambment and syntactical inversions to a more straightforward prose-like verse structure in the second part. Each part thus stands on its own and in relation to the other part; the structure performs the same singularity in duality as the first-person subject. If the poem performs an act of violence, it is not to be found in any mimetic representation of violence but rather the liberating gesture by which the poem frees readers from invalid assumptions about lyric subjectivity and objectivity.

We might say there is a dissonance between our expectations about the text and what the text actually indicates; the sheer novelty of a lyric subject representing himself as subject and object simultaneously can make us inattentive to the text to the point where we impose more well-worn interpretive scenarios on it, making it into a love poem—an unusual one to be sure, but still a more conventional poem than what we actually have in the text. We might come to expect Baudelaire to be bizarre in certain kinds of ways, and poems such as "A celle qui est trop gaie" set us up to expect him to stage sadistic violence against a lover. But in the case of "L'Héautontimorouménos," he gives us the unexpected in unexpected ways by staging the self as both subject and object, in ways that hide in plain sight, under a title that clearly indicates the textual situation. There is thus a dissonance between our expectations based on other poems we have read (by Baudelaire and in the long history of lyric love poetry) and this poem; we are not so much shocked by its novelty as unable to see that novelty. What turns out to be most unusual about the poem is not its sadism but rather its reconfiguration of subjectivity. Given the complacency of our reading strategies, it requires an act of textual violence in order to shake us out of well tread patterns of interpretation in order to see where Baudelaire's novelty actually lies in this poem. And in that sense, the *te* becomes the reader, in that we are subject to the poet's act of creative violence that stirs us from interpretive complacency and makes us reconsider the ways we align subject and object within the lyric.

The relationship to self is figured as a dissonance both in the sense that the self does violence to itself and also that the interpretation of the subjectivity as one person rather than two stands in a dissonant relationship to more easily accessible interpretations about a pair of lovers. This multiplied self that is simultaneously subject and object finds echo, in the first self-description in the poem, in the metaphor of the "faux accord." The ambiguity of unity and multiplicity is underscored in the very notion of a chord, which is perceived as a single harmonic unit although it consists of at least three discrete pitches. The word "accord," for that matter, is also multiple in meaning: the poet is the false chord, but "accord" can also be read as "agreement," suggesting that there is a false agreement between the poet and irony. While he represents the two initially as separate, they, like the "je/tu," are not really distinct, as indicated in the progression in interiorization from shaking (no penetration of one by the other) to biting (one enters the other) to being in the voice (a more complete subsumption) and on through irony's becoming equivalent with the poet's blood or life force. It is at this point, when irony has not simply affected but rather taken over and become one with the poet, that the series of "je suis . . ." statements ensues. In other words, just at the moment when the "je" is no longer present to itself that it begins naming itself as those famous pairs of opposites. Far from a doubled self, what we have is, in a sense, really no self at all. When the poet says "I am X," he has already affirmed that "'I' is irony," that it is no longer the poet who is speaking at all.[12] The poet also seems to say "I am a metaphor" and, by the rich set of contrasting metaphors, he affirms a more general contention that we might phrase, not as "I is another" à la Rimbaud but rather as "'I' is a metaphor." The only way of giving voice to the subject, then, is in a set of poetic operations such as metaphor and irony, which leads us to suggest, more radically still, "'I' am a poem," since the poet, while established via metaphor, also becomes transparent, like the "miroir" of line 19, whereby his voice is emptied of its own subjectivity in order to become the pure speaking voice of the poem itself. What speaks as a "je" by the end of the poem is not so much a speaking subject as a poem itself. This is not to say that the poem can be reduced to an autoreferential function, however, since the "I" still does remain, named under the sign of metaphor. Just at the crucial moment when we might wonder how to tell the dancer from the dance, or indeed whether "ceci n'est pas un poète," the poet remains, his subjectivity emerging through the event that is the poem itself.

The Baudelairean subject vanishes in the poem both by the equivalence between subject and irony and by the disappearance into the series of opposing metaphors, and yet we could say that this subject also thereby performs the vanishing of vanishing, since the subject *is* in fact reconstituted as this play of opposites, now removed from any traditional trappings of emotional investment that mark the lyric subject. The poem does violence, we might say, to the standard notion of a unified and individualized self in order to liberate lyric subjectivity to be conceived as a new kind of relationality. Paradoxically, by representing a *je* and a *te* as the same person, lyric subjectivity is reconfigured both as more solipsistic, since the subject-object relation is in some sense a closed circle here, and at the same time as moving beyond solipsism by expanding the overlapping roles of subject and object so that they include the subject's objective relation to itself, to another, to another figured as comparable to the self, and the poem itself as subject or object. By doing violence to the lyric poem's typical representation of subjectivity, the speaking subject lends objectivity to the poem; at the same time, in reconfiguring grammatical subjects and objects, the language of the poem acts, in its turn, on the lyric subject who is now reconceived through the linguistic configuration of the poem that produces the lyric subjectivity. This is, as I have indicated, a refusal of a mimetic model whereby the language of the poem would be a supposedly transparent representation of the lyric self. This act of violence toward the traditional conception of the lyric self is what liberates what I have been calling a "liquid" conception of self that disrupts a sense of lyric solidity. This liquidity is underscored by the imagery of the first part of the poem, which figures the poets as letting flow forth "les eaux de la souffrance," which will engender the "pleurs salés" of the object.

These images stand in contrast to that of the "sinistre miroir" as a figure of an irony which, as Starobinski has noted, as "réflexion de la réflexion [. . .] ne possède selon Baudelaire aucune valeur libératrice" ["reflection of the reflection [. . ..] does not possess any liberatory value according to Baudelaire"] (Starobinski 31). Irony is the vehicle of the subject as dissonance in the poem. It is described as "tout mon sang," another instance of a liquid containment that is then liberated to flow via the wounds implied by "la plaie et le couteau" and the other indications of torture and suffering in the latter portion of the poem. While Irony plays a starring role here, it is not quite clear in what it consists:

> elle ne semble pas avoir un sens très précis, car elle peut se rapporter à l'esprit de contradiction tel que nous le trouvons dans « La Voix » : « . . .je ris dans les deuils et pleure dans les fêtes » ou bien mettre en relief l'esprit satanique, ou enfin caractériser le remords. (Hubert 236).
>
> [it does not seem to have a very precise meaning, since it can refer to the spirit of contradiction as we find it in "La Voix": ". . .I laugh at funerals and cry at parties" or emphasize the satanic spirit, or characterize remorse.]

In this poem of doubling, Irony itself is multiple, performing, like the subject himself, a role in the poem without being defined, or, rather, defined precisely by that lack of definition. This way of reading allows us to see the reference to the lyric subject at the end of the poem as "un de ces grands abandonnés" not only as a damned subject condemned to eternal repetition of demonic laughter but also as an abandoned kind of subjectivity that reconfigures itself in relation to the poem which frees it by annihilating it by the way the poem's language constructs subject and object.[13]

We are left with a disappeared self that yet remains under the sign of its disappearance, a lyric "I" that is defined by a negation of a more stable and unified model of lyric subjectivity that nonetheless requires the persistence of an idea of that older model in order for the new subjectivity to be perceived as dissonant, as the simultaneous positing of unreconciled and irreconcilable opposites. The "faux accord" leads us to connect this model of subjectivity to the conception of dissonance that relies on notions of consonance in order to be defined as such. The "divine symphonie" cannot be annihilated without abolishing the subject's definition as a "faux accord." In so far as the divine symphony enables the emergence of the decentered and ironic lyric subject, it remains the framework within which we can see dissonance as the truth of harmony.

Another of Baudelaire's fairly early poems to feature a liquid subjectivity is "La Fontaine de sang," which decenters and reconfigures the lyric subject in a similarly multifaceted way as

"L'Héautontimorouménos," but several unique features create an extraordinary vision of a lyric subject conscious of its own dissolution:

> Il me semble parfois que mon sang coule à flots,
> Ainsi qu'une fontaine aux rythmiques sanglots.
> Je l'entends bien qui coule avec un long murmure,
> Mais je me tâte en vain pour trouver la blessure.

À travers la cité, comme dans un champ clos,
Il s'en va, transformant les pavés en îlots,
Désaltérant la soif de chaque créature,
Et partout colorant en rouge la nature.

J'ai demandé souvent à des vins captieux
D'endormir pour un jour la terreur qui me mine;
Le vin rend l'oeil plus clair et l'oreille plus fine!

J'ai cherché dans l'amour un sommeil oublieux;
Mais l'amour n'est pour moi qu'un matelas d'aiguilles
Fait pour donner à boire à ces cruelles filles! (1: 115)

[It seems to me at times my blood flows out in waves
Like a fountain that gushes in rhythmical sobs.
I hear it clearly, escaping with long murmurs,
But I feel my body in vain to find the wound.

Across the city, as in a tournament field,
It courses, making islands of the paving stones,
Satisfying the thirst of every creature
And turning the color of all nature to red.

I have often asked insidious wines
To lull to sleep for a day my wasting terror;
Wine makes the eye sharper, the ear more sensitive!

I have sought in love a forgetful sleep;
But love is to me only a bed of needles
Made to slake the thirst of those cruel prostitutes! (*Flowers* 403)]

Several elements of the poetic network that develops around dynamic consumption come together in "La Fontaine de sang." In this poem of flowing blood without a wound for a source, the liquid leaves the interior setting and flows into an undifferentiated city curiously devoid of any specifically urban features. In this simultaneously closed and open space, the poet's blood takes on a life of its own beyond his control, and it is the blood, and not the poet, that leaves the interior space and enters the city in order to displace it geographically, transforming the paving stones into islands. If drink of various kinds has until this moment in *Les Fleurs du Mal* fed poetic production, we now see the results of that feeding and the transformative power of the product, which exceeds the poet and makes him alien to himself. If his own thirst is unquenchable, the by-product of his poetic ingestion does in fact feed the creatures of the city.

By this point, the body of the poet has been used up in the process of poetic creation, as *Les Fleurs du Mal* continues its path toward the final section, "La Mort." As the body self-destructs, it leaves in its wake the poetic production that is *Les Fleurs du Mal*. In other words, the body itself comes to play a role similar to that of the fluids drunk in the poems we have been reading. The fluids are ingested and go on to form part of the body into which they are incorporated, nourishing it and transforming it by the foreign presence they introduce into the body. Likewise, the poet leaves the closed space of his domestic interior and enters the city only though the flowing medium of his blood, which becomes alien to him.[14] Once the vital fluid leaves the poet's body, overrunning the city and coloring nature, the poet's drinking becomes less fecund. In contrast to the limitless flow of the blood once released from the body, the effects of wine evoked in the next lines of the poem are limited temporally to a single day: "J'ai demandé souvent à des vins capiteux / D'endormir pour un jour la terreur qui me mine" (115) This sharpening of the senses is not, however, put to use in poetic production, and is assimilated in the closing lines of the poem to the numbing power of love as a "sommeil oublieux": "J'ai cherché dans l'amour un sommeil oublieux, / Mais l'amour n'est pour moi qu'un matelas d'aiguilles / Fait pour donner à boire à ces cruelles filles!" (115) "[I have sought in love a forgetful sleep; / But love is to me only a bed of needles / Made to slake the thirst of those cruel girls!" (403, translation amended)]. Once consumption has been succeeded by dispersal of vital energy in the form of flowing liquid, drinking becomes the horrific act of the "cruelles filles" drinking the poet's blood from a mattress of needles.[15]

The poem's liquefied self goes beyond simple questions of vaporization and centralization by the many layers at work here. First of all, the poet whose blood flows throughout the city remains a conscious perceiver while also seeing his life force dispersed beyond any unified or contained body. But the entire poem is, of course, a sort of hallucination that takes on a more vivid character in the second quatrain, where the soft "il me semble" of the first line becomes the "il s'en va," de-emphasizing the hallucinatory quality of the initial image and rendering it more real by the way in which the text represents it. The poem's language plays with containment and openness. The same kind of subject-object relationship that was operative in "L'Héautontimorouménos" is figured in the "Je l'entends," where the speaker is both subject and object to himself; this is not quite an instance of alienation since there still does seem to be a *je* fully cognizant of the blood moving beyond the container of his body, and thus the subject is still conceptually contained within the speaker. The grammar of the second quatrain performs a shift in that containment whereby the blood becomes the subject while the first-person pronoun disappears. This play of containment and boundlessness is mirrored in the geography of the second quatrain, with the boundless flowing of "à travers la cité" qualified immediately by "comme dans un champ clos."

Such confident lucidity about the flowing self on the part of the observer of the flow is figured as a nightmarish terror reinforced rather than canceled by the altered state of drunkenness, underscoring the impossibility of escape from a flowing subjectivity that, paradoxically, escapes the subject. Love and wine act on the poet in a way analogous to the functioning of language in the poem, bringing clarity to the subject about the terror of the liquefied self. But such a claim about lucidity can hardly be taken at face value, since the lucidity refers back to what the poet had identified as a hallucination: "Il me semble parfois." It is the language of the poem that has converted this lucid impression into the supposed certainty of the poet's blood flowing through the streets, thus making what had been acknowledged as a hallucination into the reality that in turn terrifies the poet. To be conscious is to be trapped in an undecidable subjectivity that hesitates between awareness of hallucination and a full engagement with the hallucination as it is created by the language of the poem that destabilizes not only the self but also the site of lucidity: Is it to be found in the wine that provides a clear vision of the poet's blood flowing, or in the realization of what the poet seemed to know at the outset, that the flowing blood is an illusion? Or is it that the subjectivity represented figuratively as the flowing blood is true in some way that transcends the distinction between the literal and the figurative so that the terror stems not from any literal vision of blood flow but of the kind of ironic self-consciousness that is aware of the liquid dissolution of the self even as it maintains enough self-integrity to hold that awareness and react to it? Once again, consciousness of the dilution of the self requires that an earlier, coherent model of the self be maintained in order to perceive the self as diluted; otherwise, there would be no measure against which the diluted self will be considered as such. This is not a mere nostalgic look back to older unified models of self but an affirmation that the unified and diluted self can only have their existence in mutually dependent dialectical relation mediated by the language of the poem, which assumes a kind of subjectivity by serving as the site of the creation of this dialectical self through the form and grammar of the poem.

The *je* returns in the tercets in a slightly more active role than it had played before when the only active verb corresponding to it was "entends," as it engages in a search in a temporality that switches to the past: "j'ai demandé" and "j'ai cherché." The past quest was unsuccessful, and the poem implies a return to the general iterative present of the flowing nightmare vision. But the last words of the poem destabilize what had seemed to be the straightforward indication of the failure of love and alcohol to induce oblivion or calm fear. "Ces cruelles filles" appear in the last line without any further context. Critics have read these words as a reference either to courtesans or, more commonly, to la Débauche and la Mort, the subject of the poem "Les deux bonnes soeurs" which precedes "La Fontaine de sang" in both editions of *Les Fleurs du Mal*.[16] What seems at first to solve a textual puzzle actually adds to the mystery. While there is presumably a partner involved in a love affair, assigning the role of *cruelles filles* to la Débauche et la Mort returns us to a solitary lyric subject, canceling any role that a lover might play here, since it would be debauchery and death that are drinking the poet's blood. The field of relations would thus switch from lyric subject and object to an intertextual relation that bypasses the lyric subject altogether by placing this poem into relation not with its lyric subject but with another poem on which this poem would depend in order to be fully meaningful. Such an interpretation is problematic to the extent that the two poems, often read as a triptych completed by "Allégorie" which follows "La Fontaine de sang," were composed separately.[17] The coherence of the poems thus depends on readerly intervention in a way that bypasses the lyric subject by highlighting the primacy of the intertextual relation, since meaningfulness now seems linked to intersubjective relations between texts rather than between text and lyric subject. Readers are otherwise faced with the risk of incoherence in the absence of clues within the poem about the referent of "ces cruelles filles"; the dissipation of the lyric subject now finds an analogue in the dispersion of meaning not just within the text but across texts, in a variation of the play of containment and uncontainment that we have seen operating in the construction of lyric subjectivity. The potential intertextual dispersion is wide-ranging; critics have seen echoes and potential sources for the language of this poem in Théophile Gautier and Shakespeare.[18] The text thus comes to have a "life of its own" that severs its strong connection to the lyric subjectivity embodied in it, all the while mirroring that flowing subjectivity in which identity is dissimulated and decentralized while not quite disappearing. The lyric subject begins to emerge, on this view, as a mere vehicle of the text's own subjectivity, a necessary, but not self-sustaining, entity that dissipates within the text, like the poet's blood, and shifts the focus to the intertextual relationships implied by the final words of the poem but also, as we begin to look for them, throughout the rest of the poem.

Once again, a parallel relationship emerges between the way dissonance operates and the way lyric subjectivity develops in Baudelaire. As I have already suggested, the new subjectivity depends on the persistence of the older model in order to be perceived as unstable and flowing. Similarly, dissonance depends on the system of harmony in which it emerged, and against which it reacts, in order to be perceived as dissonant. When we look beyond individual poems to networks of poems, an approach that is always fruitfully repaid in Baudelaire's work, we establish a framework whereby the poems become most meaningful, or even most legible, within their varying, shifting contexts. In this, they are not unlike musical chords, whose meaning emerges in the contexts in which they appear as part of a system of functional harmony within a piece, which can then be viewed historically in order to start to trace the ways in which dissonance can be "the truth of harmony." Examining the poems in relation to each other shifts the ground of subjectivity away from the lyric subject and to the poems themselves, in order to identify the ways in which the language of the poem shapes lyric subjectivity rather than being a mere by-product, transcription, or mimetic representation of a unified subject. Once again, this is not to say that the lyric subject disappears, but rather that it persists in dialectical tension with the texts through which it emerges, which it shapes, and by which it is shaped in ways that can be difficult to identify and describe precisely on account of the liquid subjectivity that this model puts in place, one that resists containment via analysis and leaves us with a remainder that only the further engagement with the poems will allow us to negotiate.

Inscribed within these considerations of subjectivity is the question of the political valence of poems such as "La Fontaine de sang." While the poem is most often read as the portrait of an anguished personal psychological state, Patrick Thériault has proposed a reading of the poem as containing coded references, "discrètes mais étonamment convergentes" ["discrete but surprisingly converging"] and which readers in the years immediately following 1848 would have recognized (Thériault 307), to keywords associated with the revolution of 1848, thus making the wound of the lyric subject assimilable "non plus à un mal métaphysique, mais à un traumatisme d'origine historico-politique" ["no longer to a metaphysical evil but to a trauma of historico-political origin"] (307) within a poem that is best read as a "lamento spleenétique faisant résonner, en sourdine, un chant révolutionnaire" ["splenetic lament that allows a revolutionary song to quietly resound"] (326) where the "cruelles filles" would be figures of the revolution, assimilated to the poet by their shared status as victims: "ensemble ces personnages offrent le tableau d'un drame tout à la fois personnel et collectif, celui, pourrait-on dire, d'un temps où plus aucun lyrisme ne coule, de source, pour animer la Poésie, l'Amour et la Révolution" ["together these characters offer the tableau of a drama that is all at once personal and collective, of a time, we could say, when no lyricism flows any longer from the source to animate Poetry, Love, and Revolution"] (331). "La Fontaine de sang" is political in a particular way in that it names the political past by not naming it, by allowing the reader to speculate on the relationship between the liquid subjectivity it more clearly portrays and the ghostly presence of the blood on the paving stones. The poem's refusal of more explicit political content draws the reader all the more into an enhanced attention to the subtleties of the poetic language here, which speaks, as I have been implying, beyond the subject, and not just as the subject's vehicle for expression.

The breakdown of the unified subject is also the breakdown of a singular meaning available in the form and language of the poem, which is itself a political consequence of the way poetry undoes the illusion of the solid bourgeois subject. The lyric subject's flowing blood becomes the flow of the text itself and its construction in such a way as to refuse a singular, unified meaning that would correspond to a singular, unified speaking subject. It is in this way that the dissolution of the subject, along with the trace of it which remains and which allows us to see it as dissolute, is deeply, but very subtly, political, in that the dissolution opens the textual space to a greater sense of agency and a greater plurality of potential interpretation. That an interpretation of the poem as directly related to the revolution of 1848 is available to us is itself a consequence of the transformation of subjectivity enacted by the poem. What is at first figured as a hallucination becomes a powerful textual reality in that the poem's language can reshape the relationship between the lyric subject and the destabilizing language of the text. The act of freeing the subject, while represented as a trauma for a lyric subject who still takes himself to be whole, is what allows access to a rich set of possible readings of the poem, as its life force, figured here as blood, overruns the bounds of an enclosed subject. The dissonance implied by the wine that brings lucidity without a precise indication of what insight is yielded by it underscores not a total indeterminacy in the poem's meaning but a call on the poem's part to identify the horizons of possible and thinkable interpretations. The lyric subject conscious of its own dissolution but unable to find the source of it shifts our attention to the ways in which the subject is filled, emptied, and refilled by words in their various configurations, within and across poems, in a model of subjectivity that is deeply informed by an autonomous artwork that is, paradoxically, at the same time rife with political stakes for those who are willing to follow the artwork where it leads.

   A particularly rich text for exploring Baudelairean subjectivity specifically within the context of esthetic reception and production is the prose poem "Le Confiteor de l'artiste." The poem has sometimes lent itself to problematically simple readings. J. A. Hiddleston notes, for instance, that it "start[s] with a spiritual intensity and vitality the élan of which cannot be maintained: the inspiration fails, the dream dissolves, the dreaded reality returns" (30). Such psychologizing readings miss the way in which the poem functions as an invitation to reconfigure art and the relation of the perceiver to it, in ways that resonate with the incomplete dissolution of the subject and the way the artwork may itself be said to lay claim to subjectivity as we have been tracing. While the language of the first paragraphs may be esthetically backward-looking in terms of presenting a romantic lyric tone, I will argue that the configuration of esthetic subjectivity in the poem as a whole invites us not simply to accept or reject the absorption of the lyric subject in the landscape he describes but rather to rearticulate the relationship between an esthetic past and present.[19] The first paragraph presents the power of the landscape to penetrate the subject, while the second contains a suggestion of drowning ("noyer son regard"), hinting at a blurring of subjective and objective relations to the point of their fusion:

> Que les fins de journées d'automne sont pénétrantes ! Ah ! pénétrantes jusqu'à la douleur ! car il est de certaines sensations délicieuses dont le vague n'exclut pas l'intensité ; et il n'est pas de pointe plus acérée que celle de l'Infini.
>
> Grand délice que celui de noyer son regard dans l'immensité du ciel et de la mer ! Solitude, silence, incomparable chasteté de l'azur ! une petite voile frissonnante à l'horizon, et qui par sa petitesse et son isolement imite mon irrémédiable existence, mélodie monotone de la houle, toutes ces choses pensent par moi, ou je pense par elles (car dans la grandeur de la rêverie, le moi se perd vite !) ; elles pensent, dis-je, mais musicalement et pittoresquement, sans arguties, sans syllogismes, sans déductions. (1: 278)

> [How penetrating are the ends of autumn days! Ah! penetrating to the verge of pain! For there are certain delicious sensations whose vagueness does not exclude intensity; and there is no sharper point than Infinity.
>
> Sheer delight to drown one's gaze in the immensity of sky and sea! Solitude, silence, incomparable chastity of the azure! a small sail trembling on the horizon, and whose smallness and isolation imitate my irremediable existence, monotonous melody of the swell—all these things think through me, or I think through them (for in the grandeur of reverie, the *self* is quickly lost!). They think, I say, but musically and pictorially, without quibblings, without syllogisms, without deductions. (*Parisian* 4)]

Maria Scott reads the poem as representing the "fail[ure] to transcend the material world by any act of the imagination" (*Baudelaire's Le Spleen* 201) and identifies the tone of the first paragraphs as Baudelaire's pastiche of his own work: "the overriding impression is of a chewing up and throwing out of fragments from the verse collection" (159). While there is certainly something of the parodic here, the esthetic vision that the poet represents as being penetrated by nature here is in more complicated dialogue with other meditations on esthetic perception within the prose poem. Fragments of earlier discourse appear here in all their discontinuity as parody but also more than that, as a call to read the earlier vision in the context of a consideration of what it would mean to have a mediated artistic vision of nature, to reflect on the penetration as itself mediated by the ways in which we conceive of the poem, and ultimately to configure the relationship between esthetic experience and reflection on that experience. That relationship is not unidirectional, an experience which is then conceived or described, but rather dialectical, in that both the immediacy of an experience and the conceptual reflection on it together create the esthetic experience in such a way that the reflection cannot be said to be merely secondary to the experience, a translation or a copy of it. Rather, esthetic experience happens in the play between the experience and reflection, neither term of which would be sufficient for constituting esthetic experience on its own.

Beyond the penetration and drowning in these first two paragraphs, there is a curious reversal of the mimetic function of art whereby the sailboat imitates the artist rather than the other way around: "une petite voile [...] imite mon irrémédiable existence." This attribution not just of any action but of a chief function of the artist blurs the boundaries of subjectivity in a precise way by claiming not just a quasi-human alterity for an object but literally a subjectivity that rivals that of the artist specifically. That same long sentence then meanders to a second key activity for esthetic perception and contemplation, thinking: "toutes ces choses pensent par moi, ou je pense par elles (car dans la grandeur de la rêverie, le moi se perd vite !) ; elles pensent, dis-je, mais musicalement et pittoresquement, sans arguties, sans syllogismes, sans déductions. » The only conjugated verbs in this paragraph (whose sentences are not all complete) are *imiter* and *penser*, which highlights the contrast or relationship between the role of the work of art and the one who would interpret it via a cognitive act. Through a kind of second-order awareness, the lyric subject is aware that the boat is imitating his own existence; is the boat thus endowed with subjectivity by some external standard or only as the projection of the lyric subject? The radical undecidability of who is thinking and who is thought is presented almost as a nonissue: either the things think or are thought, and what seems to be the essential point here, the loss of self, is presented in parentheses. But any announcement of the loss of self is self-canceling; who would be doing the affirming of the loss of self if not the self? As I have argued earlier, Baudelaire's lyric poetry cannot, paradoxically, affirm the loss of the subject despite what its surface often claims.

If the poem began with terms so well worn that they risk becoming clichés, by the middle of the poem it is not the tired familiarity of the words but rather their radical defamiliarization that is at play. What would it mean to have a non-conceptual thought, for instance? And what would it mean for things to have them? If readers are carried along on the musicality of Baudelaire's own prose here, it is easy to miss the true conceptual strangeness of the propositions in the second paragraph. Are these thoughts akin to sensory impressions? Why would the speaking subject insist on calling them thoughts in that case? And how would all of "these things" have something like sensory impressions? It is significant that the thought is represented in terms of music, since music is an asemantic form that is said to carry content, but for that content to be either intelligible or communicable requires an act of translation into words that arguably transforms the content.

The turning point in the poem is also represented in musical terms, in a shift from the "mélodie monotone" to a dissonant sonority:

> Toutefois, ces pensées, qu'elles sortent de moi ou s'élancent des choses, deviennent bientôt trop intenses. L'énergie dans la volupté crée un malaise et une souffrance positive. Mes nerfs trop tendus ne donnent plus que des vibrations criardes et douloureuses. (1: 278)
>
> [However, these thoughts, whether they emerge from me or spring from things, soon grow too intense. The force of voluptuous pleasure creates uneasiness and concrete suffering. Then my excessively taut nerves produce nothing but shrill and painful vibrations. (*Parisian* 4)]

The dissonance sounds both on its own terms and as a dissonant contrast to the harmony that had been established in the first two paragraphs, which now serves only to have better prepared the dissonance. Rather than hearing the dissonance as a mere interruption or as the indication of the failure of a contemplative esthetic experience, were we to see the dissonance as allowing us to read backward differently in the first two paragraphs? The dissonance allows us to see that what may have looked like the unity of harmoniousness in the first two paragraphs, whether that harmony is taken to be the calm of a stereotypically beautiful natural scene or the oneness of the lyric subject and the surroundings, is actually no unity at all, since it excludes the element of dissonance. What looked to be harmonious and unified was in fact simply incomplete, and the harsh sonority that completes the scene by contributing its wholeness is precisely the element that threatens the wholeness, that calls into question the entire esthetic enterprise that had been described in the first two paragraphs. If dissonance can yield this kind of insight, it can hardly be called the failure of an esthetic experience. Rather, it has revelatory potential in that it shows another sense in which dissonance can be "the truth about harmony." The objects in the poem thus think against the subject, if that subject is imagined to be a unified figure. If the self is temporarily "lost" in the poem it is only to yield subjectivity momentarily to the objects which become the vehicle of the realization of the impossibility of the kind of esthetic experience described at first in the poem. To see the immediacy of an esthetic experience transformed into the dissonance of "vibrations criardes et doloureuses" involves conceptual thought, which is dissonant with the claim that the kind of thoughts that either the subject or the objects are "sans syllogismes, sans deductions." This is not to say that it was a mere illusion that non-syllogistic thoughts could be had by objects; rather, by asserting such a thing, the poem forces the very kind of thinking that it claims is evacuated from an esthetic experience. Readers need to engage in conceptual thought in order to make sense of the claims here, but the claims, by defying clear conceptual enumeration, call us back to a kind of estheticized intellectual experience or intellectualized esthetic experience figured musically as the "vibrations criardes."

The dissonance at work in the poem reveals what the words of the poem may on first glance conceal, especially in terms of the way subjectivity is figured here. What is remarkable is not just the dissolution of the subject, the easily graspable idea of "le *moi* se perd vite," but rather the dissonant plurality of meanings that are covered over by the simple word *je*, normally taken to be a singular and unified whole self persisting over time. As Sonya Stephens argues:

> What occurs in "Le Confiteor" [...] is an oscillation between a generalized lyrical subject, first identified as the *Je* of the poet, and a second, less generalized, first person who appears—separated in time from the first (by bientôt and maintenant)—only to reject the lyrical [sic] established in the first part of the poem. [...]. Rather than a manifestation of the bipolar *moi*, this can be read as an opposition of the different personae the lyrical subject projects. (49)

The shift in the referent of the *je* might be mirrored by the temporal shift from the indefinite iterative present of the first paragraphs to the "maintenant" of the last paragraph. Notably, however, the *je* as subject pronoun disappears from the last paragraph, where there are only the objective pronouns *me* and *moi* and the possessive *mon*:

> Et maintenant la profondeur du ciel me consterne ; sa limpidité m'exaspère. L'insensibilité de la mer, l'immuabilité du spectacle, me révoltent. . . Ah ! faut-il éternellement souffrir, ou fuir éternellement le beau ? Nature, enchanteresse sans pitié, rivale toujours victorieuse, laisse-moi ! Cesse de tenter mes désirs et mon orgueil ! L'étude du beau est un duel où l'artiste crie de frayeur avant d'être vaincu. (1: 278–9)
>
> [And now the sky's depth fills me with dismay: its limpidity exasperates me. The sea's insensitivity, the scene's immutability appall me. . .Ah! Must we suffer eternally, or else eternally flee from the beautiful? Nature, sorceress without mercy, ever victorious rival, let me be! Stop tempting my desires and my pride! Studying the beautiful is a duel in which the artist shrieks with freight before being defeated. (*Parisian* 4)]

So where is the lyric subject, the *je*, ultimately located? Is it multiple? Has it disappeared? Is it generalized or personalized in this poem? There is an underlying tension here between a particular *je* that is never fully individualized and a generalized *je*, as figure of the artist, that is never fully universalized.[20] What is figured as the power of nature, in the agency that is attributed to it in this last paragraph, its ability to consternate, exasperate, and revolt the poet, can also be read as the power of the poem itself as it undoes, empties, and reconfigures the subject in nearly imperceptible ways.

The speaking subject is undone, vanquished, not so much by the immediacy of nature, as the start of the final paragraph indicates, but rather, as the third paragraph had revealed, by the *thoughts* that emanate either from things (and we note that these include not just natural phenomena but also things such as the sailboat) or the subject himself. The last paragraph enables a willful confusion between the otherwise distinct categories of nature and the beautiful. While the final sentence speaks only of the beautiful, the poet has just called out directly to a personified Nature and called her a "rivale toujours victorieuse" and asked to be delivered from the temptation of desire and pride. Another temptation lurking in this paragraph is one that would fuse Nature and beauty as if they were the same, and as if both were unmediated. If readers are lost in the immediacy of the represented contemplation of nature, it would be easy to overlook the actual origin of the speaking subject's exasperation as stemming from the mediated experience of nature as expressed through thoughts which become the subject rather than the object of the experience.

The beautiful's overwhelming intensity lies not in the natural phenomena but in reflection on it, in a reminder that art's function is not to allow for the transparent reproduction of a feeling of confronting nature but rather to reconfigure that experience through, in this case, the conceptual work of the words of the poem. Such an understanding allows us to read backward in the poem to see that, if the first sentence seems to suggest the passive swallowing up of the subject by nature, with the autumn days described as "pénétrantes," this is not a directly mimetic description but rather, already, the mediated construction of the experience through the language of the poem. The sharpness of the Infinite thus becomes not an inherent quality in the thing itself but rather a product of its representation as such. This is not to say that the experience of the Infinite as sharp and penetrating is *merely* a construction on the part of the subject, since part of what the poem performs is the reconfiguration of the subject as a relation among itself, an experience, and the language through which that experience emerges.

This approach also challenges a simpler reading of the poem as a mere example of a *failed* esthetic experience, as might otherwise be suggested by the "vanquished" artist in the final paragraph. To see failure here would only be possible if the model with which we were operating was one of domination of nature, whereby nature would submit to the design of the artist to represent it in a fully, even totalizingly, adequate way. If the artist is vanquished, it cannot be by some unmediated form of the beautiful stemming directly from nature, since no such thing has ever been figured in the poem. Luca Bevilacqua has argued that the poem is best read not as a scene of contemplating nature but rather of a landscape artist's experience of painting, so that the entire poem is about that mediated experience. He reads "Le *Confiteor*" alongside Baudelaire's remarks on painter Eugène Boudin in the *Salon de 1859*, where the painter appears "comme le modèle de l'artiste tourmenté et tenté par un rêve impossible, voire par un idéal esthétique irréalisable" (Bevilacqua 112). He draws attention to this passage in the *Salon* that criticizes the kind of unmediated mimetic expression of nature that one may be tempted at first to see represented in "Le *Confiteor*":

> Les artistes qui veulent exprimer la nature, moins les sentiments qu'elle inspire, se soumettent à une opération bizarre qui consiste à tuer en eux l'homme pensant et sentant, et malheureusement, croyez que, pour la plupart, cette opération n'a rien de bizarre ni de douloureux. (2: 660)
>
> [Artists who want to express nature, minus the emotions it inspires, submit to a bizarre operation that consists in killing in themselves the thinking and feeling man and unfortunately, you should believe that, for most of them, that operation has nothing bizarre or painful about it.]

It is best, then, to see esthetic experience, for the painter, the lyric subject, and the reader, as situated at the site of intersection between experience and conceptual reflection and posing a challenge to any attempt to see either one of those poles as dominant or as the final word in configuring esthetic experience.

On this reading, the first paragraph's evocation of the Infinite would be neither evocation of a cliché or parody of a Romantic experience of the beautiful but rather the sharpness of the concept of the Infinite as mediated (and even created) by the kinds of esthetic intervention into those concepts which makes this poem intelligible. What is essential in the poem is neither at the beginning nor at the end, neither the vagueness of the "sensations délicieuses" nor the "frayeur." It is rather in the middle, in the "vibrations criardes," the dissonance that is the truth of harmony not because dissonance cancels harmony, or reveals beautiful nature to be a psychologized nightmare, but because it allows us to see the lie of the immediacy of esthetic perception of the natural and the impulse to domination that such purported immediacy would necessitate. The poem resonates with what Adorno has to say in his *Aesthetics* lectures on the link between dissonance and the release of nature from the human tendency to domination:

> one of the substantial intentions of important works of art is not only to push nature away, to distinguish themselves from the merely natural through sublimation, but also to give nature back what belongs to it. In a sense, this happens in every dissonance—using the term in its broadest sense, beyond its limited musical meaning. One could say that every dissonance is a small remembrance of the suffering which the control over nature, and ultimately a society of domination as such, inflicts on nature, and only in the form of this suffering, only in the form of yearning—only thus can suppressed nature find its voice at all. And dissonance

therefore contains not only this aspect of an expression of negativity, of this suffering, but always at the same time the happiness of giving nature its voice, finding something not yet taken, drawing something into the work that [. . .] has not yet been domesticated, [. . .] which thus reminds us of something other than the ever-same machinery of bourgeois society in which we are all trapped. (*Aesthetics* 39–40)

The poem, through its use of structural dissonance, refigures the esthetic relationship to nature as a mediated one in ways that give the language of the poem particular power to reshape not just nature but the subject itself, so that the lyric subject is not penetrated directly by nature but rather is constituted in part by the language of the poem which brings both the subject and nature into being as co-dependent and mutually constitutive. The "intensity" figured in the first paragraph becomes that of esthetic experience, whose vagueness means that the experience remains incomplete until mediated by thoughts which, in their musical or picturesque form, are "trop intenses" and call perhaps for conceptual reflection on esthetic experience in order to make the experience meaningful, to assign some sort of sense to the "vibrations criardes et douloureuses." Such meaning would not be final or totalizing, but, rather, tentative, situated, and always subject to reformulation as esthetic experience is reconfigured in concert with the conceptual experience, in a way that refuses to give the definitive upper hand to either esthetic experience or conceptual reflection on it.

There is an extended passage in Adorno's *Aesthetic Theory* that offers, without reference to Baudelaire, an uncanny parallel to the kind of engagement with the artwork and natural beauty that we have seen operating in "Le *Confiteor* de l'artiste," as if it were providing a chance to illustrate the integral relationship between the artwork and critical reflection on it whereby neither is complete without the other. Adorno's reflections on the mediation of natural beauty in art provide an intriguing "plot" structure of its own and illuminate the ways in which Baudelaire chiefly presents not a cliché-ridden or parodic or psychologized account of the artist but rather a strikingly modern one. Or, rather, Adorno's account gives us the tools with which to return to Baudelaire's text and read its Romantic heritage differently, as containing the potential to subvert clichéd notions of oneness with nature in ways that go beyond a mere debunking of the psychological roots of such a vision and toward the kinds of complex reorganization of subjectivity that we have seen operating in the text. Adorno's theoretical reflections render more explicit the kind of shifts in the process of esthetic creation that Baudelaire's text registers and which arguably surpasses, in innovation and complexity, the kind of theorizing he did in his own critical writings on art. If Baudelaire's poem could be said to be about the failure of an esthetic engagement, it is a failure of a particular kind, a productive one, more in line with the legacy of modernism which came after him. That productive failure can, via Adorno's reflections on that modernist tradition, illuminate Baudelaire's text just as Baudelaire's poem first gives voice to this new kind of insightful "failure" for which we still lack a descriptive term adequate to the task of defining an experience that is simultaneously a failure and a portal to a redefinition of esthetic subjectivity. In what follows I will engage Adorno's text not as a supplement to Baudelaire's, nor as a key to somehow "explaining" the poem, but rather to give an account of the way, as Adorno himself recognized, art and critical reflection on it are inseparable facets of the same enterprise, always necessarily incomplete without the other. By engaging the two together, we can attempt to articulate something of the functioning of what Baudelaire, in "L'Art philosophique," called the "magie suggestive" ["suggestive magic"] that constitutes "l'art pur suivant la conception moderne" ["pure art according to the modern conception"] (2: 598). He characterizes that magic precisely in terms of subjectivity and objectivity that we have been considering; this magic contains "à la fois l'objet et le sujet, le monde extérieur à l'artiste et l'artiste lui-même" ["at once object and subject, the world external to the artist and the artist himself"] (2: 598).[21] This is an art that has no commerce with "le raisonnement, la déduction" ["reasoning, deduction"] (2: 598), which are the domain of philosophy. And yet, it would be disingenuous to deny any sort of implied conceptual content in a poem like "Le *Confiteor*," even though, and indeed because, it inscribes that kind of non-conceptual thinking, "sans syllogismes, sans déductions" ["without syllogisms, without deductions"] (1: 278). Thinking through what it would mean for an esthetic experience to be non-conceptual, and the particular kind of particular failure it has the capacity to engender, is precisely what Adorno's reflections, with their many echoes of Baudelaire's vocabulary, might help reveal.

Adorno establishes a parallel between the perception of natural beauty and esthetic perception on the basis of their shared inability to be grasped for anything more than an immediate moment:

> As indeterminate as antithetical to definitions, natural beauty is indefinable, and in this it is related to music [. . .] just as in music what is beautiful flashes up in nature only to disappear in the instant one tries to grasp it. Art does not imitate nature, not even individual instances of natural beauty, but natural beauty as such. This demonstrates not only the aporia of natural beauty but the aporia of esthetics as a whole. Its object is determined negatively, as indeterminable. It is for this reason that art requires philosophy, which interprets it in order to say what it is unable to say, whereas art is only able to say it by not saying it. (AT 72)

Adorno underscores the negative function of philosophy: it does not serve to illuminate and name, except to illuminate what cannot be named, to articulate the limit of both art and philosophy. Thus critical reflection reaches a stumbling block when it comes to thinking, as Baudelaire had called it, "musicalement et pittoresquement" ["musically and in a picturesque way"] (1: 278), and in Adorno as in Baudelaire an analogy between music and nature as they operate along these lines the possibility or impossibility of offering an account, or a translation, of the experience. There is already a sense of the desperate nature of the attempt of the critic and the artist in Adorno's characterization of the aporia of both natural beauty and esthetics: while they are not assimilable, one to the other, they lead to a similar site of impossibility.

Adorno goes on to represent the relationship between natural beauty and the subject in terms of both intensity and of a non-discursive concept:

> In art the evanescent is objectified and summoned to duration: To this extent art is concept, though not like a concept in discursive logic. The weakness of thought in the face of natural beauty, a weakness of the subject, together with the objective intensity of natural beauty demand that the enigmatic character of natural beauty be reflected in art and thereby be determined by the concept, although again not as something conceptual in itself. (AT 73)

"Le *Confiteor*" gives voice to that intensity from the very first paragraph's description of "certaines sensations délicieuses dont le vague n'exclut pas l'intensité" (1: 278). It is only when the *moi* is introduced in the third paragraph that the intensity, now not of the sensations but of thoughts, becomes "trop intenses." The "enigmatic character of natural beauty" is not quite "reflected" in Baudelaire's poem; rather, its destabilizing effect on the subject is described. Both the poem and Adorno's critical reflection attempt to voice what it would mean for esthetic experience to be "determined by the concept" but not "as something conceptual in itself"; both are particular kinds of accounts of a necessary and productive failure of conceptual analysis, if by that we mean the kind of systematizing and totalizing approach against which both Baudelaire and Adorno react. What links their approach here is an emphasis on the persistence of the concept but redefined in what for Adorno would be a tentative, situated, revisable, fragile approach to meaning. This kind of conceptuality might avoid the overwhelming nature of the Baudelairean musical and picturesque thought while resisting any claim to account thoroughly and completely for natural beauty, art, or esthetic experience.

Adorno goes on to link these questions of the representation of esthetic experience (and its representation *as* esthetic experience, in a poem) to questions of the weakening of the subject in the face of the strong subjectivity of the artwork itself: "Goethe's 'Wanderer's Night Song' is incomparable not because here the subject speaks—as in all authentic works, it is, rather, that the subject wants to fall silent by way of the work—but because through its language the poem imitates what is unutterable in the language of nature" (73). A double shift in common understandings of esthetic representation occurs here; first, it is not the subject who speaks but rather the work speaking through what is figured as the subject (the multivalent *je* that we saw operating in "Le *Confiteor*"), and second, the object of imitation is not nature itself directly but rather what cannot be said about nature. This negative expression evacuates the subject, who might even said to be "vaincu," but what we have is not failure as the endpoint but rather the potential for a reconfigured esthetic subjectivity that encompasses the work itself as well as for an approach to imitation of nature that gets us closer to the truth of representation. It does so by revealing the falsity of the notions of direct representation, direct penetration as the first paragraph of "Le *Confiteor*" describes it, in favor of an imitation of what cannot be spoken, the paradoxical articulation of an esthetic impossibility which takes on importance by the way it incites reflection on what it would mean to have art speak the impossibility of a goal it had seemed to set for itself in the imitation of nature.

Adorno's account also shares with Baudelaire's an affective account of the relationship between pain and beauty:

> The pain in the face of beauty, nowhere more visceral than in the experience of nature, is as much the longing for what beauty promises but never unveils as it is suffering at the inadequacy of the appearance, which fails beauty while wanting to make itself like it. This pain reappears in the relation to artworks. Involuntarily and unconsciously, the observer enters into a contract with the work, agreeing to submit to it on condition that it speak. (AT 73)

An important shift occurs here when the pain that had been provoked by nature "reappears" in relation to the artwork: this slide from nature to art reveals that under a model that would group natural and artistic beauty together, the pain results from both nature and art concealing the same kinds of truth in the same way. What Adorno conceptualizes and Baudelaire performs is a violent severing of the two kinds of experience of the beautiful. While both provoke pain based on the fact that they fail to "speak" to the observer in a mimetically transparent way, the poem performs, as I have suggested, a rift between the contemplation of supposedly unmediated natural beauty and esthetic experience, one that allows us to read "backward" in order to articulate a different vision of what it would mean for the artwork to "speak." While it will not yield the kind of transparency we might seek in an experience of nature (which nature itself will also fail to provide), that very failure yields insight into the esthetic experience as providing an instructive failure that shifts the ground of esthetic experience so that it lies precisely in the realm of the failure of art to produce what we thought we had wanted it to. The revulsion in the face of nature that the poet expresses allows for the chance to value the "duel" differently so that an experience of necessary "failure" and vanquishing yields to a new kind of subjectivity, one that makes room for the subjectivity of the work of art itself and for an openness to a new set of ways in which that artwork may "speak," not as transparent mimesis of nature, but as a dialectical experience of insightful failure that is adequately captured neither by the label "success" nor by "failure." This conception is worked out, rather than explicitly stated, in the poem.

What nature may have to say is, ultimately, nothing at all, or at least nothing that can be successfully mediated in language. Adorno reframes the issue of failure as one of eloquent muteness:

> If the language of nature is mute, art seeks to make this muteness eloquent; art thus exposes itself to failure through the insurmountable contradiction between the idea of making the mute eloquent, which demands a desperate effort, and the idea of what this effort would amount to, the idea of what cannot in any way be willed. (AT 78)

On this account, the speaking subject in "Le *Confiteor*" could only be vanquished inasmuch as he represents himself as a subject who wills, who actively pursues the study of the beautiful via what is arguably an excellent example of an attempt to make "the mute eloquent" that could fairly be characterized as "desperate." A perfect rendering of eloquent muteness is just as impossible as a transparent mimetic rendering of nature, so in that sense there is continuity between the older and newer esthetic models in play here. But the artwork is now situated in the space of that contradiction between two irreconcilable ideals and depends on the necessary failure of the perfect expression of eloquent muteness as a condition of possibility for the new artwork. The vanquished artist figure at the end of "Le *Confiteor*" is thus not condemned to eternal defeat, nor is he a transitional figure on the way to some kind of triumph. Rather, he is the figure of a single moment in the dialectical tension involved in reshaping what constitutes esthetic success and failure. The new model of what we might call failure-as-success does not simply dwell on or glorify esthetic failure, but rather identifies a dissonance between what we might have thought we previously understood as failure and success on their own terms rather than in an interdependent relationship.

This model allows us to pass from a clichéd representation of nature to a visceral awareness of what is at stake when the work of art is allowed to "speak" in ways that are freed from past convention, and in ways that allow us to see in the conventions the overly simplistic oppositions on which they depended. Thus the "dissonance" between the artist and the object of esthetic experience yields the truth about what had been figured as the "harmony" of that relationship. The new vision of the artwork is not a sterile one; its focus on tension frees the artwork to function differently than in a simple mimetic relationship to nature, which in turn frees nature as well. Releasing art from its mimetic relationship to nature reinforces the artwork's autonomy, which is part and parcel of the artwork's subjectivity according to Adorno: "The being-in-itself to which artworks are devoted is not the imitation of something real but rather the anticipation of a being-in-itself that does not yet exist, of an unknown that—by way of the subject—is self-determining. Artworks say that something exists in itself, without predicating anything about it" (AT 77). And it is that particular form of muteness which brings art back in proximity with nature—indeed Adorno claims that in the past 200 years "art has converged with natural beauty" (AT 77)—in ways that have shifted the grounds of that convergence away from the false one based on a mere reproductive relationship to one that emphasizes the subjectivity and autonomy of both nature and art. It is in order to realize this that the traditional lyric subject needs to be "vanquished" in order to reveal, after which he can attempt to articulate what it would mean to relate both to art and to nature in a new way, a way which was always available but not revealed as an available option until the lyric subject has been emptied and reconfigured in a new relation to the artwork.[22]

I turn now to a group of poems that engage the relation of knowledge to subjectivity in the context of a constellation that also involves the dynamic of movement and stillness. We have already seen this dynamic operating in poems where I have identified flowing movement as the motor of a change in the character of lyric subjectivity, such as "La Fontaine de sang," as well as movement figured as an act of violence, as in "A celle qui est trop gaie" or "L'Héautontimorouménos." These poems lead us toward reconfiguring subjectivity in a way that empties it out in order, not so much to grant a greater degree of agency to the poem itself so much as to recognize the agency of the poem that has always been operative, even in more conventional poems. The poems I will now explore move from movement to a kind of stillness that allows one to perceive the movement of the poem itself, an experience that Adorno describes as an effect of the contemplation of artworks. Rather than the artwork's power stemming from its supposed immediate and unmediated representation of something like nature, the power comes rather from their status as "fully mediated":

> Artworks become appearances, in the pregnant sense of the term—that is, as the appearance of an other—when the accent falls on the unreality of their own reality. Artworks have the immanent character of being an act, even if they are carved in stone, and this endows them with the quality of being something momentary and sudden. This is registered by the feeling of being overwhelmed when faced with an important work. (AT 79)

The shift in perspective that Adorno describes here, which is not so much a shift as an acknowledgment that the appearance of unmediated immediacy was never operative even in poems that seem to produce that illusion, is visible across Baudelaire's poems. As I have been claiming, what we witness in Baudelaire is not so much a simple debunking of esthetic myths of unified subjectivity and lyric harmony as, rather, of the dialectical tension that allows us to read both forward and back within the poems as we see how the dissonant element relies on a preserved notion of harmony, and, as I hope to show now, how what is perceived as movement may be a kind of stillness and vice versa. In this sense, the later poems do not cancel the earlier ones so much as they help us to read them better.

"Elévation" is a poem that seems to present a model of esthetic transcendence for the poet; it is constructed around a movement upward toward the sky and beyond:

> Au-dessus des étangs, au-dessus des vallées,
> Des montagnes, des bois, des nuages, des mers,
> Par delà le soleil, par delà les éthers,
> Par delà les confins des sphères étoilées,
>
> Mon esprit, tu te meus avec agilité,
> Et, comme un bon nageur qui se pâme dans l'onde,
> Tu sillonnes gaiement l'immensité profonde
> Avec une indicible et mâle volupté. (1: 10)
>
> [Above the lakes, above the vales,
> The mountains and the woods, the clouds, the seas,
> Beyond the sun, beyond the ether,
> Beyond the confines of the starry spheres,
>
> My soul, you move with ease,
> And like a strong swimmer in rapture in the wave
> You wing your way blithely through boundless space
> With virile joy unspeakable. (*Flowers* 21)]

The disembodied poet appears to enjoy a flight of fancy in which it is easy to get caught up as readers, to the point of not noticing the split subjectivity operating in the poem as the speaker addresses his "esprit." The addressee who moves agilely never speaks in the poem; if such an experience is possible, it is represented as ineffable by the fact that the only speaking subject seems to have no direct access to the experience he evokes as available to some aspect of himself. The poem in fact performs a weakening rather than a strengthening of the transcendent experience. From the second stanza where the speaking subject tells his spirit what it does, we move to in the third stanza to an imperative form:

> Envole-toi bien loin de ces miasmes morbides;
> Va te purifier dans l'air supérieur,
> Et bois, comme une pure et divine liqueur,
> Le feu clair qui remplit les espaces limpides. (1: 10)

> [Fly far, far away from this baneful miasma
> And purify yourself in the celestial air,
> Drink the ethereal fire of those limpid regions
> As you would the purest of heavenly nectars. (*Flowers* 21)]

And in the final stanzas, there is a shift to a generalized third person that establishes an even stronger distance between the speaking subject and the transcendent experience he is describing:

> Derrière les ennuis et les vastes chagrins
> Qui chargent de leur poids l'existence brumeuse,
> Heureux celui qui peut d'une aile vigoureuse
> S'élancer vers les champs lumineux et sereins;

> Celui dont les pensers, comme des alouettes,
> Vers les cieux le matin prennent un libre essor,
> — Qui plane sur la vie, et comprend sans effort
> Le langage des fleurs et des choses muettes! (1: 10)

> [Beyond the vast sorrows and all the vexations
> That weigh upon our lives and obscure our vision,
> Happy is he who can with his vigorous wing
> Soar up towards those fields luminous and serene,

> He whose thoughts, like skylarks,
> Toward the morning sky take flight
> — Who hovers over life and understands with ease
> The language of flowers and silent things! (*Flowers* 21)]

While these last lines are often quoted as an example of the kind of unmediated transcendent experience that is available to the speaking subject and perhaps to the reader in some of Baudelaire's poetry, the context of the poem gives little indication that the speaking subject is one of those happy ones to whom such immediate and nonverbal access to "le langage des fleurs" is accessible. The fact that the experience is presented as a generalized one rather than attributed to any particular subject by the end, along with the fact that the experience would presumably nonverbal and thus incommunicable in poetry, calls into question the possibility of the very experience it describes. The experience described is more of an absence than a presence, the evocation of an experience whose impossibility seems more affirmed than its realization, an unrealizable command to the split subject to fly away and purify itself.

In light of all that follows the second stanza, it becomes hard to read the affirmation of the spirit's agile movement as a description of experience as opposed to a wish or fantasy. Moreover, the fantasy would have a canceling effect on art, since art depends on the necessarily mediated character of our experience of nature. Even if it were possible to have an experience of effortless understanding of the mute language of flowers, poetry would have no role to play in that experience, depending as it does on the impossibility of such transparent access. In that sense we could say that, despite the movement portrayed in this poem, it enacts a kind of stillness in that it shuts down the very function of poetry as mediated esthetic experience. Rather than being an unmediated experience, the poem reveals, as Adorno put it in the passage I quoted earlier, "the unreality of [its] own reality," not only the mediated nature of the experience it represents but also the stillness of the esthetic model on which it depends, a model that ends up excluding the work of art from the experience entirely, and representing instead the negativity of an impossible and unsayable experience. Paradoxically, it may be the works that represent a greater stillness than is on offer in the language of "Elévation" that provide for the kind of movement associated with profound esthetic experience, despite what "Elévation" seems at first to portray. Poems such as "Le *Confiteor*" do not simply present a demythologized, debunked, or psychologized rewriting of esthetic experience but rather provide a way to shift the terrain of that experience that suggests a newly affirmed autonomy of the work of art that valorizes its intensity precisely by moving *beyond* the kinds of models of transcendence and unmediated communication with nature that is on display in "Elévation." These works enact the dissonance that allows us to see the fact that the harmony of unmediated esthetic experience was never where the true esthetic experience could reside to begin with, precisely because the subject's relation to art and to nature can never be unmediated. There is thus more possibility for intensity and esthetic truth within the poems that move away from an unmediated model of transcendence than in those that uphold it.

The newer esthetic model is a negative one in that it refuses unmediated experience but also on account of the terror such a model can inspire, as we saw in the *cri de frayeur* of "Le *Confiteor*" which forces a reconsideration of what it would mean for the artist to be *vaincu*. "Le *Confiteor*" proceeds from the stillness of the landscape in the first paragraphs to the moving turmoil and active duel of the final paragraphs, a literal enactment of the motion set forth by the poem in terms of the way the poem assumes a greater level of subjectivity as it empties out the lyric subject. To be unsettled by the artwork is part of the movement that it provokes, according to Adorno, and part of its moving character as an artwork, as he indicated in the reference in the passage quoted above to "the feeling of being overwhelmed when faced with an important work" (79). He goes on to affirm that "under patient contemplation artworks begin to move. To this extent they are truly afterimages of the primordial shudder in the age of reification; the terror of that age is recapitulated vis-à-vis reified objects" (79). As I have started to suggest, it may not be in poems such as "Élévation," which explicitly represent movement as the transcendent flight of the lyric subject, that we may find the best examples of poems which "begin to move." The mimesis of movement may in fact block a kind of movement that is more effectively located in poems that represent an almost paralyzing stillness. If that is the case, then those poems which may otherwise be taken to portray the absence or failure of esthetic experience enact the emergence of a more complex relationship of subjectivity and objectivity between poem and lyric subject. In their surface-level representation of failure, these poems enact success on the model that Adorno proposes, one which remaps failure and success (by naming what could be labeled failure as the very measure and condition of that success, understood differently) and movement and stillness.

Through the very terror of the speaking subject, the artwork establishes itself as autonomous because it refuses the logic of domination that was characteristic of the enlightenment relation to nature, manifest not only in its technological conquest but also by the subsuming of nature into an art form that could contain and account for it. What Adorno terms "shudder" is both a remnant of the primordial fear of nature that led to its domination and a desirable effect of esthetic experience whose absence we fear precisely because it would mean the end of esthetic experience:

> For if at one time human beings in their powerlessness against nature feared the shudder as something real, the fear is no less intense no less justified, that the shudder will dissipate. All enlightenment is accompanied by the anxiety that what set enlightenment in motion in the first place and what enlightenment ever threatens to consume may disappear: truth. [. . .] The instant of appearance in artworks is indeed the paradoxical unity or the balance between the vanishing and the preserved. (AT 80)

One could read poems such as "Élévation" as a play of vanishing and preservation of unmediated transcendence, a work that performs the necessary vanishing of that kind of experience precisely on account of the impossibility of art to create or convey such immediacy of experience. Adorno's esthetics underscore that artworks share with philosophy the impossibility of sustained unmediated experience while at the same time providing for the possibility of a momentary shudder, preserved now as the fear of its dissipation. It is in poems whose surface content figures dread and inertia that the Baudelairean artwork holds its greatest potential for "begin[ning] to move" and becoming "afterimages of the primordial shudder in the age of reification."

The "esprit" which had been figured as moving agilely in the "immensité profonde" in "Elévation" finds itself restricted and contained in the fourth "Spleen" poem, "Quand le ciel bas et lourd. . .":

> Quand le ciel bas et lourd pèse comme un couvercle
> Sur l'esprit gémissant en proie aux longs ennuis,
> Et que de l'horizon embrassant tout le cercle
> Il nous verse un jour noir plus triste que les nuits; (1: 74)

> [When the low, heavy sky weighs like a lid On the groaning spirit,
> victim of long ennui, And from the all-encircling horizon Spreads over us a day gloomier than the night; (*Flowers* 253)]

The subject-object relation between lyric subject and sky is neither one of unified communion as had been implied in "Elévation" nor one of domination of the sky by the lyric subject; rather, the poem assigns the active role to the sky that exerts force and agency merely by virtue of its weight. The status of the lyric subject is ambiguous from the start, with an unspecified third-person "esprit gémissant" presumably then associated with a collective "nous" in line four. Further transformations involve the earth changed into "un cachot humide" and the rain imitating prison bars, as spaces become increasingly confining. This restricted stasis is interrupted by a sonic event that ushers in the conclusion of the poem:

> Des cloches tout à coup sautent avec furie
> Et lancent vers le ciel un affreux hurlement,
> Ainsi que des esprits errants et sans patrie
> Qui se mettent à geindre opiniâtrement.
>
> — Et de longs corbillards, sans tambours ni musique,
> Défilent lentement dans mon âme; l'Espoir,
> Vaincu, pleure, et l'Angoisse atroce, despotique,
> Sur mon crâne incliné plante son drapeau noir. (1: 75)

> [All at once the bells leap with rage
> And hurl a frightful roar at heaven,
> Even as wandering spirits with no country
> Burst into a stubborn, whimpering cry.
>
> — And without drums or music, long hearses
> Pass by slowly in my soul; Hope, vanquished,

Weeps, and atrocious, despotic Anguish
On my bowed skull plants her black flag. (*Flowers* 253)]

The first aural image is one that endows the inanimate bells, via the act of *hurlement* which can be roaring or yelling, with a characteristic that hovers between the animal and the human but renders them animate in either case, in a move that shifts subjectivity ever further from a lyric first person and casts both the reader and the first-person subject, who will appear only in the possessive "mon" in the last line, as the passive recipient. The personalized "esprit" that was subject and object of address in "Elévation" is generalized here into the figurative and anonymous plurality of "esprits errants," present in the poem as a simile for the bells in a move that both inscribes and erases human presence in the poem. Anguish, personified, becomes the main actor in the final stanza in an act that seals the simultaneous defeat of both hope and the lyric subject.

The poem is remarkable for the contrast between the heavy "couvercle" that would seem to confine and stifle the space of the poem and the intensity of the visual, tactile, and auditory world it establishes within those confines. The contrast intensifies the esthetic experience rather than diminishing it by reducing its spatial boundaries so that the skies, which had sometimes been figured as the infinite, now come closer to the earth and circumscribe the imaginative geography of the poem. The sound of the bells projects toward the sky, but the sky is low and is, presumably, within the literally impossible spatial realm of the impersonalized "esprit" of the first stanza: How would the lid of the sky, as one physical object figured as another, weigh on the immaterial spirit? From the first stanza, then, this poem "begins to move" even, and all the more so, because its upward orientation sends the reader back down again, under the heavy sky, the pouring rain, and the bells whose upward-directed sounds presumably come crashing all the more quickly back down once they hit the heavy low-hanging sky. Rather than shutting down esthetic experience in the overwhelming experience of the triumphant Angoisse of the poem, we can read this silent, passive lyric subject as the site of precisely that overwhelming feeling that Adorno identifies as the by-product of the realization of the artwork's "immanent character of being an act," "something momentary and sudden" (AT 79). This suddenness is the "tout à coup" by which the silence of the poem is interrupted by the bells' ringing that marks that "instant of appearance" which Adorno characterizes as "the paradoxical unity or the balance between the vanishing and the preserved" (AT 80). The sound of the bells remains in the poem, but the transcendent and religious connotations of that sound have vanished except as the movement upward which returns toward the lyric subject who appears in the poem only after that sudden turning point of their pealing, summoned and constituted by that moment of preservation and vanishing.

In its own turn, that lyric subject itself is both preserved and vanished, present under the sign of the anguish that has become the sum total of identity as subject in the poem, acted on by the way in which the poem has configured the experience it describes and producing an esthetic experience in which the lyric subject remains just present enough to become the figure of anxiety. This anxiety becomes, through the process enacted by the poem, not a simple affective state of spleen but rather the anguish associated with both the presence and the potential disappearance of what Adorno calls shudder and its potential for producing esthetic truth. The poem's move toward Anguish as the lyric subject, victorious over the speaking subject, can be seen as representing not the failure of esthetic experience but as the sign of its intensified presence when art is confronted with the possibility of its own impossibility if it remains wedded to models of transcendence for its viability. It is through a negation of that model that is in no way a mere psychologizing of it that poems such as "Spleen" retain a place for the power of the artwork while at the same time performing its transformation in a way that preserves the artwork's autonomy and allows us to see it as a critique of the fiction of the unified subject. The lyric subject is undone not so much by spleen as by the power of the artwork itself to reveal unity and harmony as a lie, not in an effort to cancel esthetic experience under the sign of skepticism but rather to liberate new ways in which the artwork speaks.

A poem composed in 1861, four years after those we have just been considering, takes up the image of the *couvercle* once more, this time as the main image in poem that bears that name:

Le Couvercle

En quelque lieu qu'il aille, ou sur mer ou sur terre,
Sous un climat de flamme ou sous un soleil blanc,
Serviteur de Jésus, courtisan de Cythère,
Mendiant ténébreux ou Crésus rutilant,

Citadin, campagnard, vagabond, sédentaire,
Que son petit cerveau soit actif ou soit lent,
Partout l'homme subit la terreur du mystère,
Et ne regarde en haut qu'avec un œil tremblant.

En haut, le Ciel! Ce mur de caveau qui l'étouffe,
Plafond illuminé par un opéra bouffe
Où chaque histrion foule un sol ensanglanté;

Terreur du libertin, espoir du fol ermite;
Le Ciel! Couvercle noir de la grande marmite
Où bout l'imperceptible et vaste Humanité. (1: 141)

[The Cover

Wherever he may go, on land or sea,
Under a blazing sky or a pale sun,
Servant of Jesus, courtier of Cythera,
Somber beggar or glittering Croesus,

City-dweller, rustic, vagabond, stay-at-home,
Whether his little brain be sluggish or alert,
Everywhere man feels the terror of mystery
And looks up at heaven only with frightened eyes

Above, the Sky! that cavern wall that stifles him,
That ceiling lighted by a comic opera
Where every player treads on blood-stained soil;

Terror of the lecher, hope of the mad recluse:
The Sky! black cover of the great cauldron
In which boils vast, imperceptible Humanity. (*Flowers* 501)]

The minimal traces of individualized subjectivity that figured in "Quand le ciel . . .," the "nous" and the "mon," have yielded here to a collective and depersonalized human figure, and in the tercets, the inanimate sky takes over the role as the main subject, albeit an inert one that functions more as a setting in which little action takes place. While humanity is in some ways at the center of the poem in its collective representation in the several forms enumerated in the second quatrain, it is at the same time curiously absent except as a fearful subject of terror that echoes the "cri de frayeur" of "Le *Confiteor* de l'artiste."

One could say that the tercets perform a demystification of the transcendence typically associated with the sky in the sense of the infinite or the eternal; they reveal the "true colors" of the sky to be black rather than blue, oppressively heavy rather than light, with the "truth" of the sublime image of the sky revealed to be a pot lid, a quotidian and, worse, useful object devoid of esthetic appeal. But such a demystification is an oversimplification; what the poem accomplishes is not merely a substitution of one vision for another. The image of the sky is not simply replaced by that of the lid. Whereas in "Quand le ciel . . ." the sky had weighed down *like* a lid, in "Le Couvercle" there is a metaphoric substitution: "Le Ciel ! Couvercle noir," which suggests not merely seeing one of those terms in light of the other but also as an equivalence: the sky *is* a lid. Reading backward from this substitution of terms, we can then see that it is not the case that an artificial, made object is being put in the place of the natural and beautiful one, but rather that *both* the lid and the sky are mediated objects, that the sky that we might be tempted to take as a natural esthetic object acting upon a unified lyric subject was already mediated by the subject in ways that might have been hidden beneath the semblance of the poem and which are now revealed. That revelation, though, is not a disenchantment in the usual sense, because it invites readers to see the revelatory potential in the lid as well, as testimony to the power of art, which lies precisely in the way it mediates experience for subjects in the world to produce what Adorno would label esthetic truth. This is a truth that is not simply transcribed in the poem but enacted by it; the power of the esthetic comes not *despite* the fact that it mediates experience but precisely *because* it does so.

To see the sky as a pot lid is to enclose what had seemed expansive and intimate into a more circumscribed space, not to bring inside what was outside but rather to see the outside as limiting in ways that were concealed by a poetics of the natural and the infinite. The refusal of transcendence has, paradoxically perhaps, the potential to reveal a more powerful role for art than a transcendent model could. Whatever else the absurd surrealism of the final lines might bring—do we have a secularized hell in the suggestion of boiling humanity? How far can we lean on the metaphor before it breaks down? Where is the "stove" and who exactly is perceiving the "imperceptible" humanity?—the poem ends, as others we have been examining, on an image of movement and activity within a confined space that would otherwise suggest stillness. The movement of the boiling is concealed by the confining structure of the pot, in a way that suggests a parallel with the solidity of a poetic form such as the sonnet that can be said to conceal the movement of the poem but actually creates the conditions of its movement, its ability to re-envision esthetic experience along the lines I have been suggesting. Once again, beauty aligns itself with pain, a pain curiously devoid of any reference to the physical suffering implied by a boiling humanity. The poem preserves mystery ("Partout l'homme subit la terreur du mystère") rather than moving toward a demystification, thus inscribing mystery itself within the artwork in a way that highlights what Adorno has called its "riddle character."

And it is here, in the boiling pot, that many strands of Adorno's view of art come together in the event of the poem that acts on its readers, cruelly perhaps, as an instance of a scene of the "étude du beau" where the artist in vanquished. But from the vanquishing of the individuated artist subject may emerge crucial insight not just from the work of art but about the work of art and its relation to other kinds of experience. To bring the strands of my analysis of esthetic subjectivity together here in the boiling pot of "Le Couvercle," let us listen to Adorno on the riddle character of art as he discusses it near the beginning of his lectures entitled *Aesthetics*. He begins by positing a scenario where one is either inside or outside the work of art:

> Either one is inside a work of art and aligned with it in a living sense, in which case the question of understanding the work or of the meaning of the work does not really arise; or, on the other hand, through reflection or

development—possibly even through something like disgust or an excess of artistic experience—one is now outside the sphere of influence of art and casts one's gaze on the work. (*Aesthetics* 17)

Baudelaire's poem could be said to play with this schema of inside and outside by creating an inside, the boiling pot, that has the paradoxical effect of leading us out of the comfortable parameters of the work of art that would celebrate the infinite freedom of the sky. Enclosure under the lid means that we are jolted out of any comfortable familiarity we may have had with blue skies and the lyric subject who places them at the heart of a transcendent poetics. The container makes it impossible to be so "aligned" with the work of art that we let the critical faculty of judgment remain inactive. Like the flow of poems such as "La Fontaine de sang," the boiling water here induces that critical judgment but now within newly defined confines that invite questions about the nature of the "space" of the work of art. The incongruous final image of the poem, which even so had been prepared by the very title of the poem, places readers "outside the sphere of influence of art" and in a position explicitly to recognize its semblance as semblance.

> The moment of casting one's gaze is the catalyst of fundamental questioning: and then [...] one suddenly asks oneself abruptly: so what's it all about, what is all this? The moment one is no longer inside it, where one is no longer aligned with it, art begins to withdraw in a certain sense, to close up, and assumes what I earlier called its riddle character. (*Aesthetics* 17–18)

The closer we are to the mundane in "Le Couvercle," to the absolutely quotidian act of cooking in a covered pot, the further art withdraws from an experience of immediate comprehension. It is not that the commonplace object is somehow transfigured or infused with transcendent possibility, but rather that it transforms the container of its (equally commonplace) sonnet form in order to incite reflection on whether it may not have been the sky as traditionally figured that ends up being the commonplace, the block to esthetic potential rather than an incitement. Baudelaire's poem, like Adorno's esthetic theory, depends on our being able to ask the question "what's it all about" while also never being able to find a satisfactory answer.

Adorno's very next remark takes us back to our main focus of esthetic subjectivity by linking these questions of being inside and outside the work of art, witnessing its withdrawal, and then being led by the work of art to ask questions of what it's about in the broadest possible sense of that question, to what Adorno calls a rupture within the self.

> If there is a justification for the philosophy of art [...] then the justification for the philosophy of art lies solely in the fact that it alone can [cope with

the experience] when one has felt that rupture in oneself, when one steps out of the work and it suddenly becomes foreign and mute, and one asks oneself: what's it all about, what's the point of it, what does it say? (18)

Here too, far from proving to be the point of breakdown in esthetic experience, the disintegration of the unified self is shown to be its condition of possibility, in a move that requires cognitive reflection from the esthetic subject in order to participate fully in the process of experiencing the work of art. Neither a comfortable nor a result-oriented process, this act of reflection is what keeps alive the artwork's potential for critical reflection in a way that not only preserves but depends on the autonomy of the work of art. Critical reflection, on this view, cannot minimize or manage the foreignness of the work of art. At its best, it allows us to see the depth of that very foreignness, not just of the "modern" work of art but in works that precede the modern work, against which the modern work is sometimes thought to be reacting but which may in fact form a continuity that becomes visible to us via the critical reflection unleashed by the modern work.

Such a process of fuller esthetic perception is not possible without the critical reflection that is both made possible by and required by the split in the esthetic subject: "But if this riddle character [. . .] is truly inherent in art, then [. . .] the works of art themselves require commentary and critique for the sake of their own development and their own life" (*Aesthetics* 18). The modern artwork moves us away from a model of immediate and direct esthetic experience toward one which, through critical reflection, reveals such a model to have been mediated from the start. The new kind of sublime is both contained and not contained within an estheticized quotidian, as the fear of the sky inscribed in the poem ("Partout l'homme subit la terreur du mystère, / Et ne regarde en haut qu'avec un oeil tremblant.") melds with the potential fear of dissolution of the self in the experience of making sense of artwork, the very experience which, as we have seen, depends on the split self in order to enable critical reflection on the work of art that would at the same time complete it and reveal it as always out of our grasp because it is untotalizable. The fear on the part of generalized humanity in "Le Couvercle" in the face of "la terreur du mystère" could in that sense be the fear of self-dissolution, the uncharted search for a new articulation of subjectivity that breaks down a simple subject-object relation with the work of art. The esthetic subject is thus not quite a void, but nor is it representable in a conventional sense, as Adorno underscores: "The aesthetic subject is probably unrepresentable because, being socially mediated, it is no more empirical than the transcendental subject of philosophy" (AT 168). The space of the poem is the field of the reconfiguration of this "probably" unrepresentable subject; it is the fiction we cannot do without as we puzzle out what it means to engage with the riddle character of art.

3

Transcendence

It is perhaps tempting to see in the trajectory of Baudelaire's work a shift from an earlier model of poetic transcendence, dependent in some ways on romantic notions of the poet's privileged access to a purportedly "higher" realm beyond the mundane existence of everyday objects and material reality, to a demystified poetics that is all too painfully conscious of the ways in which the changed material conditions of the modern poet have rendered such transcendent visions obsolete or, at best, a source of nostalgia or even bemusement. Such a view implies a linear move from one conception to the other, however, which does not do justice to the complex dialectical relationship that persists in Baudelaire between transcendence and immanence. Now that we have seen how the dissonance that animates his poetry is dependent on older notions of harmony and how he reconfigures subjectivity as a mutually constitutive relation between subject and object, we are well positioned to see that this model of subjectivity also yields a transformed relationship to transcendence. Baudelaire does not simply replace that notion with a vision of poetic immanence but rather redefines the relationship of immanence and transcendence by the way in which his poems assume a certain kind of subjective agency and thereby could be said to create their own transcendence. In this chapter, then, I explore the consequences of Baudelaire's model of poetic subjectivity for the transformed power of the poetic work of art as it configures its relationship to the material world and to the lyric subject inscribed within it. Through extended readings of "Je t'adore à l'égal de la voûte nocturne," "Le Rêve d'un curieux," and "Le Crépuscule du soir" in prose, along with brief considerations of "Perte d'auréole," "Bénédiction," "A une passante," and "La soupe et les nuages," I bring together the implications of my analysis of dissonance and subjectivity for the persistence and transformation of an immanent transcendence that animates Baudelaire's poetics.

On this view, we could say that the role of the poet is both heightened and diminished. What Adorno said of Beethoven is equally true of Baudelaire:

> Beethoven's art achieves its metaphysical substantiality because he uses technique to manufacture transcendence. This is the deepest meaning of the Promethean, voluntarist, Fichtean element in him, and also of its untruth: the manipulation of transcendence, the *coercion*, the violence. (*Beethoven* 78)

By acknowledging the manufactured nature of transcendence, we assign a crucial role to the poet, who is not the passive vehicle of some kind of revelation but the technician of language who engages with art as mediation and appearance in ways that both hide and highlight that mediated, all-too-human world that the artwork constructs for the perceiver. It is here that the dialectical relation of subject and object enters in order to complicate what might seem to be a view of art that focuses exclusively on the strict control of the raw materials of the work of art by the artist. Once the artwork is brought into being, it assumes a kind of agency for itself that acts on the perceiver in a way that compels engagement, a newly invigorated form of immanent transcendence by and through the work of art. This sort of transcendence is all the more powerful, rather than less, for having shown any vertical, metaphysical transcendence to be the work of the manipulation of the form of the work of art itself. The act of violence to earlier notions of transcendence, visible especially in "Je t'adore à l'égal . . .," does not destroy it but allows a new relationship of immanence and transcendence, present but latent in other poems, to emerge and transform our relationship to the work of art.

Often identified as one of the masterpieces of Baudelaire's late poetic style, "Le Cygne" extends the poet's transformation of lyric subjectivity while also refiguring the notion of transcendent poetic experience. There is a "je" present in the poem but figured from the start as yielding its prominence to Andromaque ("Andromaque, je pense à vous !" [1: 85] ["Andromache, I think of you!" (*Flowers* 289)]) as the first of what will be a series of objects of the lyric subject's thought in the poem; the poet's "mémoire fertile" is fecund. The subject is active in ways that underscore a certain passivity, with several iterations of the verb *voir* in part one of the poem: "Je ne vois qu'en esprit tout ce camp de baraques"; "je vis [. . .] Un cygne" ["I saw a swan"]; "Je vois ce malheureux" (1: 86) ["I see that hapless bird" (289)]. Thinking regains the upper hand over seeing in the second part of the poem, a thinking that always takes as its object the seemingly infinitely multipliable figures of exile: "Je pense à mon grand cygne" ["I think of my great swan"]; "Je pense à la négresse, [. . .] à quiconque a perdu ce qui ne se retrouve / Jamais, jamais !" ["I think of the negress, [. . .] of whoever has lost that which is never found / Again ! Never!"]; "Je pense aux matelots oubliés dans une île" (1: 86-7) ["I think of the sailors forgotten on some isle" (293)]. The subject's conceptual activity leads away from himself in order to yield the subjective space of the poem to the cast of other characters, generated in the mind of the lyric subject who then remains present but as a mere vehicle for the textual existence of the creations of his mind. As Ross Chambers has argued about this poem, "the textual subject, if such there be, proves to be lacking—and to be lacking in particular the transcendent knowledge, of himself and of others, that might confer on him a status other than that of supreme ironist" (128). Neither empty vessel nor centralized plenitude, the lyric subject in "Le Cygne" preserves a remnant of an older form of lyric subjectivity as an organizing intelligence who gestures toward establishing coherence among the objects of his vision and of his imagination while resisting assimilating them into a totalizing vision. Such resistance is a rather different reading from one that would see in the poem the *impossibility* of establishing a coherent experience from the real and imagined figures in the text. The coherence of the poem lies in the way its regular form contains and orders, but just barely, what might seem like a chaos of confused imagery that gestures toward or suggests allegory in apparently transparent language without necessarily arriving there. While the lyric subject says straightforwardly that "tout pour moi devient allégorie" (1: 86) ["all for me become[s] allegory" (289)], the very formulation "pour moi" calls into question the status of the allegory, which could plausibly be read as a mere subjective impression on the part of the lyric subject rather than an interpretive model built in to the poem. What begins as a problem of establishing the status of lyric subjectivity in the poem quickly becomes one of how to read the text more broadly as that seeing and thinking subjectivity becomes duplicated by, perhaps fused with, the reader of the poem as well:

> Vainly scrutinizing the "ciel ironique et cruellement bleu" of a text that is apparently transparent but proves to be infinitely noisy, such a reader duplicates the swan's entreaties to God as he or she vainly searches the text for evidence of the presence of a controlling "author"—even one assumed to be cruelly and ingeniously unavailable to scrutiny. And such a search is likely to conclude in an assumption of authorial absence, or at least anonymity. (Chambers 128)

Chambers implies an analogy between the vertical and horizontal orientation in the poem (the glance toward the transcendent sky that simply results in a refocused concentration on what is happening on the ground) and the relationship of the lyric subject to what we might call a higher order author figure. Just as the sky refuses any answer beyond its cruel and ironic appearance, there is no transcendent author to guarantee the allegorical import of the poem's images. The infinite expansion of figures of the subject's thought is a horizontal one that would multiply examples without deepening their meaning.

And yet by drawing the reader in to this textual space that invites reflection on present and past, fiction and reality, cityscape and sky, the poem preserves esthetic experience not despite, but rather because of, the emptying out of the unified coherent subject: "As figures of unreadability, then, the becoming transparent of the urban atmosphere is of a piece with the becoming blank of the textual subject and the becoming anonymous of the city poet, no longer a numinous figure but undistinguishable henceforth from the crowd of nameless others" (Chambers 129). "Le Cygne" thus both preserves and fundamentally alters transcendence along the lines that J. M. Bernstein has identified as operating in Adorno, who develops a theory of the "formation of meaning" of the artwork that "recognizes that transcendence is, finally, not vertical but horizontal" (Bernstein "Why" 208).[1] This transcendence is accomplished by a kind of esthetic semblance that reveals "a possibility of a form of meaning, and a form of interaction between subject and object that is not identitiarian" (208). The characters in "Le Cygne" are evoked without being subsumed by the lyric subject; he thinks of them rather than becoming them, in an act of imagination that resists dominating the object but at the same time suggests a slightly permeable lyric subjectivity that allows for a play of both identity and difference with other humans and indeed, within this poem, the animal. To identify that kind of relationship between self and other is not to transcend difference but to attend to it as difference, which necessitates retaining some notion of the subject who posits that subject-object relationship without taking the further step of attempting to characterize the relationship as one of absolute identity or absolute difference. The subject-object relationship in the poem is left as the object of reflection; readers think about the speaking subject just as he thinks of these real and imagined others, without attempting to resolve or precisely define the relationship beyond one of presence to reflection and the suspension and potentially infinite expansion communicated powerfully by the ellipsis of the last line: "Aux captifs, aux vaincus ! . . . à bien d'autres encor !" (1: 87) ["Of the captives, of the vanquished! . . .of many others too!" (293)].[2] If, for Sonam Singh, "The swan in 'Le Cygne' serves to ironize a transcendental model of 'le signe'" (Singh 424), the built urban environment around which the swan is ambling "mark[s] an irrecoverable loss that incites, rather than deters, the poet's creation" (424). The new transcendence, and the altered subject-object relationship that it brings in its wake, are worked out in the poetic form of the artwork that depends on the persistence of an older model just as much as it demands the transformation of that model. Attention to the way the form accomplishes that shift in transcendence, while retaining the category itself, is the critical reflection that complements the work of art by being necessary to it but not sufficient, for establishing a totalizing interpretation of the poem.

Thinking the simultaneous persistence and transformation of transcendence and lyric subjectivity allows us a new perspective on poems such as "Perte d'auréole," a work which, according to typical readings, illustrates the debased alienation of the poet, the forced abdication of an exalted view of the poet's vocation as magus or prophet or seer in the new geographical context of an urban "mauvais lieu" (1: 352) ["house of ill fame" (*Parisian* 113)].[3] The poem tells the anecdote, via dialogue without intervening narration between a "buveur de quintessences [. . .,] mangeur d'ambroisie" (1: 352) ["drinker of quintessences [. . .,] ambrosia eater" (113)] whom we assume to be a poet, and his friend. The poet recounts the loss of his halo which fell in the mud at the side of the city street in the midst of the "chaos mouvant" (1: 352) ["shifting chaos" (113)] of the city. At his friend's suggestion that he should attempt to retrieve the halo, the poet replies:

— Ma foi ! non. Je me trouve bien ici. Vous seul, vous m'avez reconnu. D'ailleurs la dignité m'ennuie. Ensuite je pense avec joie que quelque mauvais poëte la ramassera et s'en coiffera impudemment. Faire un heureux, quelle jouissance ! et surtout un heureux qui me fera rire ! Pensez à X, ou à Z ! Hein ! comme ce sera drôle ! » (1: 352)

["Good God no! I'm fine here. You're the only one who recognized me. Besides, dignity irks me. And I'm glad to think that some bad poet will pick it up and insolently stick it on his head. Make someone happy, what a delight! and especially a happy someone I can laugh at! What about X, or Z! Right! Wouldn't that be funny!" (*Parisian* 113)]

An entirely new set of possibilities for poetry emerges if we read "Perte d'auréole" from the perspective not of the poet as subject but of the potential of the poem as simultaneously object and subject, in the context of the autonomy that Adorno claimed for the work of art and the corresponding potential for critique that it harbors when divorced from a strong notion of individual poetic subjectivity.

Régine Foloppe has underscored the self-dethroning that the poet performs in the poem as well as the way his newfound anonymity links him to others by canceling the distinction he formerly sought to uphold:

Perdant de distinction, il perd à la fois des devoirs et un empire, un statut : il se detrône. Triple glissement: [. . .] il devient le même que l'autre. Ce parti pris de communauté lui impose alors une rigeur d'autant plus grande pour garantir son identité créatrice, que celle-ci se voit alors menacée par l'imposture de "X" ou "Z," assurément habiles techniciens. D'une certaine manière alors, l'écho entre le vers et la prose écartèle proprement le poète, entre cet anonymat [. . .] et la certitude fondée de son autorité incantatoire irremplaçable. (Foloppe 278)

[In losing distinction, he loses duties and an empire and a status at the same time: he dethrones himself. A triple sliding down: [. . .] he becomes the same as the other. This preference for community imposes on him an even greater rigor to guarantee his creative identity, since that is threatened by the imposture of "X" or "Z," who are assuredly skilled technicians. Thus in a certain way, the echo between verse and prose properly makes the poet torn between that anonymity [. . .] and the certainty founded on his irreplaceable incantatory authority.]

The poet crafts what looks like a new kind of superiority over the unnamed "bad poets" and leaves what makes them bad unspecified. The text plays a curious game with anonymity here at the end, with the poet having explained that with his halo lost, "je puis maintenant me promener incognito [. . .] comme les simples mortels" (1: 352). But the poet then names other poets by not naming them, substituting X and Z for proper names. By this move he seems at least to suggest a certain interchangeability, reinforced by his newfound status as a "simple mortel," between himself and other poets. Such a move, I would argue, de-emphasizes the unified subjectivity of the poet as the site and origin of poetic activity, not in a way that debases the act of poetic creation but, rather, in a way that shifts emphasis to the work itself. "Perte d'auréole" is less about the debasing and alienation of poetry than it is about a key shift in the relation of poet to poem in this period. Without a unified poetic subject serving as the explicit or implicit creative force of the poem, the work takes on increased importance in terms of its autonomy, and subjectivity is thus reshaped as a relation to the work, which takes on increased primacy according to this model. As we recall from Adorno, it is on account of this autonomy that the artwork, even in the modern period of alienation, retains the force of critique, not due to any sort of explicit political content of the poem, but rather by the way its form constructs relationships of subjectivity and objectivity. In a dialectical move, the very alienation that disrupts the notion of the unified self has the power to reveal that such a notion of individuality was already a fiction, a bourgeois construction. In that sense, we can read the self-debasing of the poet not as, or not only as, a cynical reaction to a unappreciative bourgeois public but also as a gesture of refusal of an overemphasized individuality on the part of the poet figure that would fit all too comfortably with that same bourgeois worldview. In that sense, "Perte d'auréole" effects a kind of immanent transcendence, retaining the notion of poetic transcendence but redefining it as affiliated with the power of the artwork to overcome its previous incarnations. To say as much is hardly to refuse the power of poetry; rather, it is to affirm a central role for poetry understood via the autonomy of the work and arising from the very destruction of what we thought we had understood to be the powerful role that an earlier romanticism had carved out for it.

It is not the case, then, that a poem such as "Perte d'auréole" has a merely debunking or demystifying effect that would imply a linear progression from an "older" poetic model to be found in poems such as "Bénédiction" to a newer, more cynical refusal of poetic transcendence. Richard Klein, in his reading of those two poems, has argued that their poetics are mutually constitutive. Pointing to the presence of "yeux mortels" in the closing lines of "Bénédiction," he notes that "the success of that image suggests [. . .] that symbolic language can succeed only by naming the distance from its source. The Poem which appears to announce the Poet's apotheosis ends on a bizarre note; the accent falls strangely on the mortal longing, the dark desire, the loss reflected in human eyes" (Klein 525). The questioning of transcendence was, thus, there even in poems that seem to suggest its possibility as something beyond the human. Klein is right to suggest that part of what leads to a problematic notion of a linear push toward a supposed demystification is a hasty identification of the speaker in "Perte d'auréole" with Baudelaire himself:

> The loss of the halo reveals the illusions of a certain kind of symbolist poetry which aspired to transcend the world; "Perte d'auréole" demystifies "Bénédiction." But it would be a mistake to identify Baudelaire with the Poet-Hero of the prose poems, for his laughter at the expense of his former self, his new-found contempt for the halo, is another kind of blindness, the mystification of the demystifier. (526)

To read Baudelaire well would be to read, so to speak, between poems such as "Bénédiction" and "Perte d'auréole," giving hermeneutic priority to neither of them. The poetic space that Baudelaire forges might best be described as a betweenness, a space that resists closure by holding a tension in place which would cease to exist if our approach to the poetry were to be linear. Klein's characterization of the refusal of synthesis in Baudelaire resonates with Adorno's negative dialectics which resists Hegelian synthesis in order to maintain the active dialectic:

> It would be an error to think that, having negated the negation, we find ourselves in the presence of a new transcending synthesis. In fact we find ourselves nowhere, hovering from side to side over the space of the distance which separates two texts. Their polarity persists but now only insofar as we recognize the power of each term to become its opposite. The sign of that movement between the texts by which the same continually differentiates itself is the halo: an infinitely precious crown, a worthless commodity; a circle of pure light, the merest line drawn round a head; the index of divinity, the sign of the hollowest pretension; a symbol, an allegorical emblem—everything, nothing, more or less. (Klein 527–8)

The transcendence that is accomplished not within but between these poems reinscribes that transcendence within the human realm itself. Transcendence via the eternity figured by the sky is present only under the sign of its impossibility or its semblance, as Adorno suggests in *Negative Dialectics*: "No recollection of transcendence is possible anymore save by way of perdition: eternity appears, as such, but as diffracted through what is most perishable" (ND 360). To appeal to the sky in a metaphorical or traditionally transcendent sense is not ultimately to preserve the possibility of going beyond the realm of the human; rather, it is to reveal such a poetic use of the sky as a fully human construct, transcending the actual or supposed naiveté of a getting beyond the human by showing that the urge for that movement beyond is already inscribed in the fully human mode in which transcendent poetics emerged.

To say as much is not to degrade Baudelaire's transcendent vision or to demystify it but to say that the kind of transcendence that remains when we read between the texts preserves the category of transcendence by redefining it, rather than abolishing it by demystifying it. Just as we saw in his interventions in subjectivity both the preservation and the radical critique of bourgeois individuality, so too his notion of transcendence preserves and challenges our understanding of what such a thing might mean. Whatever it might mean, reading Baudelaire should at least reveal to us that to see his work as moving from a mystified to a demystified vision of the role of the poet is to pose the question of transcendence badly, to word it incorrectly. To incite such questions about the nature and role of the work of art is to retain a sense of its crucial importance and to engage in the back and forth between the falling under the effect of the work of art and engaging in the kind of philosophical reflection that attempts to account for or articulate that effect. It would be foolish to suggest that we "know better" than to affirm the kind of transcendence at work in poems such as "Elévation" or "Bénédiction"; what comes to the fore in the kind of reading I am proposing is a gradual emergence of a better understanding of those poems by reading them dialectically in the light of what comes after them, and vice versa. The experience of both nature and poetry is always mediated but never demystified, and understanding Baudelaire's transcendence requires a deep inquiry into the nature of that mediation since esthetic truth is inseparable from the semblance which is at the heart of the artwork.

Adorno captures this ambiguity of the transcendent in this paradoxical formula: "the transcendent is, and it is not" (ND 375). He goes on to say that "we despair of what is, and our despair spreads to the transcendental ideas that used to call a halt to despair" (375). That is to say that the transcendent remains precisely on account of its impossibility, as a manifestation of longing or regret for the impossible. The making possible of the impossible under the very sign of impossibility is, after all, a passable description of the function of art, which persists, not in spite of but because of, the impossibility of a metaphysical transcendent. Transcendence persists negatively and is transferred to the tiny remains of the former vision; the sky, we might say, becomes the underside of a pot lid. Adorno describes this as an experience of asking "can this be all?":

> Pure metaphysical experience grows unmistakably paler and more desultory in the course of the secularization process, and that softens the substantiality of the older type. Negatively, that type holds out in the demand "Can this be all?"—a demand most likely to be actualized as waiting in vain. [. . .] Idle waiting does not guarantee what we expect; it reflects the condition measured by its denial. The less of life remains, the greater the temptation for our consciousness to take the sparse and abrupt living remnants for the phenomenal absolute. (ND 375)

The "can this be all?" captures a profound disappointment while also holding out a conceptual space for something else, however small or implausible that remainder might be. Such a view of transcendence calls for a reevaluation of expectation of the horizon of metaphysics while also opening the question of what a more "horizontal," immanent transcendence might be like.

Baudelaire's "Le Rêve d'un curieux" (1860) is a poem of the "can this be all" in the context of a double space of potential possibility and impossibility, the world of the dream and of death:

Connais-tu, comme moi, la douleur savoureuse
Et de toi fais-tu dire : « Oh! L'homme singulier ! »
— J'allais mourir. C'était dans mon âme amoureuse
Désir mêlé d'horreur, un mal particulier;

Angoisse et vif espoir, sans humeur factieuse.
Plus allait se vidant le fatal sablier,
Plus ma torture était âpre et délicieuse;
Tout mon cœur s'arrachait au monde familier.

J'étais comme l'enfant avide du spectacle,
Haïssant le rideau comme on hait un obstacle . . .
Enfin la vérité froide se révéla :

J'étais mort sans surprise, et la terrible aurore
M'enveloppait. — Eh quoi! n'est-ce donc que cela ?
La toile était levée et j'attendais encore. (1: 128-9)

[Do you know as I do, delectable suffering?
And do you have them say of you: "O! the strange man!"

> — I was going to die. In my soul, full of love,
> A peculiar illness; desire mixed with horror,
>
> Anguish and bright hopes; without internal strife.
> The more the fatal hour-glass continued to flow,
> The fiercer and more delightful grew my torture;
> My heart was being torn from this familiar world.
>
> I was like a child eager for the play,
> Hating the curtain as one hates an obstacle . . .
> Finally the cold truth revealed itself:
>
> I had died and was not surprised; the awful dawn
> Enveloped me. — What! is that all there is to it?
> The curtain had risen and I was still waiting. (449)]

The poem enacts an unveiling that also poses as a sort of demystification that points up the gap between expectation and reality while leaving open the question of what an appropriate reaction would be in the face of such a distance between expectation and experience. The end suggests a curious kind of inaction within action via the lyric subject suspended in waiting at the end of the poem.[4] The waiting calms the intensity of the first part of the poem with its "désir mêlé d'horreur" and irreconcilable mix of "angoisse et vif espoir."

A simple reading would see the poem as presenting a scene of demystification: what had been expected as a grand metaphysical event turns out to be anticlimactic, with the heavy anguish-laden emotions mixed with expectant desire of the tercets giving way to a near comic sense of the banality of the event of the tercets. The literary conceit of the dream as announced in the title allows for split subjectivity that permits the lyric subject to narrate his own death, thereby becoming the subject of the experience and the one who gives it the poetic form by which we as readers have access to it. This doubling should make us alert to the ambiguity that operates in what seems like the most straightforward affirmation in the poem: "La vérité froide se révéla." Is this a truth in the demystifying sense of a contrast between the expectation and reality of what death is like? The fact that this experience and this reference to truth are inscribed both within a dream and a poem should give us pause: on what grounds could we affirm that what the lyric subject now finds to be the truth is definitive, as opposed to another experience that he now labels as truth. What kind of truth do we as readers look for in the poem? Is it a matter of identifying with the lyric subject so that we are led to a similar kind of debunking of the metaphysical import of death, replacing the divine terror with a sense of disappointment? Or is there an esthetic truth separate from the situated experiential truth articulated by the lyric subject? The fact that the poem incites us to pose such a question about a split and multiple set of meanings hidden behind what we could call the curtain of the word "vérité" suggests that we should be wary of the temptation to identify with the lyric subject in his trajectory from heightened expectancy to disappointment and continued waiting. In that sense the experience of truth comes to resemble that of death in that, by the end, we remain waiting for what we thought we had found or known when the moment of "truth" came. The poem thus enacts an overcoming of what we might have otherwise taken to be the truth of modern poetry's demystifying function and reveals a more complex reality which we can intimate but not fully expound as we find ourselves both assimilated to the lyric subject and taking our distance from him. It is that play of identity and difference which structures the poem.

The waiting that is inscribed at the end of the poem thus resonates with the act of reading poetry itself, with its eye toward esthetic truth that is both on our horizon of expectation and impossible to fulfill completely. To pursue the forging of esthetic truth is the work of the poet; Bertrand Marchal has linked the banal notion of procrastination, evident in Baudelaire's references in his correspondence to his thwarted desire to work, to more abstract questions of the illusory quality of esthetic transcendence as it is sometimes understood:

> la perte de la vérité se paie aussi d'une impuissance qui est moins circonstantielle qu'ontologique. Ce qu'on appelle la procrastination de Baudelaire n'est peut-être rien d'autre qu'une façon de restituer une forme même illusoire de transcendance ou d'au-delà qui fait que l'art est, à la limite, une activité impossible. (Marchal 139)
>
> [the loss of truth comes with an impotence that is less circumstantial than ontological. What we call Baudelaire's procrastination is perhaps nothing other than a way of restoring even an illusory form of transcendence or of a beyond that means that art is, finally, an impossible activity.]

We could say that by inscribing the word "truth" into "Le Rêve d'un curieux" Baudelaire has underscored the impossibility of affirming any such thing either at the level of the experience of death by the subject of the poem or of esthetic truth figured as a simple revealing. To ask what esthetic truth is revealed and how by the poem is to draw us nearer to the conclusion that such a thing could never simply be revealed. Rather, the form of the poem and the context of the dream bring us back to Adorno's notion of the enigmatic character of art, its resistance to precisely any attempt fully to articulate its truth by other means:

> Those who peruse art solely with comprehension make it into something straightforward, which is furthest from what it is. If one seeks to get a

closer look at a rainbow, it disappears. Understanding, however, does not extinguish the enigmaticalness of art. Even the felicitously interpreted work asks for further understanding, as if waiting for the redemptive word that would dissolve its constitutive darkening. Following artworks through in the imagination is the most complete, most deceptive surrogate for understanding, though obviously also a step toward it. (AT 122)

Reading "Le Rêve d'un curieux" or any Baudelaire poem as a simple debunking of transcendence would be to deny the enigmatic character of art, which persists even when, or especially when, the artwork seems to refuse a vision of transcendence. An esthetic truth that would be faithful to the complexity of the work of art could not come to rest in such an interpretation; rather, it would leave multiple interpretive options in suspension, which is exactly what plays out in the form of this poem. We would expect the poem to establish a relationship of some kind between the quatrains and tercets; the poem plays with that formal convention of the *point tournant* by seeming to offer the contrast between desire or dread and the deflated response of "n'est-ce donc que cela," but the poem refuses tidy conclusion by its final line ("La toile était levée et j'attendais encore") which points up the contrast between what should have been a full revelation (the raised curtain) and the suspended state of the lyric subject.

Rather than being the locus of a representation of transcendence, according to Adorno's model, the artwork produces its own transcendence, and this is a fruitful way to understand the way transcendence is transformed in Baudelaire's poetry. As I have been claiming, it is not that transcendence is canceled so much as the category remains in order to be reshaped by the modern autonomous work of art in the way in which its form operates on readers:

> Artworks [. . .] produce their own transcendence, rather than being its arena, and thereby they once again become separated from transcendence. The actual arena of transcendence in artworks is the nexus of their elements. By straining toward, as well as adapting to, this nexus, they go beyond the appearance that they are, though this transcendence may be unreal. Only in the achievement of this transcendence, not foremost and indeed probably never through meanings, are artworks spiritual. Their transcendence is their eloquence, their script, but it is a script without meaning or, more precisely, a script with broken or veiled meaning. Although this transcendence is subjectively mediated, it is manifested objectively, yet all the more desultorily. Art fails its concept when it does not achieve this transcendence; it loses the quality of being art. Equally, however, art betrays transcendence when it seeks to produce it as an effect. (AT 78)

"Le Rêve d'un curieux" is a site of transcendence insofar as it is an example of artworks that "go beyond the appearance that they are," not in order to transcend appearance but rather to understand that appearance in its full complexity, as positing a dialectical relationship with the esthetic tradition in which it intervenes and on which it depends for the construction of an oppositional meaning that would not be a mere refusal of that tradition but rather a reshaping intervention in it. The "script with broken [...] meaning" that we have in the poem is one whose parts do not easily cohere without hermeneutic remainder, so to speak: to create meaning in a way that is faithful to the puzzling complexity of a poem like "Le Rêve d'un curieux" is to remain suspended in waiting, like the lyric subject at the end of the poem with whom we identify in that implied search for meaning.

Adorno highlights the double status of transcendence in Baudelaire specifically, noting how "already in Baudelaire the transcendence of the artistic appearance is at once effected and negated. From this perspective, the deaestheticization of art is not only a stage of art's liquidation but also the direction of its development" (AT 79). For Adorno, this simultaneous effecting and negation of transcendence sees its endpoint in the eloquent muteness of the modern work of art whose representative for Adorno is Samuel Beckett, in whose works "aesthetic transcendence and disenchantment converge in the moment of falling mute" (AT 79). A similar falling mute is effected in "Le Rêve d'un curieux," where the lyric subject is caught in what seems like an eternal waiting once the words of the poem come to an end but not a conclusion in the foreordained fourteenth and last line.[5] The poem's saying of there being nothing left to say is its transcendence of appearance, the point at which the eloquent muteness of the poems sends the reader back to the enigmatic nature of the esthetic truth to be found in the poem. The muteness of the end sends us back to the rest of the poem to ask how even words can convey a sense of muteness by creating a work where "transcendence and disenchantment converge." To conceive the work of art this way is to reshape what we understand by the way in which an artwork "speaks," which Adorno characterizes as being "like elves in fairy tales: 'If you want the absolute, you shall have it, but you will not recognize it when you see it'" (AT 126). The death and/or raising of the curtain in the poem are events that disrupt the smooth flow of the more conventional meanings of hope and anguish in the face of a metaphysical event; they demystify that event but render the meaning of the poem all the more opaque by refusing to give us a continuation of a conventional discourse about death.

The poem transcends that metaphysical language by interrupting it with an enigmatic scenario. We are not left with mere meaninglessness, though; as Adorno claims, "the enigmaticalness of artworks is not all there is to them; rather, every authentic work also suggests the solution to its unsolvable enigma" (AT 127). The solution is forthcoming only at the risk of unrecognizability and via an interpretation whose inadequacy we must acknowledge and always be ready to abandon as we enter the give and take between the work of art and attempts to understand it conceptually as the way it mediates experience by creating an experience of its own. The new kind of transcendence on offer in this poem is one that transcends simplistic readings; it is an impulse, a desire, "désir mêlé d'horreur," perhaps, to understand and to be willing to wait, to arrive at an interpretation wondering if that's all there "really is" to it, to acknowledge the "vérité froide" and also be willing to abandon what hat truth seemed to be in the moment of what we experienced as understanding.

It is in one of the shortest poems of *Les Fleurs du Mal* that these questions of transcendence and disenchantment, desire mixed with horror, and the question of *la vérité froide* converge in the most complex way. "Je t'adore à l'égal de la voûte nocturne," which Jérôme Thélot aptly describes as "saturé de réflexivité" and "peut-être le plus réflexif des poèmes du livre" (Thélot 435), presents in compact form an intense interweaving of so many crucial strands of Baudelaire's poetics:

Je t'adore à l'égal de la voûte nocturne,
Ô vase de tristesse, ô grande taciturne,
Et t'aime d'autant plus, belle, que tu me fuis,
Et que tu me parais, ornement de mes nuits,
Plus ironiquement accumuler les lieues
Qui séparent mes bras des immensités bleues.

Je m'avance à l'attaque, et je grimpe aux assauts,
Comme après un cadavre un choeur de vermisseaux,
Et je chéris, ô bête implacable et cruelle!
Jusqu'à cette froideur par où tu m'es plus belle! (1: 27)

[I adore you as much as the nocturnal vault,
O vase of sadness, most taciturn one,
I love you all the more because you flee from me,
And because you appear, ornament of my nights,
More ironically to multiply the leagues
That separate my arms from the blue infinite.

I advance to attack, and I climb to assault,
Like a swarm of maggots after a cadaver,
And I cherish, implacable and cruel beast,
Even that coldness which makes you more beautiful. (*Flowers* 87)]

One could say that the main dialectical tension governing the poem is the one between transcendence and immanence and that the poetic discourse suggests accomplishing a flattening of the transcendent and immanent. But as I hope to demonstrate, any straightforward assertion about this poem is fated to fall short in terms of accounting for the enigmatic character of what happens in it. The first line suggests either a flattening of the distinction between the transcendence typically associated with an infinite night sky and the immanence of love (or simply desire) for a woman or an exaltation of that love raised to the power of the transcendent. The "equality" is undecidable and suggests an interpenetration of the two levels, immanent and transcendent, which maintains those categories by redefining them. Immanent desire is heightened by its kinship with the kind of transcendence that remains inaccessible to the poet. Unlike poems where the poet's privilege is to participate directly in transcendence by understanding and communicating with the transcendent world, here immanent desire is heightened by distance and inaccessible realms, the accumulated space between the body of the poet and the nebulous realm. That distance is the condition of possibility of adoration, which establishes itself in the ultimately unbridgeable gap between subject and object of adoration. It is that gap which prevents the object from being subsumed into the subject in a relation of total domination and reinforces a mediated relation between the two.[6]

The first part of the poem configures the subject-object relationship and the immanent-transcendent relationship co-comitantly, with an implied expansion of the literal and figurative distance between the subject and object, which are counterposed grammatically in the initial "Je t'" and then separated by the accumulated miles that separate the lyric subject from the "immensités bleues." But what to make of the fact that those accumulated miles are only the semblance of accumulation: "tu me parais [. . .] accumuler les lieues?" And are these accumulated miles to be understood as between the lyric subject and the woman or between the lyric subject and the sky? The grammar of the sentence leaves room for both possibilities, further reinforcing the flattening of distinction between the woman and the sky, the sites of immanence and transcendence. There is, then, either a clear distinction between, or complete elimination of the distinction between, the woman and the sky: either she blocks the kind of transcendence to be had from some kind of communion with the nocturnal vault, or she, by being herself just as inaccessible as that sky, is assimilated to it as the site of impossible communion either with woman or sky. Is the sky like the woman or is the woman like the sky? The two options are suspended in equal possibility here, forcing us to call into question not only a distinction between transcendence and immanence but also any kind of Platonic reading we might be tempted to perform, whereby erotic desire leads to the contemplation of "higher" things. The woman is like the sky, in her beauty and eternally receding nature, while also being distinct from the sky in a way that enables the comparative mechanisms that structure the stanza. And again, all of this may simply be the result of esthetic semblance, which is not to say a merely subjective illusion on the part of the lyric subject but rather a key element of how the work of art functions: it is via the operations of the words of the poem that the "reality" of the accumulated distance between the poet and either the woman or the sky takes shape; it is through that linguistically created distance that the lyric subject is constituted as this particular kind of subject, through the relationship of proximity or impossibility of a relationship that had seemed quite close indeed when figured as the "je t'."[7]

The second part of the poem establishes a complex play of sameness and difference with the first part, as we move from the immobility of adoration and the still image of the night sky to the startling violence of "Je m'avance à l'attaque." And yet, as Jérôme Thélot has indicated, there is an identical syntactic structure in the first and second parts of the poem, a single sentence in each case with a kind of mirror effect between "Je t'adore à l'égal [...] Je m'avance à l'atttaque":

> Par ce rigoureux parallélisme Baudelaire—consciemment—donne à entendre le sens de la seconde séquence comme identique à celui de la première. De sorte que « Je t'adore » et « Je m'avance à l'attaque » signifient la même chose : le culte religieux et le rapport sexuel sont structurellement semblables ; la prière est une opération identique à l'opération de l'amour. Sauf que la linéarité du poème indique une autre indication. Les deux parties du poème sont analogues mais non pas déplaçables. L'attaque vient *après* l'adoration, l'érotique succède au religieux—et c'est ce qu'il faut comprendre. La seconde séquence révèle le double rôle et la duplicité de l'adoration : que celle-ci n'est pas simplement le témoignage d'un culte, mais aussi une stratégie de séduction. (Thélot 444–5)

> [By this rigorous parallelism Baudelaire—consciously—gives us to understand the meaning of the second sequence as identical to that of the first, such that "Je t'adore" and "Je m'avance à l'attaque" mean the same thing: religious worship and sexual relations are structurally similar; prayer is an operation similar to the operation of love Except that the poem's linearity gives another indication. The two parts of the poem are analogous but not movable. The attack comes *after* adoration, the erotic follows the religious—and that is what we need to understand. The second sequence reveals the double role and the duplicity of adoration: it is not simply the witness of devotion, but a strategy of seduction.]

These considerations add another layer of flattening to the poem, that between adoration and seduction, if it is indeed a scene of seduction and not violence, or perhaps all seduction is to some extent violent. Would the lyric subject be the seducer, or is it that he has been seduced, by the promises of esthetic transcendence to be had in starry skies, into an attempt to procure that transcendence by an attack on the immanent body? Must one be destroyed in order to procure the other? Has the woman been killed in the process of attack? The word "cadavre" brings us quite directly into the realm of death, but it is operating here under the sign of comparison: the lyric subject attacks (but the object of attack is left unspecified in terms of explicit identification) *like* vermin attack a cadaver: is that to say vigorously? As a response to appetite? By instinct? Is the lyric subject in control of these actions even in this moment that features the most active verbs of the poem? The assimilation of the love object to a cadaver is strengthened in the final line's reference to "froideur," itself doubled in meaning via the echo of the coldness of a cadaver but more immediately signifying a figurative distance and harshness.

The lyric subject cherishes the object for her lack of proximity and attainability, as if the proximity would cancel the assimilation of the immanent object to the transcendent and demolish the relationship between immanent and transcendent on which the poem's structure is based. And in that, the lyric subject transforms in yet another way what we might have understood as immanent and transcendent, for the inaccessibility of the object, its resistance as object, is what accomplishes the leveling of sky and lover. The poem accomplishes a new kind of transcendence by refusing to represent mimetically a simple realm beyond the materiality of bodies in the world. Rather, the poem transcends typical meanings of immanence and transcendence by a voluntary confusion of the categories; the space of the poem is neither the esthetically constructed night sky nor the vaguely sketched woman's body but rather the blank space between the two sections, the "separation" that is enacted a moment after it is named in line six. The blank suggests the possibility that the woman, despite the very direct evocation of an attack, barely exists as a body. She is evoked only metaphorically ("vase de tristesse") and through her silence ("grande taciturne") and metaphorical coldness. The supposedly immanent body is figured as the hardly nameable here; it does not really make sense to speak of disenchantment in the conventional sense. Rather, the poem performs a voluntary disruption of notions of higher and lower by establishing the equivalence between body and sky and the metaphorical connotations of both. It is not that the heights are brought down to earth or that earthly material is exalted; rather, the poem transcends conventional poetic notions of space by maintaining the spatially expressed distinction between immanence and transcendence only negatively, by the absent presence of those categories on which the poem depends in order to be intelligible. The categories are present only in order to be reconfigured and called into question, not unlike the relationship we have explored between the dissonance that can only be legible in the context of a consonance that is both preserved and negated.

The poem plays with both apparent clarity and increasing complexity (as in the configuration of the subject-object relationship created and implied by the poem), and with the distinction or non-distinction of identity and difference (between the nature of the encounter, no matter how we configure the subject and object, as described in the first versus the second part of the poem). It opens not onto the infinite sky but onto an invitation to establish the terms of its enigma, figuring itself, in that sense, as a cold object akin to the sky and the woman that are inscribed within it. The poem transcends its material by passing through the esthetically constructed sky only to return to a material world that has been transformed by the poetic operations at play here, which, as I have indicated, serve to destabilize the distinction between immanence and transcendence but not in the name of eliminating those categories altogether. Both the sky and the body, and all its metaphors, become the poetic material in the sense of the "stuff" of the poem, and the poem then does creative and productive "violence" to conventional meanings and associations by reconfiguring the poetic space via the irony that multiplies meanings and brings the poem "down" to the material not by eliminating the distance from the transcendent but by multiplying the distance between the poet's arms and the "immensités bleues."

I have made repeated reference to a "woman" figured in the poem, but as I have also indicated, her presence is barely sketched. We can imply the gender from the adjective "belle," but even to call the woman a lover makes some assumptions based on the vaguest of indications in this poem which draws on some conventional associations only the better to invite their complication. One way the poem does what we could call a kind of productive violence to poetic convention is to expand the possibilities implied by the subject-object relationship beyond that of poet-lover and to perceive other possibilities.[8] One of those possibilities is to read the poem as an account of a perceiver's experience confronting a work of art. If we follow Baudelaire's notion of art as suggested here in conjunction with Adorno's idea of the autonomous work of art, what emerges is a work of art that does not exist "for" the viewer but on its own terms. As Adorno puts it in his *Aesthetics* lectures:

> Works of art have certainly preserved enough of their sacred origins that, as Benjamin once put it very aptly, they are not directly intended for an audience. No painting is there for the viewer, no symphony for the listener, nor even any drama for the audience, as they are first of all for their own sake; and only through this aspect, which must be described as a secularized theological one, so only with reference to the absolute, and not in some immediate relationship with humans, do the works exist, do they speak at all. As soon as one violates the distance that lies in them, as soon as one relates the works directly to what one wants from them, one

already "de-artifies" them and destroys the very thing one hopes to get from them. (*Aesthetics* 119)

Such a characterization of the relationship of the work of art to the perceiver is rich in possibilities for interpreting "Je t'adore . . ." If we read the subject-object relationship in the poem as that of the perceiver and the work of art, we see the play of the receding work of art, pointing not at transcendence but at the gap that separates the perceiver from whatever is figured as transcendent, to the point where it becomes impossible to name the artwork which becomes an object of desire all the more desirable for its muteness and inaccessible distance. The first part of the poem presents that situation whereby the work is "not in some immediate relationship with humans," the condition under which it can "speak at all." The remnant of the ancient sacred remains to the extent that the distance is not transgressed; if there is a sacred dimension to the poem, it is one that would refuse rather than embrace the Christian notion of the word made flesh, the flattening of the distinction between the immanent and the transcendent that could only be blasphemous to other monotheistic traditions such as Judaism and Islam which do not have a divine figure who also becomes fully immanent through taking on the flesh..

On this reading, the second part of the poem represents the movement that would constitute, in Adorno's terms, a "violat[ion] of the distance that lies in them." The attempt to possess the work of art removes it from the realm of art altogether, which on this view relies on the artwork's transcendence for it to exist as a work of art at all. It would be on account of the lyric subject's failure to possess the object in the second part of the poem that the object retains within it what the subject would have wanted to possess in the first place.[9] What seems at first to be a failed "attack" is the condition of possibility of the artwork in its ultimately inviolable coldness; what arrives to the perceiver of the work of art can never be more than a momentary understanding, a passing and uncertain moment, or what Adorno calls "shudder," about which I shall have more to say. The ambivalent status of the "attack" in this poem, unlike the much more explicit and completed sadistic violence of a poem such as "A celle qui est trop gaie," maintains the openness without which the poem would be a closed circle, a completed move from transcendence to immanence. By reducing the conceptual distance between the sky and the physical object of desire, the poem maintains the dialectical play that allows us to see the immanent and transcendent as co-determining, and created by, the structure of the work of art itself, which on this reading becomes a term in its own dialectic by being the object of desire here, which resists full possession and only on that account retains its status as a work of art. To preserve transcendence by negating it could be seen as an instance of what Adorno calls thinking "against itself" whereby metaphysics is preserved precisely by its own negation. Rodolphe Gasché underscores that "for Adorno, saving a minimal metaphysical experience for thinking is aimed at preventing the total closure of the system of immanence" (Gasché 295). To see in a poem such as "Je t'adore . . ." a descent from the ideal to the material is to close the world of poetic possibility in a way analogous to such a closure of immanence by the foreclosure of the metaphysical. In both cases, the metaphysical or transcendental remains in order to redefine itself as the kind of closure that is risked by any non-dialectical opposition between the two or any cancelation of one by the other. The poem, we might say, thinks against itself by the way its parallel syntax and form call on the reader to reconfigure the space of the poem in ways that challenge any movement "up" or "down," to use the words of the poem and their typical connotations as vehicles for thinking a dialectical relationship between immanence and transcendence differently than we otherwise may have done.

"Je t'adore . . ." is also remarkable for the way it brings to the fore questions of the relation of ethics to epistemology within the realm of poetry. I have already suggested the central importance of the subject-object relation in the poem but I have also underscored the way the poem undoes and complicates that relationship by allowing readings that render it ambiguous: is the other a lover, or the poem, or the lyric subject himself, or does it create a space where it can be all of these simultaneously? It is at this point that ethics becomes joined to epistemology, to the question of how the ethical relation can be grounded in the knowledge or non-knowledge of the other, or of the self as other. Judith Butler, in her essay "Violence, Mourning, Politics," has enumerated this relation between knowing, nonknowing, and ethical relations:

> my own foreignness to myself is, paradoxically, the source of my ethical connection with others. I am not fully known to myself, because part of what I am is the enigmatic traces of others. In this sense, I cannot know myself perfectly, or know my "difference" from others in an irreducible way. [. . .] But is there an ethical valence to my unknowingness? I am wounded, and I find that the wound itself testifies to the fact that I am impressionable, given over to the Other in ways that I cannot fully predict or control. I cannot think the question of responsibility alone, in isolation from the Other; if I do, I have taken myself out of the relational bind that frames the problem of responsibility from the start. (32–3)

"Je t'adore. . ." figures the simultaneous distance and proximity of self to other and what we could call self to other-as-self. While there appears to be a linear temporal movement from adoration to attack, the final two lines return to the coldness and inaccessibility with which the poem had opened. As I have indicated, the attack here is not necessarily accomplished; the lyric subject "advances" to attack but nothing in the poem confirms the completion of the act. If we are to read a true parallel between the two parts, the subject would remain in the posture of advancing while confirming impossibility of access; he would remain poised with his arms separated from their object, as at the end of the first part. The action of advancing would then be returned to the more passive adoration, and the alterity of the woman, or poem, or subject-as-other-to-itself would not be challenged or violated by the action of the second part but affirmed all the more strongly, with that alterity being assimilated to the more absolute alterity of the "voûte nocturne" of the first part.

Immanence, in this poem, returns us to transcendence in order to perform the immanent transcendence of a relationship that should be most intimate and best known, that of a lover or even of self to self. The poem as artwork also both comes close and withdraws in that moment of advancing that in fact becomes a multiplication of the distance separating a reader from a full and transparent reading of the poem that would exhaust the possibilities of what it "says" about subject-object relationships. All of these relationships are marked by the impossibility of full understanding, of a full "possession" that would mark the kind of totalizing, dominating approach to the world that animated the positivism and notions of progress against which Baudelaire railed. This relation of non-knowing becomes ethical in part by the other's resistance to full knowledge or assimilation or dominance. This realization allows us to rethink the simultaneous "postulations" toward the supposedly opposite poles of God and Satan according to Baudelaire, with their corresponding desires to ascend or descend. As Jérôme Thélot has argued, "Je t'adore. . ." illustrates how Baudelaire's poetry allows us to understand his more theoretical writings rather than vice versa. The complicated relation of self to other in "Je t'adore . . ." permits us to turn back to the two postulations in order to unravel them. The theoretical fragment, while written after the poem, is, according to Thélot:

> en retard sur ce poème, et moins critique, moins une pensée que lui. Il faut interpréter le fragment par le poème, non le poème par le fragment. Il n'y a pas de différence entre la postulation vers Dieu et celle vers Satan. Il n'y a pas même « deux » postulations, mais un seul désir. Il n'y a pas d'opposition entre « Dieu » et « Satan », mais un seul sacré, et seulement l'ambivalence du sacré : telle est la pensée, et telle l'expérience vécue, du poème XXIV. L'esthétique—l'éthique : ainsi se formule, en vérité, la double postulation baudelairienne. [. . .] Il n'y a pas deux amours ni deux joies, [. . .] il n'y a qu'une même expulsion d'autrui par l'image qu'on lui préfère, dans laquelle coexistent des signes formellement opposés mais structurellement identiques.
>
> La transcendance sacrée dont le poème et le désir font leur objet, qu'ils élaborent et dont ils s'enchantent, est doublement ambivalente. D'une part l'image de l'autre présente des signes divins et naturels, sublimes

et infâmes, d'autre part cette image est le fait de la violence du sujet sur autrui, et martyrise en retour le sujet lui-même. (Thélot 437–8)

[lagging behind the poem, and less critical, less a thought than it. We must interpret the fragment via the poem, and not the poem via the fragment. There is no difference between the postulation toward God and the one toward Satan. There are not even "two" postulations, but rather just one desire. There is no opposition between "God" and "Satan" but just one sacred, and only the ambivalence of the sacred: such is the thought, and such is the lived experience, of this poem. Esthetics—ethics: thus is truly formulated the Baudelairean double postulation. [. . .] There are neither two loves nor two joys, [. . .] there is only one same expulsion of the other by the image that we prefer of it, in which coexist formally opposed but structurally identical signs.

The sacred transcendence which the poem and desire make their object, which they elaborate and by which they are enchanted, is doubly ambivalent. On one hand the image of the other presents divine and natural, sublime and abominable signs; on the other hand this image is the fact of the violence of the subject toward another, and makes the subject suffer in return.]

Thélot's reading accounts for transcendence and immanence within the context of divine and secular desire but has little to say about the other potential axis of interpretation that I have proposed, namely, the way the poem implies a relationship between the work of art (the poem specifically, in this case) and the perceiver. A turn toward Adorno's discussion of shudder in esthetic experience can help enumerate the way in which esthetic experience depends on the kind of alterity to oneself that we have seen operating in the poem.

Stephanie Belmer concentrates on Adorno's characterization of shudder as "an experience of life in the emphatic sense of the term," which "is both a experience of what may pre-date or point beyond reified subjecitvity" and "occurs in response to the Other" (Belmer 30). It is "an aesthetic affect on the subject that need not be pressed into Adorno's larger project of reconciliation" (Belmer 30) that ultimately preserves alterity while providing a momentary experience of something beyond it. One could plausibly claim that the second part of "Je t'adore . . ." induces shudder in the reader by the sharp and sudden contrast with the stillness of the adoration of the immense blue sky in the first part. There is a kind of mirror effect between the movement of the lyric subject in the poem and the reader, a momentary identity via the common reaction of movement in the face of desire, an emergence of an active consciousness via a jolt inspired from outside the subject in both cases. The experience fades quickly, as we return by the end of the poem to the cold stillness of beauty. Still, the poem is activated by that momentary lunge forward, the impulse to move toward the object not in order to warm it but to retain it in its coldness and inaccessibility. In that sense it forms a contrast to the rigid frozenness not of the object but of the subject of esthetic experience in "A une passante," where the woman moves while the lyric subject is frozen, paralyzed in fascination:

> Une femme passa, d'une main fastueuse
> Soulevant, balançant le feston et l'ourlet;
>
> Agile et noble, avec sa jambe de statue.
> Moi, je buvais, crispé comme un extravagant,
> Dans son œil, ciel livide où germe l'ouragan,
> La douceur qui fascine et le plaisir qui tue. (1: 92)
>
> [A woman passed, with a glittering hand
> Raising, swinging the hem and flounces of her skirt;
>
> Agile and graceful, her leg was like a statue's.
> Tense as in a delirium, I drank
> From her eyes, pale sky where tempests germinate,
> The sweetness that enthralls and the pleasure that kills. (*Flowers* 311)]

The motion on the part of the subject in "Je t'adore..." is more paradoxical in that the movement toward the object ultimately maintains it in its otherness rather than assimilating itself to the subject. It maintains the subject-object relation, with primacy given to the object, on which the esthetic relation depends.

That sense of distance between subject and object is reinforced by the lack of closure in "Je t'adore..." While the last words "plus belle" echo the first stanza's "d'autant plus, belle," the effect is not one of a circularity that would close the poem but, as I have suggested, of an open action of attack which may or may not have reached its goal, a fact which calls into question a linear progression just as the closing words both evoke and cancel any real sense of a circular movement to closure. The question of closure can in turn yield one last insight on the status of violence in the poem, seen from the point of view of the relation of the lyric subject to art as object more generally. For Adorno, as we recall from our consideration of dissonance, acts of dissonance or violence reveal a truth that is covered up as a supposed consonance or unity in more traditional approaches to esthetics. As Lambert Zuidervaart puts it, classicism and neo-classicism "carr[y] out unification as an act of violence" for Adorno (Zuidervaart 167) so that an act of esthetic violence in a modernist text takes on the role of revealing what had been a concealed violence, an imposed unity that does violence to dissonant elements of beauty that are repressed by a classicist esthetic in ways that make it untrue. That truth is thus revealed by the act of esthetic violence enacted by the modernist work, and in "Je t'adore..." we have a literalization of that act when the lyric subject makes his attack. The poem, by its act of violence against itself in the second part, frees itself from potentially clichéd or, worse, false mimetic relations of transcendence in the starry skies of the first part and reveals attempts at neoclassical unification to do violence to the distance between subject and object that "Je t'adore..." restores in the dialectical tension between its two parts. That tension can only resolve itself by retreating into the false, which perhaps accounts for Baudelaire's frequent non-conclusive conclusions to his poems. Fidelity to the antagonistic relation between subject and object that governs both social relations and esthetic form proscribes arriving at definitive conclusion at the risk of esthetic falsehood as Adorno understands it. For him, "so long as society remains antagonistic, no artwork will achieve complete reconciliation," but "complete reconciliation remains a possibility in Adorno's esthetics. Authentic artworks promise that this possibility is still possible" (Zuidervaart 168). The dialectical tension animating "Je t'adore..." allows it to stand as a modern poem whose very evocation of purportedly eternal beauties of the nocturnal sky points to the way in which the complex metaphorical interactions of the poem, along with the complex configurations of subjects and objects in it, allow us to read that sky as mediated by the esthetic and cultural history in which it participates.

Baudelaire retains the remnant of the retrievability of the esthetic and erotic object of desire while suggesting that it may be retrievable precisely in its irretrievability, its inaccessibility as an object. This is a development in modern art that reaches its culmination, according to Adorno, in Samuel Beckett, who, as Gerhard Richter claims, "takes on the tradition not by grasping for the irretrievable and thereby creating a false sense of its retrievability, which is to say, its availability as just another element of what already is operative and thinkable in the present, but rather by letting the irretrievable speak precisely as the irretrievable" (Richter *Thinking* 66). "Je t'adore..." goes halfway toward the irretrievable by representing the lyric subject as moving toward it, yet allowing the result of that movement to remain unspecified and the longing after the cold object to remain at the end of the poem. The poem preserves and negates the traditional discourse of adoration and possession of an erotic and/or esthetic object of desire as what Hent de Vries has identified as the mode of the *in pianissimo*:

> There can be no metaphysics, no onto-theology, ethics, or esthetics in the no-man's-land between modernity and postmodernity except *in pianissimo*: that is to say, in the infinitely small—and infinitely distanced, couched in language, liquefied, and nearly liquidated—dimension of the absolute [. . .], whose minimal theology nonetheless steers clear of the (supposed) total negativism and inverted absolutism that a Habermas

(as we shall see, wrongly) ascribes to the first generation of the Frankfurt School in general and to Adorno in particular. (de Vries 24)

The negation of transcendence in a poem such as "Je t'adore . . ." is, as I hope to have shown, not a mere negation but rather a realigning of the terms of transcendence and immanence in ways that preserves them differently, and preserves the possibility of retaining the possibility of esthetic transcendence in ways that will always demand of us a kind of critical reflection on the very possibility of such a thing. That is an important part of the ironic self-consciousness that Baudelaire's particular kind of self-doubling entails. It draws us into philosophical reflection not so as to make art the servant of that reflection, a position that would have horrified the Baudelaire of the "Art philosophique" essay, but to allow us to return more richly to the work of art and to see the ways in which critical reflection is both absolutely necessary to full esthetic perception and inadequate in terms of accounting fully for it.

By passing through critical reflection we are better equipped to see how poems such as "Je t'adore . . ." allow us to read Baudelaire's own theoretical reflections on the work of art precisely because they often present a more complex and enigmatic engagement with questions of esthetic truth. A sense of what de Vries labels the *pianissimo* can be seen in some of Adorno's passing references to Baudelaire: "Baudelaire the dark has also offered sensuous enticement as the antithesis of the fraudulent sensuality of culture's façade. There is more joy in dissonance than in consonance: This metes out justice, eye for eye, to hedonism" (AT 40). Baudelaire's poetry functions as critique precisely in the way it retains and modifies the possibility of sensuous pleasure, available as momentary, provisional, and always subject to an ironic doubling that calls the very possibility of the prolongation, or even the full accomplishment, of the experience into question. What is enacted in "Je t'adore . . ." is fundamental to Baudelaire's poetics more broadly because it accomplishes the kind of preservation-in-transformation that is the hallmark of Baudelaire's participation in, and rupture with, the esthetic tradition which is his point of departure. As J. M. Bernstein puts it, "the modernist sublime is a regathering of beauty, truth and goodness: beauty beyond esthetics, truth beyond subsumption and goodness beyond categorical worthy action. In this regathering we are no longer sure where, say, sublimity ends and truth or ethical risk begins" (Bernstein, *Fate* 241). Such regathering is made possible only by a "sacrifice of beauty, which is equally the sacrifice of reason since the sacrifice of beauty is the sacrifice of the constructive moment, where the constructive moment is the sedimented moment of esthetic rationalization" (Bernstein, *Fate* 241). Such a sacrifice allows for the transformation of beauty away from the vacuous variety that it risks becoming in its stagnation and the falsity of a supposed unity and immobility. The movement of the poem, in that sense, contrasts with the stagnation and risk of vacuousness implied in the repetition of "belle...plus belle" between the first and second parts. The coldness of the beautiful object attracts the lyric subject, but is only transformed into esthetic action by a violence that presumably attempts to move from adoration to transformation of the object by an action that simultaneously eliminates and reinforces the distance between that subject and object.

Critical self-reflection as it is prompted by "Je t'adore . . .," where as readers we move from passive contemplation of a "beautiful" poem to an evaluation of what is at stake in the transformation of beauty that it performs, is what allows art to preserve both its critical function and its brief acknowledgment of the possibility of a world different from the alienated one it has become:

> That the world, which, as Baudelaire wrote, has lost its fragrance and since then its color, could have them restored by art strikes only the artless as possible. This further convulses the possibility of art, though without bringing it down. [. . .] The injustice committed by all cheerful art, especially by entertainment, is probably an injustice to the dead; to accumulated, speechless pain. Still, black art bears features that would, if they were definitive, set their seal on historical despair; to the extent that change is always still possible they too may be ephemeral. (AT 40)

The reorientation of the relationship of art to goodness, truth, and beauty which art's critical function implies is worked out in Baudelaire via a simultaneous transformation of subject-object relations and the dialectical interplay of transcendence and immanence. I turn now to "Le Crépsucule du soir" in prose in order to consider a poem where the subject-object relation is not human to human but human to non-human, including the natural world and the poem itself as subject and object. What "Crépuscule" shares with "Je t'adore" is the irreducibly dialectical relationship that animates the reconfiguration of both subjectivity and transcendence at work in Baudelaire's poetry.

Beyond its status as one of the poems that exists in both verse and prose versions, "Le Crépuscule du soir" is distinctive for its two very different prose poem versions, the first being little more than an anecdote in a similar vein as "Le Mauvais vitrier," about two friends of the speaking subject. The definitive version is significantly richer and, I would argue, more complex than its verse equivalent; it brings together several strands of the relationship among dissonance, subjectivity, and transcendence that we have been pursuing. The poem resists any individualized expression of a lyric subject; the speaking subject's only use of the first person singular comes later in the poem, to invoke his memory of the friends he describes. Just as the twilight represents a liminal moment, an ambiguous temporality belonging fully neither to night nor to day, the first paragraphs establish a series of antithetical, paradoxical, or contradictory set of relations between the temporal and spatial settings and the interior state of those who inhabit it.

> Le jour tombe. Un grand apaisement se fait dans les pauvres esprits fatigués du labeur de la journée ; et leurs pensées prennent maintenant les couleurs tendres et indécises du crépuscule.
> Cependant du haut de la montagne arrive à mon balcon, à travers les nues transparentes du soir, un grand hurlement, composé d'une foule de cris discordants, que l'espace transforme en une lugubre harmonie, comme celle de la marée qui monte ou d'une tempête qui s'éveille. (1: 311)

> [Daylight falls. A great calming forms in pitiable minds wearied by the day's toil; and their thoughts now absorb twilight's tender and indistinct tints.
> Meanwhile, a great howling, composed of a multitude of discordant shouts, reaches my balcony from the mountaintop, through the evening's transparent clouds, and transformed by the space into a dismal harmony, like a rising tide or an awakening storm. (*Parisian* 50)]

The abstract and inanimate *jour* is the main actor in the first paragraph as it falls and then plays what is characterized as a determining role in the thoughts of those within its temporal realm. The thoughts of the *pauvres esprits* are formed by the day in what would appear to be a poem that has decentered the human subject in favor of the agency of the non-human world of light as affected by the turning of the planet. Indeed, Nikolaj Lübecker, in an insightful reading of the poem, has argued that it "invites us to think human beings as dynamic mediations of their environments" (690).[10] But it is not so easy to get beyond lyric subjectivity in such a way that we can affirm the mediation of the subjects by their environment that would come to replace its opposite, the mediation of the environment by the subject. I would argue that the poem imposes a dialectical reading of the relation between subject and object, human and spatiotemporal environment, by frustrating any desire to read the poem as affirming either pole of those dichotomies as dominant; such resolution of the tension that the poem crafts violates the dissonance it carefully constructs.

We might notice, for instance, that the simple indication of the day "falling" represents a complex play between human subject and spatiotemporal situation. The day "falls" only figuratively; to speak of it this way is to assign it agency, but it is also to impose a human category on a temporal construct that cannot be said in any literally meaningful sense to "fall." Furthermore, in terms of that expression, day is equivalent to night, which also can be said to "fall," a fact which reduces the opposition to a similarity, which is highlighted in the word "crépuscule" itself, which, as a term of intermediality, can refer either to the moment before full dawn or full nightfall. This tension between opposites structures the entirety of these paragraphs, as the "grand apaisement" of the first paragraph finds both an echo and its opposite in the "grand hurlement" of the second.[11] The falling day of the first paragraph is echoed via contrast in the "marée qui monte" of the second, while the "esprits fatigués" of the first paragraph find an echo in the "tempête qui s'éveille." These last two examples go a step further in establishing the blurred boundaries that guide the poem, since they also serve, beyond establishing these contrasts, to eliminate the space that separates the human beings from their surroundings, as the "hurlement composé d'une foule de cris discordants" comes presumably, but not necessarily, from a collective humanity "du haut de la montagne." The sound is likened to the natural sounds of nonliving water in the tides or storms. Furthermore, there is dissonance in the sonic possibilities on offer in the comparison, with the language of the poem, which moves swiftly from the tide to the storm via the conjunction "ou," concealing what are in fact two very different sounds, the first rhythmic, regular, and peaceful, the other sporadic and violent.

In short, the lyric language of these paragraphs masks a dissonance of which harmony is one of the terms in the opposition, as the "cris discordants" are transformed *by the space* into "une lugubre harmonie." The sonic world arrives to the speaking subject via yet another paradoxical aspect of the landscape/soundscape, "les nues transparentes," a destabilizing image of typically opaque structures that allow not visual imagery but rather sounds to pass through, altering the basic meaning of what we typically think of as transparency. It may appear at first that the landscape/soundscape has more agency that any human subjectivity here, with the speaking subject serving as a mere passive vehicle to which the sounds arrive (and not even to him, but rather to his balcony). But it is not so easy to claim a non-anthropomorphic reading of the poem once we consider that the dissonance it constructs, as well as the subjectivity it reshapes, are both an effect of language, of the play of opposites that are at the same time similarities, of the voluntary confusion between rising and falling and between the literal and the metaphorical. If agency is reconfigured here, it is above all to accord heightened subjectivity not to the landscape/soundscape but rather to the poem itself, the effects of language through which the setting is created and by which it is always mediated. In that sense, both the speaking subject and the setting, and, similarly, the reader of the poem, can all be taken as constructed to some extent by the artwork itself, which transcends the nature/city opposition by its implicit demonstration that both nature and the built environment are themselves constructions by subjects who are themselves in part constructed by the artwork. It is in that sense that the artwork calls to us, compels us to interpretation, and, through that interpretation, reminds us that no interpretation will ever be completely sufficient or complete. At best, it allows us to see the dialectical tension, present in so many of the textual details of a poem like "Crépuscule du soir," which propel the artwork and maintain its vitality.

The third paragraph both clarifies the spatial situation of the poem and maintains its tension by continuing to destabilize the very low-high opposition on which it nonetheless depends:

> Quels sont les infortunés que le soir ne calme pas, et qui prennent, comme les hiboux, la venue de la nuit pour un signal de sabbat ? Cette sinistre ululation nous arrive du noir hospice perché sur la montagne ; et, le soir, en fumant et en contemplant le repos de l'immense vallée, hérissée de maisons dont chaque fenêtre dit : « C'est ici la paix maintenant ; c'est ici la joie de la famille ! » je puis, quand le vent souffle de là-haut, bercer ma pensée étonnée à cette imitation des harmonies de l'enfer. (1: 311)

> [Who are the hapless ones not calmed by evening, and who, like owls, take the night's arrival as a sign of witches' Sabbath? Their ominous ululation reaches us from the dark asylum perched on the mountain. And in the evening, when the wind blows from above, I can lull my mind astonished at this imitation of hell's harmonies, smoking and contemplating the stillness of the immense valley which bristles with houses whose every window says, "Here is peace, here is family joy!" (*Parisian* 50)]

The glance upward in this poem, toward the same realm of the "nues transparentes," reveals not an infinite beyond but rather the invisible but troublingly audible bodily world of the sick. The point of comparison is not heavenly music but "les harmonies de l'enfer," a phrase whose referent is anything but clear: While "heavenly music" can call to mind at least some stereotyped auditory imagery, what would sounds labeled, not even "infernal music," but "infernal harmonies" sound like? Are we to suppose an equal and opposite sound, so that what is harmony in hell is what would elsewhere be considered dissonance? Or, if we hark back to the wider and indeed more precise notion of harmony that implies a necessary tension between consonance and dissonance, would this be some different configuration of that tension rather than a simple relabeling of one as the other? The word was carefully considered, since an earlier variant of the end of the paragraph reads: ". . . souffle de Fourvières [sic], bercer ma pensée étonnée à ce redoutable écho de l'Enfer" ["blows from Fourvières, to lull my mind astonished at this fearsome echo of Hell"] (1: 1328). The definitive version removes the geographical specificity of Fourvière (and of the capitalized proper noun "Enfer" as well) and transforms what had been a mere echo of the (nonspecified) sound of an echo into a specifically musical reference, transcending earthly music not by projecting it into ideal spheres but by evoking a necessarily inconceivable sound, an expression with no clear referent except the literal ones of the cries of bodily suffering. Furthermore, the definitive version changes echo to "imitation," which performs a further inversion of the more typical reference to earthly music being an imitation of the music of the spheres.

While it is conventionally the work of art that is understood to be an imitation of nature, here it is the all too "natural" cries of the suffering that are figured as imitation, in yet one more transformation of the conventions of art and nature so that the least "artful" sounds, ones that are assimilated to the level of the animal cries of "ululation," bring imitation down from the level of art to that of the non-human. But still, the imitation is characterized as the appropriate vehicle for the kind of tranquil contemplation typically associated with art, since the lyric subject is situated at the midpoint not of heaven and hell but of the bourgeois domestic tranquility from below and the simultaneous sinister ululations from above. The poem transcends conventional notions of artistic contemplation by characterizing it as arising from the understated simultaneity of the metaphorical "speech" of the houses affirming peace in the imagined words the subject imputes to them and the infernal harmonies. The lyric subject's experience is literally determined by the way the wind blows, but he seems to find calm in those imitation infernal harmonies from on high that lack the terror one might think they would inspire. The poem seems to seek a transcendence of the opposition of celestial harmony and earthly realms not by excluding one from the realm of the other but rather by setting the subject precisely at the heart of their intersection, where dissonance is most available to him. Still, it is perhaps not quite accurate to characterize his experience as esthetic; he seems more a passive vehicle of the impressions from above and below, a closed world in terms of access to his full subjectivity. In that sense, the poem stages a refusal of the kind of interiority or sublime terror that might be the experience of the romantic lyric subject. Far from posing as the opposite of that kind of subject, the lyric subject in this poem evokes that model only, not to reject it, but to stand curiously aloof from it, a figure among others in the landscape/soundscape, compelling interpretation of the pieces of a world that seem coherent in their incoherence, harmonious in their series of dissonant relationships and conceptual play with literal and figurative constructions of a mental world.

The anecdotes of the middle paragraphs of the poem continue, in a sometimes ludic mode, the play of up and down, rising and falling, that we have noted in the falling day and the rising storm of the first paragraphs. In these "down to earth" anecdotes, the poet retains both the presence of questions of transcendence via this spatial orientation and the presence of sickness which had dominated the first paragraphs. The human subjects in the middle paragraphs are, like the lyric subject, passive: the friends whose story we read are made (psychologically) sick by the twilight:

Le crépuscule excite les fous. — Je me souviens que j'ai eu deux amis que le crépuscule rendait tout malades. L'un méconnaissait alors tous les rapports d'amitié et de politesse, et maltraitait, comme un sauvage, le premier venu. Je l'ai vu jeter à la tête d'un maître d'hôtel un excellent poulet, dans lequel il croyait voir je ne sais quel insultant hiéroglyphe. Le soir, précurseur des voluptés profondes, lui gâtait les choses les plus succulentes. (1: 311)

[Twlight agitates madmen. –I remember two of my friends whom twilight would make quite ill. The first one would then neglect all friendly and polite ties, and abuse the first-comer, like a savage. I saw him throw an excellent chicken, which he believed to be some insulting hieroglyph, at a headwaiter's face. The evening, herald of profound voluptuous pleasures, spoiled the most succulent things for him. (*Parisian* 50)]

The thrown chicken is much less frequently discussed in Baudelaire criticism than the flower pot which the narrator throws down on to the glazier's head in "Le Mauvais vitrier." The cooked chicken is thrown up rather than down, and indeed toward the head of the recipient, the metaphorical site of mind where words and symbols are processed and become meaningful. The act of throwing the chicken becomes perhaps a caricature of the kind of skyward gestures and cries one might expect to see in lyric poetry. Such a reading might be of questionable plausibility were it not for the "hiéroglyphe" that the friend thinks he sees in it, which is precisely the image Baudelaire uses elsewhere to evoke poetic transcendence. In the *Réflexions sur quelques-uns de mes contemporains*, Baudelaire claims that Hugo's poetry translates the pleasures transmitted

> par l'être visible, par la nature inanimée, ou dite inanimée ; non seulement, la figure d'un être extérieur à l'homme, végétal ou minéral, mais aussi sa physionomie, son regard, sa tristesse, sa douceur [. . .] ; enfin, en d'autres termes, tout ce qu'il y a d'humain dans n'importe quoi, et aussi tout ce qu'il y a de divin, de sacré ou de diabolique.
> Ceux qui ne sont pas poètes ne comprennent pas ces choses. (2: 132)

[by visible being, by inanimate nature, or what we call inanimate ; not only, the figure of a being external to man, vegetal or mineral, but also its physiognomy, its gaze, its sadness, its sweetness [. . .]; finally, in other words, all there is that is human in whatever it may be, and also all that is divine, sacred, or diabolical.
Those who are not poets do not understand these things.]

Shortly thereafter, Baudelaire evokes the hieroglyph: "tout est hiéroglyphique, et nous savons que les symboles ne sont obscurs que d'une manière relative, c'est-à-dire selon la pureté, la bonne volonté ou la clairvoyance native des âmes. Or qu'est-ce qu'un poëte (je prends le mot dans son acception la plus large), si ce n'est un traducteur, un déchiffreur ?" ["everything is a hieroglyph, and we know that symbols are only obscure in a relative way, that is according to the purity, the good will or the native clairvoyance of souls. Now what is a poet (I'm taking the word in its broadest meaning), if not a translator, a decipherer?"] (2: 133). The totality of the poetic world thus includes both the human and the divine, in a way that simultaneously both preserves the transcendent world and reduces the distinction between the immanent and transcendent by the fact that "*tout est hiéroglyphique*" (my emphasis). The poet's role as translator suggests the potential imperfection of poetic language or its inability completely to communicate the kind of transcendence that is at hand in the divine, the diabolical, or even in the immanent.

While one could see this as a failure of poetic language, it is also the condition of its possibility as well as what permits it to avoid the domination implied by a totality. The multiplicity of interpretations allows art to retain its enigmatic character, its otherness that resists full assimilation by the poet or anyone else. There is thus more to transcendence than meets the eye, and perhaps more to the immanent world of objects as well. In light of Baudelaire's comments, it is hard not to read significance in the reference to the "hiéroglyphe" in "Crépuscule du soir." While it is possible that the use of the word could merely be ironic in order to heighten the comic effect, the context of the earlier paragraphs and their play with high and low, sky and city, suggest something more, as does the commentary on the human and divine and diabolical realms extending to all reality and not just to the "poetic" world. The hieroglyph, in other words, is the meeting place of experiential reality and the mediated linguistic experience, the hieroglyph becoming itself a kind of hieroglyph, an invitation to look to see what lurks behind that word and what kind of reality it hides. The word takes on all the more importance given the fact that the reference to the hieroglyph was not present in the original version of the chicken-throwing anecdote. The chicken thrower in the grips of insanity is painted as seeing what may not be there in the chicken when he sees in it "je ne sais quel insultant hiéroglyphe." Here, the insane man is akin to the poet as seer, about whom the lyric subject knows that he sees something in it but knows not what. Rather than gazing at the clouds, he focuses attention on the immanent world of humble, even comic, objects, and ironically, the lyric subject, who is often figured as a poet in the prose poems, is put in a role analogous to the misunderstanding public, looking at the visionary, not knowing exactly what he sees in the object of contemplation, and dismissing him as insane.

To take the chicken throwing so seriously is perhaps to miss the comic absurdity of the scene, but in light of the frame in which the anecdote is cast in the definitive version of the poem, it can hardly be merely comic or simple parody. The similarity to the pot-throwing in "Le mauvais vitrier," which has been seen as an implicit poetics, should be enough to encourage a multifaceted reading of the scene as more than an off-the-cuff anecdote. The very fact that we can plausibly ask these questions about this scene in its larger context suggests the porous distinction between immanent and transcendent reality as it is constructed here: a mere parody would simply dismiss, or at least momentarily poke fun at, the notion of transcendence by morphing it into a "natural" material object thrown aloft confrontationally to the reader just as much as to the headwaiter. But the very act of imagining it as a kind of hieroglyph suggests that there cannot *not* be a transcendent meaning to that natural object, that it shares with the more conventionally transcendent the fact that we can have no unmediated access to it. By reconfiguring the field of possible meanings, the natural material object here becomes the vehicle of an immanent transcendence, a site where the poem forces a rereading and reinterpreting of both immanence and transcendence, of the serious and the comic, and invites us to rethink the placement of the poet in all of this: is the lyric subject the poet, with his summary judgment about the insanity of his friend? Or, as I have suggested, is it more plausible to see the friend as a figure of the poet, proffering a provocative gesture that is misconstrued as insane by the lyric subject? The lyric subject ultimately remarks laconically that the unfortunate incident made his friend miss out on, or spoiled, "les choses les plus succulentes," a phrasing which, like so much else in the poem, plays with literal and figurative meanings. Did he trade his chicken dinner for nothing, or should we think of the lyric subject of "Le Mauvais vitrier" posing, in his final question, the rhetorical question: "Mais qu'importe l'éternité de la damnation à qui a trouvé dans une seconde l'infini de la jouissance ?" (1: 287) ["But what does an eternity of damnation matter to someone who has experienced for one second the infinity of delight?" (*Parisian* 15)], which a reader reading the prose poems in published order would already have encountered before, fourteen poems back?[12]

The freedom of the space of the artwork as "Le Crépuscule du soir" constructs it resists the imposition of singular meanings carried through the spaces and objects of the poem and presents the lyric subject as something less than the determiner of all meaning and perception but something more than the passive quasi-agent at the mercy of a foreign and hostile space in which he is acted upon. The poem has the potential to actualize the freedom of the work of art, but without a guarantee that such a freedom will indeed come to be realized. The openness to the possibility of that kind of failure is part and parcel of a non-totalizing approach to the work of art and to the questions it inspires while necessarily remaining mute about definitive answers, since the alternative would remove the work from the domain of art altogether.

After the middle three paragraphs which recount the anecdotes, the lyric voice returns in the final three paragraphs which, like the first three paragraphs, were a later addition to the first published version of the poem. The additions create a symmetrical ABA-type form, but one in which the scenes that transpire in the middle third encourage us to read the return of the lyric voice differently in the final third, not as a mere regression to a romantic lyricism that might first be implied by the first lines of that return: "Ô nuit ! ô rafraîchissantes ténèbres ! vous êtes pour moi le signal d'une fête intérieure, vous êtes la délivrance d'une angoisse !" (1: 312) ["O night! O refreshing darkness! For me you signal an inward celebration, you are the liberation from anguish" (*Parisian* 51)]. The potentially hermetic interior world of contemplation is complicated in the following paragraph by the intriguing reversal effected by the use of the verb "imitate":

Les lueurs roses qui traînent encore à l'horizon comme l'agonie du jour sous l'oppression victorieuse de sa nuit, les feux des candélabres qui font des taches d'un rouge opaque sur les dernières gloires du couchant, les lourdes draperies qu'une main invisible attire des profondeurs de l'Orient, imitent tous les sentiments compliqués qui luttent dans le cœur de l'homme aux heures solennelles de la vie. (1: 312)

[The pink glows still lingering on the horizon like the day dying under its night's victorious subjugation, the fires of candelabra forming spots of opaque red on the sunset's final glories, the heavy draperies drawn by an invisible hand from the depths of the East, imitate all the complicated feelings struggling in a person's heart during life's solemn hours. (*Parisian* 51)]

Here it is not the lyric subject who imitates nature but rather the natural scene (evoked via the substitution of manmade interior objects such as the candelabra and the drapes, both evoked metaphorically to describe elements of the natural sky) that imitates the interior life of human beings. Such a move temporally displaces agency onto the natural world, which abandons the role of passive object of knowledge in order to take on not just any active role but that of one of the most significant functions of art, imitation of the phenomenal world. Within the context of the poem, the imitation of those feelings becomes an actual creation of the feelings, dependent as they are on the twilight sky that gives rise to them, but only within the esthetic domain of an imitation rather than a direct relationship of causation. Still, the lyric subject remains as the one giving voice to, and thereby creating, this series of substitutions and equivalences among the twilight sky, the objects of a domestic interior, and the (necessarily metaphorical) "interior" state of the human subject. The poem cannot negate subjectivity, and presents an intriguing counterpoint to those poems of urban shock and paralysis such as "A une passante." It invites us to question the mediated and mediating relationship among nature, the built world of commodities, and the subject who constitutes and is constituted by them. The scene is hardly a bucolic one, and the possibility that the lyric subject will, like his friends, slip either into madness or into "l'inquiétude d'un malaise perpétuel" (1: 312) ["the anxiety of a perpetual disquiet" (*Parisian* 51)] remains, but the inscription of imitation in the poem realigns the subject in a dialectical relationship both to the natural and the built worlds. The voice that calls out "Crépuscule, comme vous êtes doux et tendre !" (1: 312) ["Twilight, how gentle and tender you are!" (*Parisian* 51)] cannot be taken as one of innocence and removal from contemporary reality in favor of some timeless eternal return of the twilight, but nor is lyricism completely discredited in this poem which, moments earlier, led the reader to contemplate a thrown chicken. While it is nature that imitates here, for the imitation to be recognized as such requires its perception by the lyric subject, by whose linguistic mediation the imitation is brought into being.

The final paragraph compares the sky to a dancer's dress whose transparent outer layer allows us to see not beyond the dress but rather to another part of the dress itself:

> On dirait encore une de ces robes étranges de danseuses, où une gaze transparente et sombre laisse entrevoir les splendeurs amorties d'une jupe éclatante, comme sous le noir présent transperce le délicieux passé ; et les étoiles vacillantes d'or et d'argent, dont elle est semée, représentent ces feux de la fantaisie qui ne s'allument bien que sous le deuil profond de la Nuit. (1: 312)

> [Or it appears like a strange dancing dress, whose transparent and dark gauze reveals a glimpse of the muted splendors of a brilliant skirt, just as the delectable past might pierce through the gloomy present. While the trembling gold, and silver stars, sprinkled over it, represent those fires of fantasy which ignite well only under the deep mourning of the Night. (*Parisian* 51)]

The apparently simple comparison hides a multitude of layered complexity. The metaphor is a tentative one: the sky is not a dress; rather, one *would say* it is a dress, which reinforces the status of the metaphor as resulting from the perceptual imagination of the lyric subject. The dress is and is not transparent; its gauze outer layer, while described as transparent, is not fully so, and what it allows the viewer to see is not the body of the dancer but the inner layer of the dress. We never get beyond the drape to the body that the drape is covering; the "splendeurs" are not that of the body which in other Baudelaire poems offers the possibility of transcendence; here, the splendors to be had are those of the dress itself, an object whose transparency reveals more of the object itself rather than anything beyond or even under it.

If the sky is comparable to the dress, what the sky (or clouds) would reveal is more sky, a rewriting of the transcendent as immanent but which is immediately extended into yet another comparison, this time to the past that is visible through the present. The metaphorical association continues to be spun out in what begins to look like the potentially endless series of associations in the last lines of "Le Cygne." The strength of the metaphorical valence gradually weakens, from "on dirait..." to the comparative "comme" to the stars that "représentent" the subject's flights of mental fancy. This final return to the inner mental world is marked by an increasingly prosaic description; gone are the lyrical apostrophes and exclamations that marked the start of this final section. The stars do not so much inspire transcendent thought as serve to represent them figuratively, with no suggestion of a vertical relation between what might even be psychotic flights of fancy, if we recall the mental imbalance of the two friends evoked in the middle section. And yet, we might say that lyric prose has, by the end of the poem, transcended itself, transcended the potential lie of the transcendent or transparent relationship between the sky and the mind, all the better to reveal the mediation that has been at work all along in positing that relationship. The poem could well be said to be like a garment which reveals another layer of the same garment, which is still to hold out for poetry a revelatory function, entirely transformed by its own processes in a way that does not exclude the external world but rather depends on it as the vehicle of the poem's operations and of the mediation that the poem could not accomplish without that mediated relationship.

The poem's play with natural objects, made objects, and a subjectivity that inscribes itself as an agent that is formed by those objects just as much as it forms them, allows us to ask about what may be hiding in plain sight, like the inner material of the dress that is revealed by the transparent gauze of the outer material. The poem takes on a certain degree of agency by allowing the production of transcendent meanings that remain immanent while at the same time transcending the ordinary status of both the ordinary objects and the potentially clichéd approach to supposedly transcendent sites of meaning such as the twilight sky. By the juxtaposition of its spaces as well as of the lyric and the prosaic, the poem creates a dynamic play of its elements that highlights the dialectical nature of the mutually determining and determined relationship between the immanent and transcendent. In place of the dichotomy between the contemplation of the clouds and the comedy of the lyric subject sent back to eat his soup in "La soupe et les nuages," for instance, the tightly constructed, but potentially disorienting, form of "Le Crépsucule du soir" refuses to untangle the sky from the chicken, the contemplating poet from the world of action and suffering that is present in the poem. The lyricism to which we return does not ring hollow; it challenges the reader to reveal fuller meanings inherent in that lyricism by showing that any dichotomizing approach to it risks totalization and therefore falsity, if it does not define lyricism as being in a dialectical relation to what seems at first to oppose it. If we are not attentive to the dialectical moment, we risk missing immanent transcendence altogether and retaining a model of lyricism that harks back unconvincingly to earlier forms of transcendence or to a cynical refusal of any role for lyric poetry whatsoever in the alienated world of high capitalism, both of which Baudelaire's poetry refuses. A subjectivity formed via supposedly pure interiority, a contemplation without reference to the empirical world, risks entry into pure fantasy. The parting image of stars not in the sky but on the dress, which represent the "feux de la fantaisie" illuminated well only at night, evokes a more totalizing darkness that stands opposed to the twilight that guided the rest of the poem; this last word given over to individual fancy can hardly seem fully convincing as a preferable state, and is a far less rich, and maybe even less true, light than the dialectical twilight in which the poem forms its reality.

Commodified reality, and even commodified nature, is never far in this poem, as one last look at the chicken-throwing scene can attest. It takes place in a restaurant, where the organic object has been turned into a commodity for sale on the bourgeois market. What bothers the friend about the chicken is that he saw in it some sort of "insultant hiéroglyphe." Rob Halpern has noted, in an analysis of Baudelaire but not of this particular poem, that Marx writes in *Capital* that value "transforms every product of labor into a social hieroglyphic" (quoted in Halpern "Dark" 3). The twilight, we remember from the poem, had "spoiled the most succulent things" for this friend, as if the lucidity of twilight made the commodified food unpalatable. If, as I had suggested earlier, the reference to the hieroglyph suggests a reading of the scene whereby the poet figure is not the lyric subject but perhaps this friend, based on Baudelaire's association of deciphering hieroglyphs with the poet, then one plausible reading of this scene is that the poet's gesture is one of rebellion. The poem would suggest a refusal of commodity culture and supposedly succulent pleasures in favor of a poetics of negation that risks being seen as insanity by the lyric subject as, in this case, a representative of mainstream bourgeois opinion who then retreats from the scene into an attempt to cultivate interiority from the peace of his domestic space. The space of this poem, by contrast, refuses to confirm unilateral readings about the role of the poet, or even which of those two characters might be most plausibly said to be playing that role. The work exists in that space between reason and insanity, "crazy" action in the marketplace and an equally suspect attempt at withdrawal from it. To expect a didactic conclusion akin to the kinds that are indeed present in some Baudelaire poems such as "L'Albatros" is to retreat from the modernism that intensifies rather than cheapening or discounting the power of poetry in Baudelaire, a power that is located in what Adorno called "the space between discursive barbarism and poetic euphemism that remains to artworks" (AT 32). The power of a poem like "Crépuscule du soir," and indeed what I have been calling its agency, is that it both depends on and transcends models of poetry that reduce it to a mere commodity or which attempt to ignore the changed circumstances of the lyric altogether by failing to make sufficient interpretive space for the central role of a dissonance that both depends on and negates earlier models of harmony. It is not, Adorno writes in the same passage, "for art to pursue the results of ordinary knowledge" (AT 32), an approach as misguided, he writes, as seeing art as what it never was, "a language of pure feeling, [. . .] a language of the affirmation of the soul" (32). "Le Crépuscule du soir" performs the negation of what never was, forms a dissonance not in order to reject poetry but to reveal a potential in it that had been present but hidden in earlier poetry, the dissonance that is the truth of harmony, the immanence that makes a new kind of dialectical transcendence visible.

Coda and Conclusion

If what I have been claiming about the insistently dialectical nature of Baudelaire's poetry is true, a tidy conclusion would be not only impossible but also a violation of the spirit of the endless play of tensions that animates all of Baudelaire. What I hope to have shown is that a new mode of thinking about the nature and role of the artwork in modernity, one which approaches the question through a reconsideration of dissonance in conjunction with a reconfiguration of relations of subject and object common to both the artwork and to conceptual reflection, emerges in Baudelaire's poetry and is taken up by Adorno's theory of esthetics. Read together, both register a key shift in the nature and role of lyric subjectivity which poses important questions not just for esthetics but also for epistemological questions about the way esthetic and conceptual experience mediate perception of the external world and the human subject's relation to it. This reoriented subjectivity depends on both the persistence and the negation of older models of esthetic transcendence, reorienting them in light of new ways of thinking about objects in their relation to subjects. Born to an important extent from the alienation of high capitalist modernity, this reorientation nonetheless carries potential for implicit critique of that modernity by carving out a role for the persistence of past models of subjectivity and transcendence under the sign of dissonance.

In a critique of Adorno's esthetics that claims that they are "costly," Michel de Beistegui claims that

> they lead, at best, to a kind of utopianism, a messianic promise of reconciliation that generates an individual as well as collective mood that oscillates between hope and melancholy, and forces the ultimate goal of human action and nature, namely, happiness, into a forever postponed future. The hopes, expectation, and promises once ascribed to religion (and then political praxis) are now transposed to art: faced with the "original sin" of philosophy, art is announced as "redemption," "salvation," "expiation," and "promise," with the following significant difference that the redemption in question is impossible. (Beistegui 56–7)

What Beistegui signals as the core of Adorno's esthetics could apply to Baudelaire as well, a certain fascination with the metaphor of original sin and the occasional desire for what turns out to be an impossible redemption.[1] While it is open to question whether such a "promise of reconciliation" can indeed be branded utopian, I would argue that what Beistegui identifies as a weakness of Adorno's approach is precisely one of its key strengths. Adorno holds out a strong critical role for art in relation to philosophy that is born from art's autonomy, its refusal simply to take up philosophical questions by other means. I have argued that Baudelaire's poetry functions to challenge the potentially totalizing, systematizing impulses of philosophical conceptualization, not in order to refuse conceptual thought entirely but rather to provide the impetus to find new ways of thinking through and about art and its role in mediating the perceiver's relation to, and construction of, the world seen as a complex interaction of subject and object.

The impossibility of a redemptive project whereby art would bring philosophy to its fulfillment is precisely what animates and invigorates, via a dissonant relationship, the role of modern art. That role does not necessarily lead to melancholic brooding over the impossibility of reconciliation, as Beistegui implies, but rather contains a new potential for art, in the sense of an energy that is held in suspense and whose very suspension animates the artwork and puts into play the dynamic tension between a conceptual approach to enumerating what is at stake in a given artwork and the way in which the artwork always surpasses the conceptual approach, challenging us to return again and again to the artwork rather than coming to rest in the finality of a definitive interpretation. It is under the sign of the negative, and of the impossibility of resting in definitive negation that Baudelaire accomplishes this animated potential of the artwork that is, paradoxically, most visible in moments of suspension. Perhaps the best illustration of this is "Le Goût du néant":

Morne esprit, autrefois amoureux de la lutte,
L'Espoir, dont l'éperon attisait ton ardeur,
Ne veut plus t'enfourcher ! Couche-toi sans pudeur,
Vieux cheval dont le pied à chaque obstacle butte.

Résigne-toi, mon cœur ; dors ton sommeil de brute.

Esprit vaincu, fourbu ! Pour toi, vieux maraudeur,
L'amour n'a plus de goût, non plus que la dispute;
Adieu donc, chants du cuivre et soupirs de la flûte !
Plaisirs, ne tentez plus un cœur sombre et boudeur !

Le Printemps adorable a perdu son odeur !

Et le Temps m'engloutit minute par minute,
Comme la neige immense un corps pris de roideur;

— Je contemple d'en haut le globe en sa rondeur
Et je n'y cherche plus l'abri d'une cahute.

Avalanche, veux-tu m'emporter dans ta chute? (1: 76)

[Dejected soul, once anxious for the strife,
Hope, whose spur fanned your ardor into flame,
No longer wishes to mount you! Lie down shamelessly,
Old horse who stumbles over every rut.

Resign yourself, my heart; sleep your brutish sleep.

Conquered, foundered spirit! For you, old jade,
Love has no more relish, no more than war;
Farewell then, songs of the brass and sighs of the flute!
Pleasure, tempt no more a dark, sullen heart!

Adorable spring has lost its fragrance!

And Time engulfs me minute by minute,
As the immense snow a stiffening corpse;
I survey from above the roundness of the globe
And I no longer seek there the shelter of a hut.

Avalanche, will you sweep me along in your fall? (*Flowers* 257)]

As in "L'Héautontimorouménos," the poem begins with a je-tu relationship that is revealed to be a doubled subject addressing himself, enlarging the perspective by the end so that he is somehow removed from the scene he is contemplating, held in suspension in that moment of contemplation and initiating a new je-tu relationship via direct address to the avalanche in the final line. The poem remains suspended in the desire for oblivion, a desire on the part of the subject to be acted upon by a force of nature that, presumably, remains deaf to his desire. To reduce the subject to nothingness would mean the death of art, as would an exaltation of the subject to some kind of plenitude of being. The desire for annihilation represents, paradoxically, the impossibility of the kind of resignation that the poet had called for in line 5, and sets in motion an esthetics of waiting for an impossible event that prefigures the works of Samuel Beckett. Far from an esthetics of futility and perpetually frustrated hopes, what Baudelaire creates is a space for poetry as the dynamic working out of an impermanent subjectivity that is a stranger to itself and which is constituted by the artwork in ways that the reader is invited to complete by the imperative to interpretation.

The necessary failure of a desire for nothingness shifts the role of the esthetic, transcending older models of wholeness and subjectivity by compelling new approaches to what an esthetics of what Adorno calls "dark art" (AT 39) would mean as it holds out, despite everything, the chance for new modes of esthetic experience: "Art indicts superfluous poverty by voluntarily undergoing its own; but it indicts asceticism as well and cannot establish it as its own norm" (AT 40). What poems such as "Le Goût du néant" challenge us to do is to refuse both older models of subjectivity and transcendence and also avoid a simplistic refusal of any sort of potential esthetic experience at all. Adorno makes passing reference to this poem in order to indict the view "that the world which, as Baudelaire wrote, has lost its fragrance and since then its color, could have them restored by art strikes only the artless as possible" (AT 40). And yet these older models can be transcended in ways that both Baudelaire's poetry and Adorno's esthetics point to and which hold out the potential for what Adorno calls "a livable world" that recognizes and integrates darkness rather than refusing it in the name of a politically suspect affirmation:

> Ever since Baudelaire the dark has also offered sensuous enticement as the antithesis of the fraudulent sensuality of culture's façade. [. . .] The caustic discordant moment, dynamically honed, is differentiated in itself as well as from the affirmative and becomes alluring; and this allure, scarcely less than revulsion for the imbecility of positive thinking draws modern art into a no-man's-land that is the plenipotentiary of a livable world. (AT 40)[2]

Any desire on the reader's part to be "swept away" by the poem as the subject wishes to be swept away by the avalanche is thwarted by the imperative to contemplation inscribed in the poem and also activated by the way the poem, by the very way in which it constructs the desire for nothingness, raises questions that require a turn toward the conceptual. The process is without synthesis, without end, as the conceptual soon shows its limits and returns us to the experience of the artwork which necessarily surpasses conceptual attempts to grasp it.

Far from melancholy or frustration, this dynamic of esthetic experience and esthetic reflection is what animates any approach to art that takes it seriously and refuses to reduce it to definitive meaning. An openness to potentially infinite shifts in the meaning that can be made from a poem reveals the historical mediation of meaning without reducing the artwork to a mere product of its time. Such a renewed sense of vitality of art and its interpretation as itself a dynamic and integral part of the experience of art is arguably only made possible by the dissonance of the modern artwork that highlights the complex subject-object relation between the lyric subject, the poem, and by extension the reader, that was always there but often hidden or elided in poems more invested in preserving the illusion of a whole and inviolable lyric subject. What modern art releases, in the historical interplay with the kinds of meanings and interpretations available to us at any given historical moment, is the tremendous esthetic potential of an art that seems, on only the most restrictive or totalizing views of art, to be frozen or impotent of trapped in something like the death of art.[3] Such a view of the new potential in art as it reveals itself in Baudelaire and characterized by Adorno is in no way an attempt at redeeming art; rather, it insists on this new potential for art being actualized only because art can never be redemptive in the usual sense.[4]

Waiting for an impossible event in the context of looking toward death also figures in the sonnet "Le Rêve d'un curieux," with its lyric subject who witnesses his own death in a dream, as we saw in chapter three. The poem stages something like the surprise of disillusionment, but by now we should be suspicious of the kind of linear readings, from enchantment to disenchantment, that surface readings of Baudelaire tend to confirm at first glance.[5] In fact it is only because of the persistence of an older set of metaphysical expectations that the poem's experience is made possible; rather than sloughing off expectations, the lyric subject is still waiting, despite the supposed revelation of the unspectacular experience of death. To wait in the face of that revelation is to preserve metaphysics under the sign of negation, to transcend linear models in order to engage the dialectical tension inherent in the persistence of metaphysics. Adorno writes in *Negative Dialectics* about the experience of the "can this be all?":

> Pure metaphysical experience grows unmistakably paler and more desultory in the course of the secularization process, and that softens the substantiality of the older type. Negatively, that type holds out in the demand "Can this be all?" [. . .] Nothing could be as truly alive if something that transcends life were not promised also; no straining of the concept leads beyond that. The transcendent is, and it is not. We despair of what is, and our despair spreads to the transcendental ideas that used to call a halt to despair. That the infinite world of infinite agony might be encompassed by a divine cosmic plan must impress anyone not engaged in the world's business as the kind of madness that goes so well with positive normalcy. (ND 375)

To wait is to be open to metaphysical experience in full recognition of its emptiness, to seek an experience of that very emptiness, which registers as the doubled, ironic experience of a transcendent which is and is not, which is, we might say, precisely through its not being.[6] Baudelaire inaugurates a poetics of waiting, not because we know or believe that something will come but precisely because we know it will not. It is not so much a waiting for *nothing* (in both the sense of purposeless waiting and a waiting for nothingness) as a waiting as a negation of older kinds of transcendent experience that nevertheless holds out a role for some kind of esthetic transcendence via negation. Death is not an event in this poem so much as the condition of realization of it as a non-transcendent event, a false transcendence that is to be worked through in order to return to the work of art as the site of a new kind of esthetic experience. This esthetic experience transcends the falseness of an older kind that depended on a metaphysics of transcendence no less than on linear models of teleological progress and the affirmation of the world as it is supposedly given. To wait, still, is to be receptive to being acted upon by the work of art, to be constituted as a subject by the work of art at the same time that one is bringing its meaning into being historically through reflection. The modern work of art thus retains its power not despite the negation of harmony and transcendence but because of it.

To be left waiting after disappointment from a metaphysical experience that turned out to be other than what one had expected could be taken as emblematic of the esthetic paradigm I have been suggesting is operative in Baudelaire generally. His work depends on the transcendence of the expectation of a harmonious esthetic experience in a way that does not simply demystify or cynically deny the power of idealist poetics. Rather, the subject who continues to wait remains open to new kinds of meaning to be generated from those same experiences, new ways of inscribing them in the context of the modern, ironic, dissonant subjectivity that enters into relationship with the work of art and is constituted by it. The waiting is potentially infinite and strikes a balance between an active and passive subject, affirming the wait rather than abandoning the attempt to experience the transcendent. Ross Chambers has described *Le Spleen de Paris* as the "very epitome of Baudelairean *poiesis*" insofar as it is "a work in progress that denies the possibility of progress" (Chambers 154–5); it is emblematic as well, for Chambers, of "the body of [Baudelaire's] writing understood as a *Nachlass*, unfinished and unfinishable" (155). The works are in a state of perpetual becoming through the collaboration of historically situated readers open, like the lyric subject, to be acted upon by the text in a mutually constitutive way, to transcend disappointment by embracing the work of interpretation as dialectical and therefore never-ending, a perpetual falling not just into history but into the play of samenesses and differences that separate Baudelaire's time from our own. The subject of "Le Rêve d'un curieux" lives on after what he took to be a powerful experience ended up lacking in the power to move him; that is not to say the experience was meaningless. It remains to the artwork not to serve as a record of transcendent experience but a vehicle for making meaning from the new configuration of dissonance, subjectivity, and transcendence that comes from having realized the untruth of an esthetics of unity and harmony. In that sense, esthetics too lives on, as Adorno said of philosophy, "because the moment to realize it was missed" (ND 3).

To say that Baudelaire's work is unfinished, in both the usual sense and the more extended sense of perpetually subject to new interpretive interventions based in large part on its ironic character, is to make it impossible to make definitive statements about it as a whole. This does not mean, however, that we should be content to view only small corners of the work as somehow representative of that whole, as tempting as that may be in the case of the radical novelty of poems such as those of the *Tableaux parisiens* or certain prose poems. In a series of lectures on dialectics in 1958, Adorno returned to his debate with Benjamin on Baudelaire, and while he admits that when he returned to them, "the details of Benjamin's argument struck me as rather more plausible now" (*Introduction* 89), he is still ultimately critical of Benjamin, now chiefly because of his privileging of the part at the expense of the whole:

> Where we are interested in the relationship between Baudelaire's lyric poetry and the age of high capitalism [. . .] we cannot merely content ourselves with seizing on individual features of a capitalist reality, as these appeared before the eyes of Baudelaire, and adducing them in order to explain the content of his work. Rather, we must try in this connection to derive the commodity character, which does indeed play a quite central role in Baudelaire, from the structure of society as a whole and the attempt to perceive the subjective reflection of the commodity form in this poetry itself, rather than contenting ourselves with individual motivations here. (*Introduction* 89–90)

Adorno offers these comments on Baudelaire in the context of reflections on the role of whole and part in dialectical thought which, he underscores, "is not one of mere subsumption. [. . .] Rather, it is a dynamic relation, one where both moments reciprocally produce one another rather than just being given alongside one another in a reified and, so to speak, timeless manner" (*Introduction* 88). This approach to thought stands in resistance to both the instrumentalization of thinking and what Adorno calls identity thinking, or a subsuming of an object under a concept that is mistakenly taken as coextensive with that object, a totalizing kind of thought. And it is when philosophy is forced to confront the necessary mediation of thought by language that the esthetic plays a crucial role in understanding dialectical thought.

An early essay of Adorno's from the 1930s, "Theses on the Language of the Philosopher," already establishes the crucial importance of esthetics:

> The growing significance of the philosophical critique of language can be formulated as the onset of a convergence between art and knowledge. While philosophy has to turn itself towards the unmediated unity of language and truth—thought up to now only esthetically—and must

measure its truth dialectically against language, art wins the character of knowledge: its language is esthetic, and only then harmonious, if it is "true": when its words are in accordance with the objective historical condition. ("Theses" 38–9)

I hope to have shown how Baudelaire's words could be said to be "in accordance with the objective historical condition" in ways that construct knowledge esthetically, through the functioning of the autonomous work of art, ways that are manifest in the entirety of Baudelaire's poetic corpus and not just in those poems that are situated explicitly in the modern city. What I hope to have established as a dialectical approach to lyric subjectivity in Baudelaire is a subjectivity produced by the sociohistorical world of high capitalism but which acts at the same time as a mode of resistance to it on account of the ways in which it complicates relationships of subjects and objects. I hope to have demonstrated some of the ways in which Baudelaire's poetry works out, not in conceptual form but in the very form and content of the poems themselves, new ways of configuring subjects and objects, a project he himself identified as the heart of what he labeled, to recall a passage I have cited above, "l'art pur suivant la conception moderne" ["pure art according to the modern conception"], which is to create "une magie suggestive contenant à la fois l'objet et le sujet, le monde extérieur à l'artiste et l'artiste lui-même" ["a suggestive magic containing at the same time object and subject, the world external t the artist and the artist himself"] (2: 598). By refusing a simple model of subsumption or domination of the object by the unified subject, Baudelaire opens poetry as a dialectical space where subject-object relations are in a constant state of becoming other than they were, without a projected stopping point of synthesis. The divided self brought into being in part by the material conditions of the lyric poet in high capitalism produces a way of constructing that world that provides implicit resistance to notions of linear progress perceived by a unified subject. The dissonance at the heart of Baudelairean subjectivity, constructed through language which mediates all thought in processes that become particularly visible in poetry and its interpretation, leads us to see the non-identity or non-correspondence between words and concepts that dominated older models of poetic transcendence. This allows us in turn to put a seemingly endless set of Baudelaire's poems in constellations, reading them both with and against each other in order better to articulate the way meaning is produced through doubleness and dissonance rather than despite that doubleness and dissonance. By reading this way, across earlier and later poems, in verse and in prose, we keep alive the dialectical interplay of part and whole which informs dialectical thinking and literary interpretation alike.

Baudelaire's work on language, the way in which the poetry allows us to see the dissonance that animates the transformation of subjectivity that he accomplishes and from which we can begin to establish his esthetics, is laden with philosophical significance precisely on account of the way that esthetics necessarily intervenes in the work of thought which is dependent on language for its expression. A similar breakdown in harmony occurs both in Baudelaire's poetry as it looks back on, depends on, but also reconfigures a poetics of harmony, and in models of philosophy that, like older esthetics, uphold what turns out to be a problematic model of subject-object relations. Reconfiguring the subject in relation to the object unmasks the fiction of a unified self and frees up a more complex and dynamic understanding of subject-object relations that has, as I hope to have shown, two kinds of potential: one, a release from the relation of domination that results from a traditional approach to subject-object relations which sees the latter as something to be mastered, dominated, and even subsumed by the former, and two, the persistence of the subject rather than its obliteration, the affirmation of the role of the thinking and creating human subject in mediating its own relationship to the world rather than being dissolved as a mere object. While language mediates thought, it always does so via the active engagement of the thinker, and meaning is created in both art and thought as the result of the self-reflexive intervention of a subject with its own language, in relation to a lived world perceived as dynamic, creating and created by the subject via the kind of intervention in language that poetry allows and indeed even requires.

To see objects otherwise, as static and separable from the whole, is to fall into a trap that Adorno identifies with Descartes:

> We can only arrive at this *clara et distincta perceptio* in the first place if the objects of knowledge are indeed static, distinct and clearly delimited in themselves, if they are so isolated from all others that they can be separated from the whole and can be treated as individual objects without violating their intrinsic truth. (*Introduction* 102–3)

The reason we need to reject the Cartesian relation of subject and object, on Adorno's view, is because "objects are dynamic and contradictory in themselves and, precisely by virtue of this contradictory character, are actually bound up within all other objects as well" (*Introduction* 102–3). This view of objects aligns them with the ironic and contradictory character we have identified with the Baudelairean lyric subject as well, which further blurs the boundaries between subjects and objects by seeing both as divided against themselves. Since, as I have argued, we can't simply abandon subject-object relations entirely, since conceiving our relationship to the world and to language depends on that relationship, what Baudelaire's poetry invites us to do is to reconfigure those relationships by seeing a fuller range of dialectical interplay between them. It is in that way that we avoid a universalist poetics while at the same time guarding against equally simplistic models that would see poetry as a mere product and reflection of its sociohistoric context. It is through poetry's work on language that we can begin to understand what is at stake in an esthetic reconfiguration of our mediated relation to the world we both inhabit and create.

Another way of saying this, perhaps, is that the most fruitful model of subjectivity in Baudelaire may be found, as is often the case with him, less in his critical or autobiographical writings than in his poems, which themselves play a crucial role in positing and mediating philosophically oriented questions in which artworks incisively intervene. In this case, while I have suggested that the vaporization and centralization of the self is a helpful guide to Baudelairean subjectivity if we understand it as a dialectical tension between those poles, I would claim that, ultimately, the notion of the irony-infused "faux accord" in the "divine symphonie" is the richer model. Existing in unresolved and unresolvable dissonance, the self is constituted negatively, not by its total absence or its complete disappearance into words or discourse, but by its negation of the divine insofar as the divinity is a figure of oneness or harmony. As I have suggested, it is only by retaining the notion of oneness, now constituted only via negation, that the subject as dissonant is able to emerge as the truth of a subject-object relation that that risks being falsely constituted and oversimplified as a unified lyric subject whose first-person "I" fails to acknowledge the way that language mediates the I's relation to itself and to the objects that constitute and are constituted by it. The I/you of the lyric subject as *faux accord*, subject and object of its own actions, remains suspended in dialectical tension between a subjectivity turned inward and against itself and one constituted as and through its own objects, as the series of objects to which the lyric subject assimilates itself in "Spleen: J'ai plus de souvenirs . . .": "Je suis un cimetière abhorré de la lune [. . .] Je suis un vieux boudoir [. . .]" (1: 73) ["I am a cemetery abhorred by the moon [. . .] I am an old boudoir" (*Flowers* 249)]. The precarious boundary between the lyric self and the world it inhabits and via whose language it is mediated is what allows for the work of art to play a role in the constitution of subjectivity, exercising its autonomy by its ability to captivate readers by impelling us to an interpretive act that leads us to philosophical concerns only to lead us back again to the work of art in its ability always to surpass attempts by conceptual thought to subsume the work of art, to exercise that non-dialectical power of the artwork as object that Adorno theorizes as identity thinking. In its place, Adorno proposes, in his essay "On Subject and Object," a relationship of non-domination that he even goes so far as to label peace:

> Were speculation concerning the state of reconciliation allowed, then it would be impossible to conceive that state as either the undifferentiated unity of subject and object or their hostile antithesis: rather it would

be the communication of what is differentiated. Only then would the concept of communication, as an objective concept, come into its own. [...] In its proper place, even epistemologically, the relationship of subject and object would lie in a peace achieved between human beings as well as between them and their Other. Peace is the state of differentiation without domination with the differentiated participating in each other. (*Critical* 247)

This peace is not to be confused with stasis or resolution. A dissonant relationship is not a hostile one, and in fact one could say that the peace that Adorno evokes here comes precisely from tension rather than a suspect or false resolution of it.

The mutual "participati[on] in each other" underscores the persistence of a transformed subjectivity that forms itself in knowledge of the fact that it is constituted by the object while still maintaining an identity for itself that stems from that constitution. This subjectivity is what holds the world together for Adorno:

The idealist construction of the subject founders on its falsely taking subject to be objective in the sense of something existing in-itself, precisely what it is not: measured against the standard of entities, the subject is condemned to nothingness. Subject is all the more the less it is, and all the less the more it believes itself to exist, to be for itself something objective. As an essential moment, however, it is ineradicable. Upon the elimination of the subjective moment the object would come apart diffusely like the fleeting stirrings and twinklings of subjective life. (*Critical* 257)

Seen in this light, Baudelaire's poetry represents an ever-renewed invitation to work out the consequences of the renewed subjectivity it enacts and to plumb the depths of the way that subjectivity engages questions of both ethics and epistemology as these become inseparable from esthetics, springing as they do, paradoxically, from the autonomy of the artwork and its own construal as acting upon the perceiver.

Esthetics are thus reshaped by their negation of the older, false, harmonious model of relation of subject to object, to which the Baudelairean poem does several kinds of violence in order to surpass it and maintain a relationship of negation to it, one shot through with the esthetic and political power of an irony whereby to exist ironically is, as Terry Eagleton puts it, "to live a discrepancy between inward and external, ambiguously suspended between one's negating subjectivity and the world it confronts" (Eagleton 1990, 181).[7] The constellations that emerge from Baudelaire's dissonant subjectivity point to something beyond our immediate grasp, which both calls for critical reflection and points to the way that critical reflection will always send us back to the poems, because they always surpass reflection's ability to account for them fully. The poems point implicitly to something that can't be reduced and simplified at a conceptual level, something to which we need to keep returning in a series of reconfigurations of his poems. Those poems invite new ways of seeing at the same time as their perpetual reconstitution guards against a static view of his poetics in its relation to the world from which it springs and which it in turn creates. As reading subjects, we too are reconfigured by the ways in which these poems, as a kind of subjects in their own right, act upon us and call out for an ever-renewed attempt to make and re-make sense of the world from which they spring and which they play a crucial role in forming.

NOTES

Introduction

1 Baudelaire *Œuvres complètes* 1: 683. Further references will be given in the text with volume and page number. Translations from *Les Fleurs du Mal* are from William Aggeler's *The Flowers of Evil*. All other translations from French, unless otherwise noted, are my own.

2 *Aesthetic Theory* 187. Further references will be given in the text with the abbreviation AT.

3 For more on the Adorno-Benjamin exchange, see Susan Buck-Morss 60 ff.

4 For a concise exposition of some key differences between Benjamin and Adorno on the question of language and the non-identical, see Stern 56–7. See also Barbara Johnson 111–19 on the debate between Adorno and Benjamin over the status of representation and interpretation: "It quickly becomes apparent to [Benjamin's] best interpreters [. . .] that, far from adding mere 'captions' to realities, Benjamin is transforming what counts as 'real.' Even captions become allegorical texts, and the question of reading reality 'like a text' becomes a question of what reading a text is like" (Johnson 114).

5 See also Kathy Kiloh: "Adorno reads Benjamin's efforts to focus attention on the things themselves as a reorientation of thought towards the object that prematurely and erroneously declares the dominance of the subject to be over once and for all. This is a dangerous move according to Adorno, as Benjamin ignores the very real possibility that it could lead to a further reification of the subject, which is then devoid of any ability to form a critical perspective on the world" (107).

6 See for instance Peter Nicholls's recent indication that "what Benjamin doesn't really explore is the way in which the failure of a transcendental horizon brings with it more than just the pathos of historical decline" (Nicholls 435).

7 See Terry Eagleton: "There are, perhaps, two different Adornos, the one somewhat more defeatist than the other. It is possible to read his work as a retreat from the nightmare of history into the aesthetic, and there is enough in his writings to make this a plausible view. It is the most easily caricatured side of his thought: Beckett and Schoenberg as the solution to world starvation and threatened nuclear destruction. [. . .] This Adorno asks us simply to subsist

in the near-tolerable strain of an absurdist, self-imploding thought, a thought before which all hubristic system-builders must humble themselves [. . .]. But there is also the other Adorno who still hopes that we might go through the aesthetic and come out in some unnameable place on the other side, the theorist for whom the aesthetic offers a paradigm, rather than a displacement of emancipatory political thought" (*Ideology* 360).

8   Richter goes on to say that "we begin to think with Adorno when we engage his textual production in a way that does not merely reconstruct this or that development of a concept. Rather, to think with Adorno also means to accept the invitation to learn what he calls 'the art of reading'" (*Thinking* 6).

9   J. M. Bernstein points to the similarity and difference between nature and art in Adorno's conception of them: "the internal complexion of the artwork must be conceived as, somehow, intrinsically meaningful, as meaningful in itself (and thus not given meaning by what is external to or different from it). As much as anything, natural beauty instigates and so models such a notion of intrinsic meaningfulness. If that modeling were sufficient, art would not be necessary" (Bernstein "Dead" 151).

10 I address epistemological concerns in Baudelaire at greater length in *Poetry's Knowing Ignorance* 37–49.

11 See Françoise Meltzer on this: "It is not enough to acknowledge Baudelaire's contradictions—he acknowledges them himself. My own attempt, rather, is to understand the lack of understanding in Baudelaire, to try to explicate how he does not see what he nonetheless records" (Meltzer 8).

12 The quote from Adorno is from *Lectures on Negative Dialectics* 74.

13 See Peter Uwe Hohendahl "The Epehmeral."

14 See Donald Burke on Adorno's conception of autonomous art as a corrective to both *l'art pour l'art* and committed art: "In two distant passages from the final section of *Aesthetic Theory* entitled "Society," Adorno formulates a position between *l'art pour l'art* and committed art, both of which Adorno construes as ideological. Adorno claims that *l'art pour l'art*'s concept of beauty all too easily lends itself to commodification and kitsch (AT 237), whereas he criticized committed art for communicating maxims—which is ultimately authoritarian (AT 242). For Adorno, authentic autonomous art is the third element of a triad, of which *l'art pour l'art* and committed art are the antithetical remainders. Autonomous art is not midway between two extremes, but rather a self-conscious art aware of its embeddedness in the dialectic of the relations and forces of production, prefiguring a state of reconciliation that is beyond the scope of art to actualize: 'Art's double character—its autonomy and *fait social*—is expressed ever and again in the palpable dependencies and conflicts between the two spheres (AT 229)'" (Burke 254).

15 See also Fredric Jameson: "The central tension in Adorno's aesthetics is that between his formal project of desubjectifying the analysis of aesthetic phenomena and his commitment [. . .] to the description of aesthetic *experience*: some last remnant of absolutely subjective categories which the desubjectifying impulse cannot wish to dissolve. What happens, of course,

is that under these circumstances aesthetic experience retreats into the ineffable and the unsayable: since anything that can be said or formulated or thematized about it at once falls into the force field of the desubjectifying dialectic and is transformed into symptoms and evidence of *objective* processes" (*Late* 123).

16 Cf. Françoise Meltzer on Baudelaire's relationship to the past: "Baudelaire's crisis is the rejection of modernity in the sense of the new at the expense of memory. He may talk of *le moderne* and be enraptured by the productions of contemporary art and literature; but he emphatically neither wants nor acknowledges the erasure of the past. Indeed, as the past is increasingly wiped out around him, Baudelaire becomes obsessed with memory, even as he grows even more fearful of a death that, in its annihilation of consciousness, closely parallels the eradication of history that the new Paris professes to accomplish" (241).

Chapter 1

1 Baudelaire *Flowers* 263 Translations of Baudelaire's verse poems are from Aggeler; further references will be indicated in the text.

2 I explore Baudelaire's amodernity in greater depth in *The Fall out of Redemption*.

3 On dissonance in "Le Mauvais vitrier" see Boutin: "Baudelaire ends 'Le Mauvais Vitrier' with a tension between the spontaneous fury of the speaker's cry and the appeal to an esthetic ideal, 'la vie en beau,' in such a way as to draw attention to the incompatibility of the dissonance of the cry and the harmonizing impulse of the urban picturesque" (104).

4 Attention to dissonance also highlights the paradoxical aspect of truth's complexity as Adorno understands it. Berthold Hoeckner describes Adorno's notion of truth as "the moment of simultaneous appearance *and* disappearance, of presence *and* absence, part *and* whole. The logic of contradiction upon which he built his negative dialectics cannot exist without invoking what is contradicted. This paradox is Adorno's trope of truth" (15–16).

5 Daniel Melnick suggests a parallel between "destabilizing chromaticism," "apocalyptic gestures at moments of climax and cadence," and the demonic in his study of dissonance and modern fiction, in the context of a brief discussion of Chopin: "Chopin makes more overt what Schumann struggles with: the demonic power of will to possess the spirit, to be a means of aesthetic exploration that threatens to explode aesthetic balance, to promise transcendent power as it drives the transcendent into silence" (33).

6 Jocelynne Loncke signals the view endorsed by several critics that indicates, on the basis of a manuscript list of titles where Beethoven figures, that Beethoven was the inspiration for the poem that was eventually entitled "La Musique" (Loncke 30). Claude Pichois disputes this attribution in his notes to the Pléiade edition (1, 964).

7   Esthetic and political emancipation are, of course, deeply intertwined for Adorno. He makes this explicit, for example, with reference to the relationship of the new music to Romanticism: "Romanticism must not simply be rejected by new music [. . .]. If new music is antithetical to Romanticism, this is only so as to make the Romantic fully conscious of itself. Above all, then, the goal of new music must be the complete liberation of the human subject. For thanks to the bourgeois controls on Romantic composition, [. . .] this liberation had been hampered in the expression of suffering by expressive conventions whose musical language was permeated until recently with a variety of residues" (Adorno *Sound* 121).

8   See also Lydia Goehr's commentary on the way shock forces a rethinking of the relationship between the old and the new in Adorno: "the tendency of the new in New Music also registers the tendency of the new, by extension, in the music of the tradition, say in a late Beethoven string quartet. What the sociological registering of shock does here is undermine our attempt to quarantine New Music as a way to show our loyalty to the tradition. It subverts the conservative rationalization. Not only do we recognize our deception in thinking the tradition never presented anything new. We also come to see the illusion in claiming that, because it is natural, true, and immutable, our tradition could not be other than it is" (Goehr 232).

9   I address this idiosyncratic adaptation of metaphysical and theological concepts more extensively in *The Fall Out of Redemption*.

10 As Baudelaire writes in *Richard Wagner et Tannhäuser à Paris*, in music, as in painting, and the written word, "il y a toujours une lacune complétée par l'imagination de l'auditeur" ["there is always a lacuna completed by the imagination of the hearer"] (2: 782).

11 Adorno relates the reshaping of the relationship of part and whole in modernist esthetics to social conceptions of totality that resonate with Baudelaire's critique of bourgeois approaches to art: "The mistake of traditional esthetics is that it exalts the relationship of the whole to the parts to one of entire wholeness, to totality, and hoists it in triumph over the heterogeneous as a banner of illusory positivity. [. . .] As the sermon goes, society once enjoyed a blessed closure where every artwork had its place, function, and legitimation and therefore enjoyed its own closure, whereas today everything is constructed in emptiness and artworks are internally condemned to failure. [. . .] On no account does an artwork require an a priori order in which it is received, protected, and accepted. If today nothing is harmonious, this is because harmony was false from the beginning" (AT 158).

12 See Dorothy Kelley's reading of the poem as enacting "the undoing of the equation of woman with nature" (Kelly 197) showing that what seems at first to be the "natural" association of woman and nature in Baudelaire turns out to be a product of the artifice that we call culture, "an artificial social state that has become second nature, which, like the woman's dress and gaiety, is an artifice unaware of itself" (202).

13 Baudelaire *Parisian* 12. Further references to Edward Kaplan's translations will be given in parentheses in the text.

14 See Maria Scott's "Baudelaire's Canine Allegories" for a reading of the poem, via a Rabelaisian intertext, which sees it as "invit[ing] the reader to embark on a search for covert meanings" (110) here and in the prose poems more broadly.

15 As Weber puts it: "Dans la mesure où, lorsqu'il rit d'un public mangeur d'excréments, le lecteur réduit lui-même le poème à un facile jeu de reconnaissance image/sens, il prend place, du même coup, parmi le public-canaille dont il croit se distinguer" ["Insofar as, when he laughs at a public who eats excrement, the reader himself reduces the poem to a facile game of image/meaning recognition, he takes his place at the same time among the riffraff public from which he thought he had distinguished himself"] (Weber 245).

16 As Ulrich Plass has remarked: "According to Adorno, certain kinds of poetry are capable of articulating subjectivity in a negative form that approximates the psychological and social structure of ego-weakness: the ego yields to the objectivity of language which in itself is senseless. Surprisingly, Adorno views this loss of control [. . .] in esthetically positive terms [. . .]. What is *merely* negative in a social context [. . .] becomes positive or [. . .] negative in a *productive* way in literature, because literature provides a medium for experience and reflection on modernity implicitly pitted against the instrumental rationality exemplified by what Adorno calls 'identity thinking'" (Plass xvii).

17 "Irrespect de l'autre et irrespect du langage vont de pair, et, ensemble, montrent l'artiste semblable à son contraire, à son public bourgeois. « N'avez-vous pas remarqué souvent que rien ne ressemble plus au parfait bourgeois que l'artiste de génie concentré ? »" (Thélot 24). The passage quoted is from "Quelques caricaturistes étrangers" ["Disrespect of the other and disrespect of language go together and show the artist to be similar to his opposite, to his bourgeois public. 'Have you not often noticed that nothing resemble the perfect bourgeois more than the artist of concentrated genius?'"] (Baudelaire 2: 572). See also Steve Murphy's reading that suggests that blame would fall to the poet rather than the dog for offering it something it is not in a position to appreciate (Murphy 72).

Chapter 2

1 Portions of Chapter 2 appeared in "Digesting Les Fleurs du Mal: Imaginative Spaces and Liquid Modernity in Baudelaire," in *Nineteenth-Century French Studies* 37, no. 1–2 (Fall–Winter 2008–2009): 30–41, http://doi.org/10.1353/ncf.0.0044 (reproduced with permission).

2 See also Jean-Michel Maulpoix's characterization of the lyric subject as "rien d'autre que l'arbitre de ce jeu instable entre tu et il, entre elle et moi, entre la présence immédiate de celui ou de celle à qui l'on s'adresse, et l'éloignement de cette figure imaginaire que l'on ne peut que rêver de ressaisir dans la langue. Le « je » lyrique est un lieu articulatoire qui subsiste ou qui se reconstitue par-

delà la « disparition élocutoire du poète »" ["nothing other than the referee of this unstable game between you and he, between she and me, between the immediate presence of him or her to whom one speaks, and the distancing of this imaginary figure that one can only dream of capturing in language. The lyric 'I' is an articulatory space that subsists or reconstitutes itself beyond the 'elocutory disappearance of the poet.'"] (Maulpoix "Quatrième" 155).

3 Martin Jay reminds us of the suspicion aroused in Adorno in claims of recuperating some kind of purported unity of subject and object, on the grounds that such a unity cancels thought as he understands it: "For Adorno, any philosophy which lamented the lost origins of humanity's wholeness with the world or identified utopia with its future realization was not merely misguided, but potentially pernicious as well. For the obliteration of the distinction between subject and object would effectively mean the loss of the capacity for reflection that was no less its result than the alienation bemoaned by Marxist Humanists and others" (Jay 64).

4 Peter Gordon elaborates the implications of Adorno's view: "each and every subject is *already also* an object. This is so because, notwithstanding the subject's capacity to conceptualize the world, the subject is *also* a worldly being and therefore at the mercy of its own material conditions (its corporeality, its sensual relation to its surroundings, its dependency on the human collective, and so forth). But this means that the relation between subject and object can never exhibit a thoroughgoing reciprocity: [. . .] Every object is an object even when it is not an object-for-a-subject, but *every* subject is necessarily *also* an object. [. . .] Adorno also claims that the primacy of the object is not only a social or materialist phenomenon; this primacy is in fact *logically presupposed* in the very concept of experience" (Gordon *Existence* 127–8).

5 Such a view of the subject calls into question Walter Benjamin's assertion in a note that "Il n'y a vraisemblablement aucun poète lyrique avant Baudelaire qui compte dans son œuvre autant de poèmes où le « je » ait complètement disparu" ["There is likely no lyric poet before Baudelaire who has in his works so many poems where the 'I' has completely disappeared"] (Benjamin 634).

6 The part-whole relation plays an important part in dialectical thought more generally for Adorno: "The dialectical conception also insists upon a relation of tension between [. . .] the whole and the parts [. . .]. The relation of whole and part in the dialectic is not one of mere subsumption. [. . .] Rather, it is a dynamic relation, one where both moments reciprocally produce one another rather than just being given alongside one another in a reified and, so to speak, timeless manner" (Adorno, *Introduction* 87–8). Dialectical thought thus refuses any attempt to synthesize part and whole in favor of maintaining them perpetually in tension.

7 Jean-Pierre Richard sees the drinking of blood in Baudelaire as the affirmation of life and the remedy to an otherwise inevitable paralysis: "Boire le sang tout chaud, c'est boire aux sources de la vie. Le sang sera donc le signe même de l'expansion, l'antithèse vivante de toutes les paralysies" ["To drink hot blood is to drink at the source of life. Blood will thus be the very sign of expansion, the living antithesis of all paralysis"] (118).

8   On the affinities between Adorno and deconstruction, see, for instance Terry Eagleton: "The parallels between deconstruction and Adorno are particularly striking. Long before the current fashion, Adorno was insisting on the power of those heterogeneous fragments that slip through the conceptual net, rejecting all philosophy of identity, refusing class consciousness as objectionable 'positive,' and denying the intentionality of signification. Indeed there is hardly a theme in contemporary deconstruction that is not richly elaborated in his work" (Eagleton Benjamin 141). See also Ryan 73–80.

9   The approach I am enumerating here with reference to Adorno can, I hope, provide an alternative to another current approach to rethinking the subjectivity of works of art, that of Graham Harman. He claims that "rather than emphasize the social conditions that gave rise to any given work, we ought to do the contrary, and look at how works reverse or shape what might have been expected in their time and place [. . .]. To call someone 'a product of their time and place' is never a compliment; neither should it be a compliment when aimed at a literary work" (Harman 201). I would claim that Harman develops a false dichotomy here that can be corrected by seeing the work of art in a dialectical relation to its social condition; it is never a simple either/or question of a work shaping or being shaped by is context; the real interest is in articulating the specifics of how it is always both.

10 On the subjectivity of the work of art, see also Mitchell Gell's "What Do Pictures Want," where he defines agency as any persons or things "who/which are seen as initiating causal consequences" (16).

11 The most influential readings of this poem have been Paul de Man's deconstructive reading of Baudelairean irony and Leo Bersani's psychoanalytic approach More recently, Debarati Sanyal has proposed a reading of the poem through the lens of trauma theory, arguing that "the poem 'acts out' a process of interiorization, wherein a incompatibility between self and world reveals incompatible registers within the self" (Sanyal 33).

12 Per Buvik, who responds to de Man's reading by noting the distinction between the ironic and the comic as separate categories in Baudelaire, reminds us that "selon le poète, l'homme *est* par définition ironique" ["according to the poet, man *is* by definition ironic"] (Buvik 92). We could extend this further and say that, in this poem, man *is* irony.

13 Deborah Harter sees in the plural of "ces grands abadonnés" an inscription of the lyric subject ina community, an interpretation consistent with my reading of the lyric subject as broken down an posited in complex relation to others as subjects and objects: "From a narrative 'je' dominant in the first six stanzas, lost in the agony of its own duplicity, comes in these lines a proclamation of community, a clear statement of brotherhood along those (or at least between those two) who find themselves 'out of tune' with the divine symphony from which their conditions would seem to have departed" (Harter 37).

14 In this way the poet invests not only the text but also nature and the city themselves with vital life-energy. Contemporary ecocritical approaches emphasize a similar interplay between subject, setting, and text: "David Abram maintains that our relationship with texts is 'wholly animistic,' since the articulate subjectivity that was once experienced in nature is shifted to

the written word. At one time nature spoke; now texts do [. . .]. As cultural artifacts, texts embody human (or ostensibly divine) subjects, but stand conspicuously outside nature, whose status as subject therefore becomes problematical" (Manes 18).

15   By now, the poetic process has itself become the flowing object, as one cannot read this poem in isolation if one wishes to find a referent for "ces cruelles filles." Only in relation to the preceding poem, "Les Deux bonnes sœurs," does this reference become meaningful, since the latter speaks of "La Débauche et la Mort" (114), who are likely the daughters referenced in "La Fontaine de Sang." See Pichois' notes in Baudelaire 1: 1064.

16   See 1: 1064, note 4.

17   See Thériault 313.

18   See the notes in Antoine Adam's edition of *Les Fleurs du Mal* 413–14 for echoes in Gautier's novella *Avatar* and his novel *Mademoiselle de Maupin*. See Baudelaire 1: 1063–4 for Claude Pichois' indication of Shakespeare's *Julius Caesar* and its reference to Caesar's recounting of a dream in which his statue bled (Act II, scene 2).

19   Laurent Jenny has underscored the way the poem's reworkings of both temporality and subjectivity are intertwined: " « Le *Confiteor* de l'artiste » nous achemine aux confins d'une fictonnalisation du Je. Tant que l'énonciation demeure temporellement indéfinie [. . .], elle apparaît aussi extensible à tout autre [. . .]. Mais que la mise en situation du Je tende à se temporaliser [. . .] et alors nous voyons prendre forme un moi fictif dont l'expérience n'est plus offerte à un partage actuel, mais rapportée, et posée comme ontologiquement indépendante à la fois du sujet parlant et du destinataire" ["'Le *Confiteor* de l'artiste' leads us to the confines of a fictionalization of the I. As long as the enunciation remains temporarily indefinite [. . .], it also appears extendable to all others [. . .]. But the situating of the I tends to temporalize itself [. . .] and thus we see taking shape a fictive self whose experience is no longer offered to a current sharing, but sent back, and posed as ontologically independent at the same time from the speaking subject and from the receiver"] (100–1).

20   See Laurent Jenny's comments on the moment in the poem's third paragraph where the *je* appears at the same time as the first temporal markers: "Le statut indécis des déictiques « bientôt » et « maintenant », qui hésitent entre valeur actuelle et valeur générique, maintient l'énonciation dans l'ambiguïté" ["The undecided status of the deictic markers 'soon' and 'now,' which float between current and general value, maintains the enunciation in ambiguity"] (101).

21   This take on what Baudelaire calls the "modern conception" of art itself points to a connection with Romanticism via the ideas of Schelling's *System of Transcendental Idealism* that Baudelaire may have read in French translation (see 2: 1378, n.1).

22   See Rob Halpern's insightful reading of the poem in light of Adorno, where he argues that "surrender to the historical conditions that enable and constrain the work may mean risking a kind of figural annihilation of both artist and artwork alike, a kind of poetic disfiguration of the lyric self that encodes other

forms of real social violence. This dialectical tension penetrates and motivates Baudelaire's late innovation. Indeed, Baudelaire the prose poet is a consummate dialectician" (Halpern *Politics* 282). His reading goes on to show that "while the poem illustrates the artist's historical defeat before those [historical] forces, its very existence as a poem simultaneously testifies against its own conclusion. This is the socio-esthetic paradox 'Le Confiteor' depicts" (303).

Chapter 3

1   Sonam Singh sees in this horizontality evidence against Walter Benjamin's reading of the poem; "Melancholy is not overcome, but its resounding echoes draw the mind to an ethical concern outside its parish. In this narrative submission to the historical and geographical vastness and hetereogeneity of the world; in the speculative outward, not upward, projection of correspondences into obscure consummations; in the endless displacement of origins; and in an anticlimax of unknowability (". . .") rather than a confident universal truth [. . .] Baudelaire marks his crucial difference from Benjamin. Here there is no angelic view, no cogent meta-narrative; the poet's vision and knowledge give out at an early distal, temporal, and historical range, and in this sputtering in the face of an earth ridiculous and sublime the poem acquires its distinctive conceptual power" (Singh 424).

2   Similarly, Richard Burton notes: "The poem's emblematic victims both are and are not himself: he does not attempt to absorb them into himself or lose himself in them; subject and object are, for once, maintained in a state of tremulous equilibrium that enables both to exist *individually and in relationship to each other*" (Burton 165).

3   Richard Klein, for instance, argues that "'Perte d'auréole' allows itself to be read as a *determined* negation of the poetic experience narrated in 'Bénédiction'" (Klein 517).

4   I consider "Le Rêve d'un curieux" in light of the impossibility of a sense of an ending in *The Fall out of Redemption* 114–17.

5   It is interesting to note that the dedicatee of the poem, Félix Nadar, recounted one of his last conversations with Baudelaire, who was already stricken with aphasia, as including an ambiguous gesture toward the sky coupled with a repetition of the only word Baudelaire could still speak in what was otherwise his muteness: "Nous disputions de l'immortalité de l'âme. 'Voyons, comment peux-tu croire en Dieu?' répétais-je. Baudelaire [. . .] me montra le ciel. Devant nous, au-dessus de nous, c'était, embrasant toute la nue, [. . .] la pompe splendide du soleil couchant. 'Crénom ! oh, crénom ! » protestait-il, encore me reprochait-il, indigné, à grands coups de poing vers le ciel" ["We were arguing over the immortality of the soul. 'Say, how can you believe in God,' I repeated to him. Baudelaire [. . .] showed me the sky. In front of us, above us, there was, inflaming the whole sky, [. . .] the splendid pomp of the sunset. 'Crénom! Oh, crénom!' he protested, he said in reproach, indignant, shaking his fist at the sky"] (quoted in Chérix 444–5).

6   There are echoes here of Adorno's notion of reconciliation of subject-object in which subject and object continue to mediate each other, maintaining their separate and mutually constituting relationship rather than dissolving into the other. On this, see Kathy Kiloh: "Reconciliation would not collapse subject and object into a state of undifferentiated immanence; instead, subject would continue to mediate object, and vice versa. Mediation would increase, bringing subject and object into greater proximity with one another. The continued separation of subject and object would impede rather than facilitate the domination of the subject over the object, and resist the subject's claim to possess the alien through knowledge of it" (Kiloh 115–16).

7   Susan Blood highlights the way that, in Baudelaire's poetry, violence lingers over, but cannot cancel, either the subject or the subject-object relation: "Although the relationship between an 'I' and a 'you' is common in lyric poetry, in Baudelaire it is experienced as both an obsession and an embarrassment, one which he attempts to cover over with violence. [. . .] The violence of the poetic contract cannot be purged by a 'purer' violence, one which would eliminate the other by destroying the self" (Blood 9).

8   This kind of productive violence also characterizes the act of thinking for Adorno: "His strategy is thus to identify moments that disrupt, interrupt, and disturb thought, viewing in such disturbances not mere embarrassments or obstacles to be overcome but conditions of possibility for genuine thought to unfold. [. . .] Emphatic or genuine thinking in the Adornean sense thus names the mode of thought that registers the ways in which it allows itself to become affected, even interrupted, by what is not already included in it" (Richter *Thinking* 29–30).

9   There are echoes here of Baudelaire's comment to Madame Sabatier after she had agreed to take him as her lover: "Il y a quelques jours, tu étais une divinité, ce qui est si commode, ce qui est si beau, si inviolable. Te voilà femme maintenant" ["A few days ago, you were a divinity, which is so convenient, so beautiful, so inviolable. Now there you are, a woman"] (*Correspondance* 1: 425).

10 Lübecker expands this analysis in *Twenty-First-Century Symbolism*: "The challenge posed by Baudelaire's poem ['Le Crépuscule du soir'] precisely lies with how it disturbs our desire to think agency in individual and individualizing terms. It highlights that Baudelaire's poem leaves little space for what might be called the fiction of the autonomous, liberal subject, that it instead suggests that the characters (who are obviously there) must be thought of as temporary 'individual-environments'" (*Twenty-First-Century* 86).

11 For more on these structural echoes, see Chesters.

12 On Baudelaire's "poetics of not mattering," see Whidden 233–5.

Coda and Conclusion

1   I elaborate the consequences of Baudelaire's refusal of the possibility of redemption, in his esthetics and poetry as well as in the work of some of his important interpreters, including Walter Benjamin and Benjamin Fondane, in *The Fall out of Redemption*.

2. Adorno's comments echo Georges Blin's earlier commentary on "Le Rêve d'un curieux": "Selon de nouveaux paradoxes, c'est quand le vouloir-vivre se trouve ainsi mis en veilleuse, c'est quand triomphe le « goût du Neant » que la vie devient ici-bas vivable" ["According to new paradoxes, it is when the will to live finds itself thus put on hold and when the 'taste for nothingness' triumphs that life here below becomes livable"] (Blin 180).

3. As Gerhard Schweppenhäuser indicates, for Adorno, "it would be false to pursue affirmative metaphysics and start from changeless, eternal essences, but just as false to squander the epistemological gain brought by the initiation of a negative metaphysics" (Schweppenhäuser 76).

4. For a reading of "Le Goût du néant" that appeals to Lyotard as "a corrective to Adorno's stern and pessimistic judgment" on art, see Eliassen.

5. Alan Toumayan hints at the complexity inherent in this poem when he indicates that, "as the example of ["Le Rêve d'un curieux"] suggests, Baudelaire's identification of the elements and basic dynamic of subjectivity, which he often examines in anomalies, dysfunctions, and pathologies, his prescient deconstructions of totalization and negativity and concomitant examinations of the themes of the other and of the outside through such concepts as inspiration, incompletion and excess, awaiting, powerlessness, and other modalities of the weakness of negativity, his analyses of subjectivity through alternatives and complications to autonomy and identity, augur the modernism of such writers as Bataille, Blanchot, and Beckett" (Toumayan 142–3).

6. An aphorism of Emil Cioran's expresses the same paradox: "Dieu *est,* même s'il n'est pas" ["God *is,* even if he is not"] (Cioran 1386).

7. See also Claire Colebrook on an irony which "is not a device *within language* used to reflect upon meaning but is a certain way of living or existing toward meaning in general" (Colebrook 4).

WORKS CITED

Acquisto, Joseph. *The Fall Out of Redemption: Writing and Thinking Beyond Salvation in Baudelaire, Cioran, Fondane, Agamben, and Nancy.* Bloomsbury, 2015.
Acquisto, Joseph. *Poetry's Knowing Ignorance.* Bloomsbury, 2020.
Adorno, Theodor. "The Actuality of Philosophy." *Telos* 31 (Spring 1977), 120–33.
Adorno, Theodor. "Aesthetic Theory." Tr. Robert Hullot-Kentor. U of Minnesota P, 1997.
Adorno, Theodor. Aesthetics. Tr. Wieland Hoban. Polity, 2018.
Adorno, Theodor. *Beethoven: The Philosophy of Music.* Tr. Edmund Jephcott. Stanford University Press, 1998.
Adorno, Theodor. *Critical Methods.* Tr. Henry W. Pickford. Columbia UP, 1998.
Adorno, Theodor. *An Introduction to Dialectics.* Polity, 2017.
Adorno, Theodor. *Lectures on Negative Dialectics.* Polity, 2008.
Adorno, Theodor. *Notes to Literature.* Tr. Shierry Weber Nicholsen. Columbia UP, 1991–2.
Adorno, Theodor W. *Philosophy of New Music.* Ed. Robert Hullot-Kentor. University of Minnesota Press, 2006.
Adorno, Theodor. *Sound Figures.* Tr. Rodney Livingstone. Stanford UP, 1999.
Adorno, Theodor. "Theses on the Language of the Philosopher," in Donald Burke et al., *Adorno and the Need in Thinking.* U of Toronto P, 2007, 35–40.
Adorno, Theodor and Walter Benajmin. *The Complete Correspondence 1928–1940.* Ed. Henri Lonitz, tr. Nicholas Walker. Harvard UP, 1999.
Angermann, Asaf. "The Ghosts of Normativity: Temporality and Recurrence in Adorno's Ethics of Dissonance." *The Germanic Review* 90:4 (2015), 260–72.
Baudelaire, Charles. *Correspondance.* Gallimard, 1973.
Baudelaire, Charles. *Les Fleurs du Mal.* Ed. Antoine Adam. Classiques Garnier, 1961.
Baudelaire, Charles. *The Flowers of Evil.* Tr. William Aggeler. Academy Library Guild, 1954.
Baudelaire, Charles. *Œuvres complètes.* Gallimard, 1975.
Baudelaire, Charles. *The Parisian Prowler.* Tr. Edward Kaplan. U of Georgia P, 1997.
Bauman, Zygmunt. *Liquid Modernity.* Polity Press, 2000.
Beckett, Samuel. *Molloy, Malone Dies, The Unnameable.* Calder, 1994.
Beistegui, Miguel. *Aesthetics after Metaphysics.* Routledge, 2015.
Belmer, Stephanie. "Emmanuel Levinas and Theodor Adorno on Ethics and Aesthetics." *Angelaki* 24:5 (October 2019), 29–43.

Benjamin, Walter. *Baudelaire*. Ed établie par Giorgio Agamben, Barbara Chitussi et Clemens-Carl Härle. La fabrique, 2013.
Bernstein, J. M. "The Dead Speaking of Stones," in Fred Rush, ed., *The Cambridge Companion to Critical Theory*. Cambridge UP, 2004, 139-64.
Bernstein, J. M. *The Fate of Art: Aesthetic Alienation from Kant to Derrida and Adorno*. Penn State UP, 1992.
Bernstein, J. M. "Why Rescue Semblance? Metaphysical Experience and the Possibility of Ethics," in Tom Huhn and Lambert Zuidervaart, eds., *The Semblance of Subjectivity: Essays in Adorno's Aesthetic Theory*. The MIT Press, 1997, 177-212.
Bersani, Leo. *Baudelaire and Freud*. U of California P, 1977.
Bevilacqua, Luca. "Le 'Confiteor' du peintre." *L'Année Baudelaire* 17 (2013), 97-113.
Blin, Georges. *Baudelaire*. Gallimard, 1939.
Blood, Susan. *Baudelaire and the Aesthetics of Bad Faith*. Stanford UP, 1997.
Bonnefoy, Yves. "L'enjeu occidental de la poésie," in Marc Fumaroli, ed., *Identité littéraire de l'Europe*. Presses Universitaires de France, 2000, 205-21.
Boutin, Aimée. *City of Noise: Sound and Nineteenth-Century Paris*. U of Illinois P, 2015.
Bowie, Andrew. Adorno and the Ends of Art. Polity, 2013.
Buck-Morss, Susan. *The Origin of Negative Dialectics*. Free Press, 1979.
Burke, Donald A. "Adorno's Aesthetics of Reconciliation: Negative Presentation of Utopia or Post-metaphysical Pipe-Dream?" in Donald Burke et al., eds., *Adorno and the Need in Thinking*. U of Toronto P, 2007, 233-60.
Burton, Richard D. E. *Baudelaire In 1859*. Cambridge UP, 1988.
Butler, Judith. "Violence, Mourning, Politics." *Studies in gender and Sexuality* 49:1 (2003), 9-37.
Buvik, Per. "La notion baudelairienne de l'ironie." *Revue Romane* 31:1 (1996), 87-98.
Chambers, Ross. *An Atmospherics of the City: Baudelaire and the Poetics of Noise*, Fordham UP, 2015.
Chérix, Robert-Benoit. *Commentaire des Fleurs du mal*. Droz, 1962.
Chesters, Graham. "The Transformation of a Prose-Poem: Baudelaire's 'Crépuscule du soir.'" in Malcolm Bowie, Alison Fairlie et Alison Finch, ed., *Baudelaire, Mallarmé, Valéry: New Essays in Honour of Lloyd Austin*, Cambridge UP, 1982, 24-37.
Chua, Daniel. *The "Galitzin" Quartets of Beethoven*. Princeton UP, 1995.
Cioran, Emil. *Œuvres*. Gallimard, 1995.
Colebrook, Claire. *Irony in the Work of Philosophy*. U of Nebraska P, 2002.
Collot, Michel. "Le sujet lyrique hors de soi," in Dominique Rabaté, ed., *Figures du style lyrique*. Presses Universitaires de France, 1996, 113-25.
Cornille, Jean-Louis Fin de Baudelaire. *Autopsie d'une œuvre sans nom*. Hermann, 2009.
DalMolin, Jean-Louis "'Tout entière': A Mystifying Totality," in William J. Thompson, ed., *Understanding Les Fleurs du Mal*. Vanderbilt UP, 1997, 86-94.
de Man, Paul. *Blindness and Insight*. U of Minnesota Press, 1983.
De Vries, Hent. *Minimal Theologies: Critiques of Secular Reason in Adorno and Levinas*. Johns Hopkins UP, 2019.

Eagleton, Terry. *The Ideology of the Aesthetic*. Basil Blackwell, 1990.
Eagleton, Terry. *Walter Benjamin or Towards a Revolutionary Criticism*. Verso, 2009.
Eliassen, Knut Ove. "The Anaesthesia of Charles Baudelaire's 'Le Goût du néant,'" in Michael Syrotinski and Ian Machlachlan, eds., *Sensual Reading: New Approaches to Reading and Its Relations to the Senses*. Bucknell UP, 2001, 248-70.
Evans, Margery. "Soubresaut or Dissonance? An Aspect of the Musicality of Baudelaire's 'Petits Poèmes en prose,'" *The Modern Language Review* 83:2 (April 1988), 314-21.
Farina, Mario. *Adorno's Aesthetics as a Literary Theory of Art*. Palgrave Macmillan, 2020.
Felski, Rita. "Context Stinks!" *New Literary History* 42 (2011): 573-91.
Fleming, Paul. "The Secret Adorno." *Qui Parle* 15:1 (Fall/Winter 2004), 97-114.
Foloppe, Régine. *Baudelaire et la vérité poétique*. L'Harmattan, 2019.
Gasché, Rodolphe. *The Honor of Thinking: Critique, Theory, Philosophy*. Stanford UP, 2007.
Gell, Mitchell. *What Do Pictures Want?*. U of Chicago P, 2004.
Goehr, Lydia. "Dissonant Works and the Listening Public," in Tom Huhn, ed., *The Cambridge Companion to Adorno*. Cambridge UP, 2004, 222-47.
Gordon, Peter. *Adorno and Existence*. Harvard University Press, 2018.
Halpern, Rob. "Baudelaire's 'Dark Zone': The Poème en Prose as Social Hierolyph; or The Beginning and the End of Commodity Aesthetics." *Modernist Cultures* 4 (2009), 1-23.
Halpern, Rob. *The Politics of Autonomy: Social Engagement and Aesthetic Value from the Romantic Fragment to the Poème en Prose*. Dissertation, U of California Santa Cruz, 2006.
Harman, Graham. "The Well-Wrought Broke n Hammer: Object-Oriented Literary Criticism." *New Literary History* 43:2 (Spring 2012), 183-203.
Harter, Deborah. "Divided Selves, Ironic Counterparts: Intertextual Doubling in Baudelaire's 'L'Héautontimorouménos' and Poe's 'The Haunted Palace,'" *Comparative Literature Studies* 26:1 (1989), 28-38.
Hiddleston, J. A. *Baudelaire and Le Spleen de Paris*. Clarendon Press, 1987.
Hoeckner, Berthold. *Programming the Absolute: Nineteenth-century German Music and the Hermeneutics of the Moment*. Princeton UP, 2002.
Hohendahl, Peter Uwe. *The Fleeting Promise of Art: Adorno's Aesthetic Theory Revisited*. Cornell UP, 2013.
Hohendhal, Peter Uwe. "The Ephemeral and the Absolute: Provisional Notes to Adorno's Aesthetic Theory," in Gerhard Richter, ed., *Language without Soil: Adorno and Late Philosophical Modernity*. Fordham UP, 2010, 206-226.
Hubert, J.-D. *L'esthétique des Fleurs du mal*. Pierre Cailler, 1953.
Hulatt, Owen. *Adorno's Theory of Philosophical and Aesthetic Truth*. Columbia UP, 2016.
Jameson, Fredric. *The Benjamin Files*. Verso, 2020.
Jameson, Fredric. *Late Marxism: Adorno or The Persistence of The Dialectic*. Verso, 2007.
Jay, Martin. *Adorno*. Harvard UP, 1984.

Jenny, Laurent. "Fictions du moi et figurations du moi," in Dominique Rabaté, ed., *Figures du style lyrique*. Presses Universitaires de France, 1996, 99-111.

Johnson, Barbara. *Mother Tongues: Sexuality, Trials, Motherhood, Translation*. Harvard UP, 2003.

Kaufman, Robert. "Difficulty in Modern Poetry and Aesthetics," in Jonathan Culler and Kevin Lamb, eds., *Just Being Difficult? Academic Writing in the Public Arena*. Stanford UP, 2003, 139-56.

Kaufman, Robert. "Lyric Commodity Critique, Benjamin Adorno Marx, Baudelaire Baudelaire Baudelaire." *PMLA/Publications of The Modern Language Association of America* 123:1 (2008), 207-15.

Kelly, Dorothy. "Toxic Doxa in Baudelaire: 'A celle qui est trop gaie' and 'Une charogne.'" *Symposium* 66:4 (2012), 194-205.

Kiloh, Kathy. "The Linguistic Image: Mediation and Immediacy in Adorno and Benjamin," in Donald Burke et al., eds., *Adorno and the Need in Thinking*. U of Toronto P, 2007, 103-29.

Klein, Richard. "Bénédiction / Perte d'auréole : Parables of Interpretation." *Modern Language Notes* 85 (May 1970), 515-28.

Laforgue, Pierre. "Sur la rhétorique du lyrisme dans les années 1850 : Le Flacon de Baudelaire." *Poétique* 126 (2001), 245-52.

Loncke, Jocelynne. *Baudelaire et la musique*. Nizet, 1975.

Lübecker, Nikolaj. "Twenty-First Century Baudelaire? Affectivity and Ecology in 'Le Crépuscule du soir'." *Modernism/Modernity* 27:4 (November 2020), 689-706.

Lübecker, Nikolaj. *Twenty-First-Century Symbolism: Verlaine, Baudelaire, Mallarmé*. Liverpool UP, 2022.

Mallarmé, Stéphane. *Œuvres complètes*. Gallimard, 1998-2003.

Manes, "Nature and Silence," in Cheryll Glotfelty and Harold Fromm, eds., *The Ecocriticism Reader: Landmarks in Literary Ecology*. U of Georgia P, 1996, 15-29.

Marchal, Bertrand. "Baudelaire, Barbier, Gautier et le mauvais moine." *L'Année Baudelaire* 6 (2002), 127-41.

Maulpoix, Jean-Michel. "La Quatrième personne du singulier," in Dominique Rabaté, *Figures du sujet lyrique*. Presses Universitaires d France, 2005, 147-60.

McCall, Corey. "Against the Reification of History: Benjamin and Adorno on Baudelaire," in Corey McCall and Nathan Ross, eds., *Benjamin, Adorno, and the Experience of Literature*. Routledge, 2018, 19-36.

Melnick, Daniel. *Fullness of Dissonance: Modern Fiction and the Aesthetics of Music*. Fairleigh Dickinson UP, 1994.

Meltzer, Françoise. *Seeing Double: Baudelaire's Modernity*. U of Chicago P, 2011.

Mitchell, W. J. T. *What Do Pictures Want*. U of Chicago P, 2004.

Murphy, Steve. *Logiques du dernier Baudelaire*. Champion, 2007.

Nicholls, Peter. "Mud and Meytaphysics: The Matter of Modernism." *Forum for Modern Language Studies* 56:4 (2021?), 427-44.

Nicholsen, Shierry Weber. *Exact Imagination, Late Work: On Adorno's Aesthetics*. The MIT Press, 1997.

North, Michael. "The Afterlife of Modernism." *New Literary History* 50:1 (Winter 2019), 91-112.

Plass, Ulrich. *Language and History in Theodor W. Adorno's Notes to Literature.* Routledge, 2007.

Richard, Jean-Pierre. *Poésie et profondeur.* Editions du Seuil, 1955.

Richter, Gerhard. *Afterness.* Columbia UP, 2011.

Richter, Gerhard. "Introduction," in Gerhard Richter, ed., *Language without Soil: Adorno and Late Philosophical Modernity.* Fordham UP, 2010, 1-9.

Richter, Gerhard. *Thinking with Adorno: The Uncoercive Gaze.* Fordham UP, 2019.

Ryan, Michael. *Marxism and Deconstruction: A Critical Articulation.* Johns Hopkins UP, 1982.

Said, Edward. *Music at the Limits.* Columbia UP, 2008.

Sanyal, Debarati. *The Violence of Modernity.* Johns Hopkins UP, 2006.

Schweppenhäuser, Gerhard. *Theodor W. Adorno: An Introduction.* Tr. J. Rolleston. Duke UP, 2009.

Scott, Maria "Baudelaire's Canine Allegories: 'Le Chien et le flacon' and 'Les Bons Chiens.'" *Nineteenth-Century French Studies* 33:1 & 2 (Fall-Winter 2004-5), 107-18.

Scott, Maria. *Baudelaire's Le Spleen de Paris: Shifting Perspectives.* Routledge, 2018.

Singh, Sonam. "Baudelaire without Benjamin: Contingency, History, Modernity." *Comparative Literature* 64:4 (2012), 407-28.

Starobinski, Jean. *La mélancolie au miroir.* Gallimard, 1989.

Stephens, Sonya. *Baudelaire's Prose Poems: The Practice and Politics of Irony.* Oxford UP, 1999.

Stern, Alexander. "Guilt and Mourning," in Peter E. Gordon, Espen Hammer, and Max Pensky, eds., *A Companion to Adorno.* John Wiley & Sons, Inc., 2020, 51-66.

Thélot, Jérôme. *Baudelaire: Violence et poésie.* Gallimard, 1993.

Thériault, Patrick. "'La Fontaine de Sang' de Baudelaire: Veine secrète et inspiration rouge." *Revue d'Histoire littéraire de la France* 119:2 (April-June 2019), 305-32.

Toumayan, Alain Paul. "Levinas and French Literature," in Donald Wehrs and David Haney, eds., *Levinas and Nineteenth-Century Literature.* U of Delaware P, 2009, 126-47.

Vaillant, Alain. *Baudelaire, poète comique.* Presses Universitaires de Rennes, 2007.

Waddell, Nathan. *Moonlighting: Beethoven and Literary Modernism.* Oxford UP, 2019.

Weber, Julien. "Aux frontières de l'esthétique: Le grotesque baudelairien." *Nottingham French Studies* 58:2 (2019), 237-48.

Wellmer, Albrecht. "Truth, Semblance, Reconciliation: Adorno's Aesthetic Redemption of Modernity." *Telos* 62 (December 1984), 89-115.

Whidden, Seth. *Reading Baudelaire's Le Spleen de Paris and the Nineteenth-Century Prose Poem.* Oxford UP, 2022.

Wu, Colleen Shu-Ching. "Oneself as Subject in Dickinson's Poetry: Adorno and Heidegger." *Style* 49:3 (2015), 334-53.

Zuidervaart, Lambert. *Adorno's Aesthetic Theory: The Redemption of Illusion.* The MIT Press, 1991.

INDEX

Note: Page numbers followed by "n" refer to notes.

"A celle qui est trop gaie"
  (Baudelaire) 36, 52, 56, 58–60,
  109, 139
"Actuality of Philosophy, The"
  (Adorno) 23
Adam, Antoine 64
Adorno, T., *see also individual entries*
  "Actuality of Philosophy, The" 23
  on advanced consciousness 26
  Aesthetic Theory 2, 4, 6–8, 15–18,
    20, 22, 24–5, 32–4, 38, 46–7,
    65, 68–70, 77, 78, 81–2, 103–4,
    108, 109, 115, 118–20, 131–3,
    138–9, 145, 158, 162, 172 n.14
  on artwork 2–4, 7, 9
  critique of Benjamin 4
  dialectical thinking about
    subjectivity 74
  Dialectic of Enlightenment 36–7
  "Essay as Form, The" 17
  on esthetic truth 17, 50, 69, 85,
    112, 116, 118, 128, 130–3, 145
  on identity thinking 5–6, 75, 165,
    168, 175 n.16
  on *l'art pour l'art* 20, 21, 77,
    172 n.14
  Negative Dialectics 75–7, 85,
    128–9, 163, 164
  Notes on Literature 7
  "On Lyric Poetry and Society" 5
  "On Subject and Object" 168–9
  remarks on Beethoven 43
  Sound Figures 43–4
  on subject–object relations 1, 4–6,
    14, 15, 20, 21, 26, 28, 32, 35,
    67, 69, 76, 77, 93, 114, 120,
    124, 135, 138–41, 143, 146,
    162, 166–8, 180 n.6, 180 n.7
  "Theses on the Language of the
    Philosopher" 164–5
  on unity of form and content 35
advanced consciousness 26
Aesthetic Theory (AT) 2, 4, 6–8,
  15–18, 20, 22, 24–5, 32–4, 38,
  46–7, 65, 68–70, 77, 78, 81–2,
  103–4, 108, 109, 115, 118–20,
  131–3, 138–9, 145, 158, 162,
  172 n.14
agency 177 n.10
alienation 40, 70
"Allégorie" (Baudelaire) 95
Angermann, Asaf 38
animality 1
art pensif 23
artwork 2–3, 7–11, 18
  artistic truth *vs.* philosophical
    truth 18–20
  authenticity 85
  autonomous 77–8, 172 n.14
  autonomy of 4, 5, 21, 32–3
  co-enactment of 19
  and critical reflection, chronological
    relationship between 24
  enigmatic 24–5
  fragility of 19
  knowledge of 22
  and philosophy, affinity
    between 23–4
  quasi-mystical characteristic of 13
  rationality 16
  and subjectivity, interplay
    between 13–15, 83–4

INDEX

unity of 36, 44–6
"Assommons les pauvres" (Baudelaire) 36
"A une passante" (Baudelaire) 4, 121, 143, 155

Banville, Théodore de 42, 151
Barbereau, Auguste 76
Baudelaire, Charles, *see also individual entries*
   "A celle qui est trop gaie" 36, 52, 56, 58–60, 109, 139
   aesthetic project 49
   "Allégorie" 95
   on *art pensif* 23
   on artwork 2–3, 13–15, 18
   "Assommons les pauvres" 36
   "A une passante" 4, 121, 143, 155
   "Bénédiction" 121, 127, 128
   "Confession" 27, 58–61
   "Crépuscule du soir" 149, 152, 158
   critique of bourgeois approaches to art 174 n.11
   on duality 10–15
   "Elévation" 27, 110–15, 128
   engagement with Beethoven 37, 40–4, 46, 47
   on homo duplex 10, 12–13, 73
   "J'aime le souvenir. . ." 79
   "Je t'adore à l'égal de la voûte nocturne" 28, 121, 122, 140–6
   "La Débauche et la Mort" 15, 178 n.15
   "La Fontaine de sang" 27, 73, 91, 92, 95, 96, 109, 119
   "L'Albatros" 157
   "La Mort" 93
   "L'Art philosophique" 105, 145
   "La soupe et les nuages" 121, 156
   "Le chien et le flacon" 62, 63, 70–2
   "Le *Confiteor* de l'artiste" 27, 73, 97, 100, 102, 103, 105, 107, 108, 112, 178 n.19
   "Le Couvercle" 27, 73, 116–20
   "Le Crépuscule du soir" 4, 28, 121, 146, 153, 156, 158
   "Le Cygne" 4, 122–4, 156
   "Le Flacon" 4, 27, 52, 55, 62–4, 67, 69–72, 80
   "Le Flambeau vivant" 57
   "Le Gâteau" 36
   "Le Goût du néant" 160–1, 181 n.4
   "Le Mauvais vitrier" 36, 146, 151, 153, 173 n.3
   "Le Peintre de la vie moderne" 76
   "Le Rêve d'un curieux" 121, 129–33, 163, 164
   "Les deux bonnes soeurs" 95, 178 n.15
   Les paradis artificiels 50
   Le Spleen de Paris/Petits poèmes en prose 41, 164
   "L'Héautontimorouménos" 4, 27, 29–30, 73, 76, 79, 85–7, 89, 91–2, 109, 161
   metaphysics 51
   on method of thinking 7, 8
   modernity 18, 28, 30
   Notes nouvelles sur Edgar Poe 44–5
   "Perte d'auréole" 4, 34, 121, 125–7
   "Que diras-tu ce soir . . ." 56–7
   "Réversibilité" 57
   Richard Wagner et Tannhäuser à Paris 174 n.10
   "Sed non satiata" 79
   "Spleen" 114, 116
   "Tout entière" 27, 52–4, 56–8
   "Une martyre" 36, 69
Bauman, Zygmunt 79
beauty 42, 45, 48–50, 62, 142, 143
   natural, and subjectivity 105, 106
   and pain, relationship between 107–8
   transformation of 145
Beckett, Samuel 133, 144, 161
Beethoven, Ludwig van 8, 33, 49, 122
   engagement with Baudelaire 37, 40–4, 46, 47
Beistegui, Michel de 25, 159–60
Belmer, Stephanie 142
"Bénédiction" (Baudelaire) 121, 127, 128

Benjamin, Walter   3, 5, 165, 176 n.5, 180 n.1
  Adorno's critique of   4
  Marxist approach to thought and social critique   6
Bernstein, J. M.   8, 22, 23, 75, 124, 145, 172 n.9
Bersani, Leo   177 n.11
Bevilacqua, Luca   102
Blin, Georges   181 n.2
Blood, Susan   180 n.7
Bonnefoy, Yves   79
Boudin, Eugène   102
bourgeois self   74, 75
  centralization of   82–3
Bowie, Andrew   13
Burton, Richard   12–13, 179 n.2
Butler, Judith
  "Violence, Mourning, Politics"   140
Buvik, Per   177 n.12

Capital (Marx)   157
capitalism   157
centralization of the self   70, 73, 74, 78, 82–3, 93, 168
Chambers, Ross   123, 164
Chua, Daniel   47
Cioran, Emil   181 n.6
classicism   44
Colebrook, Claire   181 n.7
commodified reality   157
commodity culture   157
"Confession" (Baudelaire)   27, 58–61
consonance   29, 30, 37, 38, 40, 41, 43, 50, 51, 75, 83, 91, 137, 143, 145, 149
constellation   9, 23–5, 84, 109, 166, 169
Cornille, Louis   75
"Crépuscule du soir" (Baudelaire)   149, 152, 158
critical reflection   3, 15, 16, 22–5, 47, 104–6, 120, 124, 145, 169
critical self-reflection   146
critical theory   6
cross-temporal networks   26

DalMolin, Eliane   54–5
deconstructionist approach   80
de Man, Paul   177 n.11
depravation, accusation of   42
Descartes, R.   167
de Vries, Hent   144–5
Dialectic of Enlightenment (Adorno)   36–7
discordance   30
disenchantment   10, 26, 34, 37, 118, 133, 134, 137, 163
disparition élocutoire du poète   80
dissonance   2–4, 8–10, 25–7, 29–72
  act of resistance   34
  between artist and object of esthetic experience   108–9
  autonomy of artwork   32–3
  dissonant sonority   50, 99–100
  esthetic   21
  "faux accord"   34–5
  of modernity   30–2, 37, 41–2, 44
  and music   39–44, 99–100
  proto-modernist aesthetics of   40
  as revealer of dialectical tension   37
  structural   103–4
  subjectivity   4, 26, 29–30, 36, 88–9, 164, 169
  as truth about harmony   29, 33–41, 43, 46–51, 54, 75, 96, 100, 109
  unity of artwork   44–6
  unity of form and content   35–6
duality   10–14
Dupont, Pierre   21

Eagleton, Terry   82–3, 169, 171–2 n.7, 177 n.8
ego-weakness   80
  psychological and social structure of   175 n.16
Eichendorff, Joseph von   26, 31, 80
"Elévation" (Baudelaire)   27, 110–15, 128
ephemerality   13
epistemology   1, 6, 12, 15, 28, 38, 40, 140, 159, 169, 172 n.10, 181 n.3
equality   135

"Essay as Form, The" (Adorno)   17
esthetic truth   17, 50, 69, 85, 112, 116, 118, 128, 130–3, 145
eternal transitoriness   18, 19
Evans, Margery   40–1

failure   108
Fall out of Redemption, The   180 n.1
Farina, Mario   35
"faux accord"   26, 30, 34–5, 51, 88, 89, 91, 168
Felski, Rita   25–6
flâneur   4, 79
Fleming, Peter   31–2
Foloppe, Régine   125–6
Fondane, Benjamin   180 n.1
fragmentation   40, 53–4
    of the self   78
frustration   162

Gasché, Rodolphe   139–40
Gautier, Théophile   21, 95
genius   85
Goehr, Lydia   51, 174 n.8
Goethe, J. W. von
    'Wanderer's Night Song'   106–7
Gordon, Peter   176 n.4

Halpern, Rob   10, 157, 178–9 n.12
Harman, Graham   177 n.9
harmony   25, 164
    dissonance as truth about   26, 29, 33–41, 43, 46–50, 54, 75, 96, 100, 109
    structural, of music   39–40
    tonal   83
    Western system of   30
Harter, Deborah   177 n.13
hermeneutics   78
Hiddleston, J. A.   97
hieroglyphs   151–2, 157
historicity   13
Hoeckner, Berthold   173 n.4
Hoffman, E. T. A.   42
Hohendahl, Peter Uwe   17, 19–20
homo duplex   10, 12–13, 73
Hubert, J.-D.   55–6
Hulatt, Owen   7, 15, 16

identity thinking   5–6, 75, 165, 168, 175 n.16
imagination   83–5
imitation   150, 154
immanent transcendence   28, 121, 122, 126, 129, 135–42, 153, 156, 157
immanent-transcendent relationships   28, 121, 135
incomprehensibility   22
Infinite   103
irony   89–91
Islam   139

"J'aime le souvenir. . ." (Baudelaire)   79
Jameson, Fredric   172–3 n.15
Jay, Martin   176 n.3
Jenny, Laurent   178 n.19, 178 n.20
"Je t'adore à l'égal de la voûte nocturne" (Baudelaire)   28, 121, 122, 140–6
"joie de descendre"   26
Judaism   139

Kaufman, Robert   3, 15
Kelley, Dorothy   174 n.12
Kiloh, Kathy   171 n.5, 180 n.6
Klein, Richard   127, 179 n.3

"La Débauche et la Mort" (Baudelaire)   178 n.15
"La Fontaine de sang" (Baudelaire)   27, 73, 91, 92, 95, 96, 109, 119
Laforgue, Pierre   66
"L'Albatros" (Baudelaire)   157
"La Mort" (Baudelaire)   93
"La Musique"   173 n.6
landscape/soundscape   148
"L'Art philosophique" (Baudelaire)   105, 145
l'art pour l'art   20, 21, 77, 172 n.14
"La soupe et les nuages" (Baudelaire)   121, 156
"Le chien et le flacon" (Baudelaire)   62, 63, 70–2

"Le *Confiteor* de l'artiste"
    (Baudelaire) 27, 73, 97, 100,
    102, 103, 105, 107, 108, 112,
    178 n.19
"Le Couvercle" (Baudelaire) 27, 73,
    116–20
"Le Crépuscule du soir"
    (Baudelaire) 4, 28, 121, 146,
    153, 156, 158
"Le Cygne" (Baudelaire) 4, 122–
    4, 156
"Le Flacon" (Baudelaire) 4, 27, 52,
    55, 62–4, 67, 69–72, 80
"Le Flambeau vivant"
    (Baudelaire) 57
"Le Gâteau" (Baudelaire) 36
"Le Goût du néant"
    (Baudelaire) 160–1,
    181 n.4
"Le Mauvais vitrier" (Baudelaire)
    36, 146, 151, 153, 173 n.3
"Le Peintre de la vie moderne"
    (Baudelaire) 76
"Le Rêve d'un curieux"
    (Baudelaire) 121, 129–33,
    163, 164
Le Salon de 1859 83, 102, 103
"Les deux bonnes soeurs"
    (Baudelaire) 95, 178 n.15
Les Fleurs du Mal 27, 29, 56, 64, 78,
    88, 92, 93, 95, 134
Les paradis artificiels (Baudelaire)
    50
Le Spleen de Paris (Baudelaire) 164
"L'Héautontimorouménos"
    (Baudelaire) 4, 27, 29–30, 73,
    76, 79, 85–7, 89, 91–2, 109
linear model of artistic
    development 10
liquefied self 93–4
liquidation 78–80, 133
liquid modernity 79
literary criticism 4, 6
Loncke, Jocelynne 42, 173 n.6
Lübecker, Nikolaj 147, 180 n.10
lucidity 94
lyric poetry and society, relationship
    between 5–6

lyric subjectivity 2, 26–9, 31, 32, 52,
    56, 71, 73, 74, 82, 85, 87, 88,
    90, 91, 95, 96, 109, 122–5, 147,
    159, 166

Mallarmé, Stéphane 32
Marchal, Bertrand 131
Mars, Victor de 87–8
Marx, K. 3
    Capital 157
mass culture 6
Maulpoix, Jean-Michel 29, 175 n.2
melancholy 43, 49, 160, 162
Melnick, Daniel 173 n.5
Meltzer, Françoise 41–2, 172 n.11,
    173 n.16
mental imbalance 156
metaphysics 1, 49, 51, 56, 58, 75,
    80, 96, 122, 130, 133, 139, 140,
    144, 163, 174 n.9
    affirmative 181 n.3
    language 133
    of transcendence 122, 129, 164
Michelangelo 46
modernism/modernity 14, 18,
    28, 104
    afterlife of 3
    dissonance of 30–2, 37, 41–2, 44
    esthetic 31
    liquid 79
    metaphysical 80
    poetic 29–31
    postmodernity 79, 144
Mozart 39, 40
multiplicity 89–90
music
    dissonance and 39–44, 100–1
    structural harmonic logic of
        39–40
musicology 6

Nadar, Félix 179 n.5
nature 13
negative dialectics 127
Negative Dialectics (Adorno) 75–7,
    85, 128–9, 163, 164
Nicholls, Peter 171 n.6
Nicholsen, Shierry Weber 14, 67

nonhuman actors 26
non-identity 15, 17, 21, 75, 166, 171 n.4
North, Michael 3
Notes nouvelles sur Edgar Poe (Baudelaire) 44–5
Notes on Literature (Adorno) 7

objectivity 5, 14, 31, 32, 73, 88, 90, 105, 113, 126, 175 n.16
"On Lyric Poetry and Society" (Adorno) 5
"On Subject and Object" (Adorno) 168–9

part-whole relation 176 n.6
passion 49
"Perte d'auréole" (Baudelaire) 4, 34, 121, 125–7
Petits Poèmes (Baudelaire) 41
philosophy, negative function of 105–6
Pichois, Claude 61–2, 64, 69
Plass, Ulrich 22, 80, 175 n.16
Platonism 55–6
Poe, Edgar Allan 21, 26, 29, 42, 44–5, 47
postmodernity 79, 144
postulations simultanées 12–13
psychological disturbance 42
psychology 1, 33, 42, 48, 96, 97, 103, 104, 112, 116, 150
  ego-weakness 175 n.16

"Que diras-tu ce soir . . ." (Baudelaire) 56–7

radical defamiliarization 99
reconciliation of subject-object 180 n.6
Réflexions sur quelques-uns de mes contemporains (Banville) 42, 151
reification 80
Rembrandt 46
resistance 34, 35
"Réversibilité" (Baudelaire) 57
Richard, Jean-Pierre 176 n.7

Richard Wagner et Tannhäuser à Paris (Baudelaire) 174 n.10
Richter, Gerhard 7, 8, 16, 24, 144, 172 n.8
romanticism 37, 44, 74, 80, 82, 103, 126, 174 n.7, 178 n.21

Said, Edward 41
Sanyal, Debarati 177 n.11
Schweppenhäuser, Gerhard 181 n.3
Scott, Maria 98
  "Baudelaire's Canine Allegories" 175 n.14
"Sed non satiata" (Baudelaire) 79
self-canceling 99
self-consciousness 21, 94, 172 n.14
self-integrity 94
Shakespeare, W. 95
shudder 15, 74, 113, 139, 142
similarity 16–17
Singh, Sonam 179 n.1
society and lyric poetry, relationship between 5–6
sociology 6, 36, 39, 174 n.8
Sound Figures (Adorno) 43–4
spirituality 1
"Spleen" (Baudelaire) 114, 116
Starobinski, Jean 88, 90
subjectivity 4, 8, 25, 73–120
  artwork 83–4
  and artwork, interplay between 13–15
  complications of 76
  configuration of 9
  dialectical 74, 76
  dissonant 4, 26, 29–30, 36, 88–9, 164, 169
  esthetic 10, 11, 97, 105, 107, 118–20
  flow of 81
  liquid 91, 96
  lyric 2, 26–9, 31, 32, 52, 56, 71, 73, 74, 82, 85, 87, 88, 90, 91, 95, 96, 109, 122–5, 147, 159, 166
  poetic 27, 32, 63, 67–9, 72, 73, 82, 121, 125
  societal 32

subject–object relations 1, 4–6, 14, 15, 20, 21, 26, 28, 32, 35, 67, 69, 76, 77, 93, 98, 114, 120, 124, 135, 138–41, 143, 146, 162, 166–8, 180 n.6, 180 n.7

"Tableaux parisiens" 79, 164
temporality 10, 25, 94, 146, 178 n.19
Thélot, Jérome 71, 134, 142
Thériault, Patrick 96
"Theses on the Language of the Philosopher" (Adorno) 164–5
Toumayan, Alan 181 n.5
"Tout entière" (Baudelaire) 27, 52–4, 56–8
transcendence 4, 9–10, 25–8, 121–58
  artistic 10
  demystification of 117
  dissonance and 37, 49, 56, 121
  immanent 28, 121, 122, 126, 129, 135–42, 153, 156, 157
  immanent-transcendent relationships 28, 135
  manufactured nature of 122
  metaphorical 128
  metaphysics of 122, 129, 164
  negation of 145
  poetic 121, 126, 127, 151, 166
  refusal of 118
  transcendent idealism 40
truth 49
  artistic *vs.* philosophical 18–20

esthetic 17, 50, 69, 85, 112, 116, 118, 128, 130–3, 145

ululation 150
"Une martyre" (Baudelaire) 36, 69
unity 89, 145
  of artwork 36, 44–6
  of form and content 35–6
  of the "I" 74–5
Unnamable, The 2

Vaillant, Alain 12, 23
vaporization of the self 70, 73, 74, 78, 83, 93, 168
versification 30
violence
  esthetic 143, 144
  mimetic representation of 88
"Violence, Mourning, Politics" (Butler) 140

Wagner, Richard 37
'Wanderer's Night Song' (Goethe) 106–7
Weber, Julien 62–3, 175 n.15
Wellmer, Albrecht 35–6
wholeness 54, 58, 78, 100, 162, 174 n.11, 176 n.3
woman, as caricature of transcendent unity of God 55–6
Wu, Colleen Shu-Ching 81

Zuidervaart, Lambert 143

www.ingramcontent.com/pod-product-compliance
Lightning Source LLC
Chambersburg PA
CBHW052045300426
44117CB00012B/1978